Exploring the Bible
THE DICKINSON SERIES

INTRODUCING THE
NEW TESTAMENT

STUDENT TEXT
SECOND EDITION

REV. ANNE ROBERTSON

MASSACHUSETTS BIBLE SOCIETY
One Book, Many Voices

Massachusetts Bible Society
199 Herrick Road
Newton Centre, MA 02459

Book design by Thomas Bergeron
www.thomasbergeron.com
Typeface: Jenson Pro, Gill Sans

ISBN-13: 978-0-9882481-8-2

SECOND EDITION

PHOTOGRAPHY CREDITS

Image #1 (p. 45) Session 2, The Good Samaritan © 2002 by Stephen Sawyer, used with permission; Image #2 (p. 47) Session 2, Image of coin featuring Caesar Augustus used courtesy of Classical Numismatic Group, Inc., source: www.cngcoins.com; Image #3 (p. 55) Session 2, Photo of sheep and goats courtesy of Azeem Baloch; Image #4 (p. 64) Session 3, Photo of Melchizedek icon courtesy of Tetcu Mircea Rares; Image #5 (p. 74) Session 3, Photo from Trafalgar Square passion play: a miracle © Stephen Craven; Image #6 (p. 81) Session 3, Son of God © Vicki Thomas, Prophetic Artist, used with permission; Image #7 (p. 83) Session 3, Christ Our Light, Donald Jackson (artist, scribe) © 2002, The Saint John's Bible, Saint John's University, Collegeville, Minnesota USA, used with permission, all rights reserved; Image #8 (p. 85) Session 3, Photo of the Dome of the Rock by Carlos Rebolledo; Image #9 (p. 109) Session 4, Paul of Tarsus composite created by experts of the Landeskriminalamt of North Rhine-Westphalia using historical sources, proposed by Dusseldorf historian Michael Hesemann; Image #10 (p. 123) Session 4, Photo of the tel at the site of ancient Lystra © Jane Britnell, used with permission; Image #11 (p. 125) Session 4, Photo of Roman amphitheater at Ephesus by Rennett Stowe; Image #12 (p. 127) Session 4, Image of Saint Lydia of Thyatira, source: www.eikonografos.com, used with permission; Image #13 (p. 151) Session 5, Photo of Midnight Song, bronze sculpture by Tom White, Tom White Studios, Inc., source: www.tomwhitestudio.com; Image #14 (p. 170) Session 6, "Jesus' followers continued to meet and chose Matthias to replace Judas Iscariot' — from Bible Stories for Children, used with permission, source: www.africanpastors.org; Image #15 (p. 191) Session 6, Cartoon, "I can't stand to listen to anyone else preach . . ." © 1994 Mary Chambers, source: www.leadershipjournal.net/cartoons; Image #16 (p. 232) Appendix 2, Altar Frontal at St. Peter's Episcopal Church-on-the-Canal, Buzzards Bay, MA, photo by Charlotte Daigle, used with permission

For my mother
Joan Ruth Robertson Thompson
May 26, 1932–October 18, 2012

Your hymns rocked me to sleep.
Your love and faith formed my own.
Your life showed me Christ.
I sing now for you.
With you.
One.

"The glory that you have given me I have given them, so that they may be one, as we are one, I in them and you in me, that they may become completely one, so that the world may know that you have sent me and have loved them even as you have loved me."

John 17:22–23

ACKNOWLEDGMENTS

This course is the last in the three-course series *Exploring the Bible: The Dickinson Series*. As with the previous courses, I have to first acknowledge Dr. Charles Dickinson, whose gifts of time, expertise, and treasure have made this entire series possible. You can read more about him on p. v and can watch a brief video about his hopes for this series on the exploringthebible.org website.

Special thanks go to Rev. John Stendahl, our Board President and Pastor of the Lutheran Church of the Newtons in Newton Centre, MA. John has a special heart for interfaith work and, with his keen theological mind, was able to help me shape the material in Appendix 4, "Who Killed Jesus?" I am indebted to him for (I hope!) keeping me out of hot water in that section.

To be sure the material presented here is in keeping with the best scholarship, Dr. Wayne Meeks, Woolsey Professor Emeritus of Religious Studies at Yale, was kind enough to review the material for accuracy. I am grateful for his corrections, suggestions, and overall support.

I also continue to be indebted to the following congregations and group facilitators who have served as pilot groups to test the effectiveness of both the Student Text and the class sessions outlined in the Leader's Guide: Dr. Ellen Porter Honnet and Jacqui James at the First Unitarian Society of Newton (West Newton, MA); Lynne Osborn at St. Matthew's United Methodist Church (Acton, MA); Aurelio Ramirez at the Lutheran Church of the Newtons (Newton, MA); Frances Taylor, Director of Faith Formation at Sacred Heart Parish (Lynn, MA); and Rev. Dr. Thomas D. Wintle at First Parish Church (Weston, MA). They had to deal with this material in its raw, unedited form, and their feedback has been critical to shaping this final product.

Our production team continues their awesome work, from editor Nancy Fitzgerald, copyeditor Jennifer Hackett, proofreader Maria Boyer, and designer Thomas Bergeron, to the amazing staff I am privileged to work with at the Massachusetts Bible Society: Jocelyn Bergeron, Michael Colyott, and Frank Stevens. The MBS Trustees and retired editing professional Ms. Cynthia Thompson are also to be commended for their work in offering feedback on the materials and reaching out to find appropriate places to offer and endorse these courses.

IN GRATITUDE,

Anne Robertson

INTRODUCING EXPLORING THE BIBLE: THE DICKINSON SERIES

Exploring the Bible: The Dickinson Series is a series of three, six-week courses that leads to a Certificate in Biblical Literacy from the historic Massachusetts Bible Society.

Each of the three courses is designed to fit six ninety-minute sessions with a group of eight to fifteen people. The Massachusetts Bible Society provides training, materials, and ongoing support for those who would like to run the program in their local churches or communities. Those leading the courses are not expected to be biblical experts or pastors. They are those gifted and trained to facilitate a warm, welcoming, and open group environment where the material can be presented and discussed with respect for all participants.

The courses can be done informally or for either CEU or certificate credit. For the details of doing the courses for credit visit exploringthebible.org/getting-credit.

THE EXPLORING THE BIBLE PROGRAM

Three Courses: A Bird's-Eye View

I. **What Is the Bible?** A broad overview of the Bible, including chapters on how to select a Bible suitable for your needs, how the Bible is organized, how the collection of books that comprise the Bible were chosen, different ways that people approach the text, and what archaeology has to tell us about the text and its stories.

II. *Introducing the Old Testament.* A look at the best-known stories, most influential passages, and unforgettable characters that comprise the Old Testament. What are the primary themes and narratives? What are the characteristics of ancient Hebrew literature and the mindset of people in the ancient Near East? Explore both the writings themselves and the historical contexts that gave them birth.

III. *Introducing the New Testament.* Learn about Jesus as a man, as a Jewish rabbi, and as the Christ of Christian faith. Explore first-century Nazareth, what ancient letter-writing practices can tell us about Paul's letters, and the wild apocalypse of Revelation.

Online Resources

Join us for discussion on the Exploring the Bible Facebook page and follow us on Twitter @ExploreBible to swap questions and experiences with others across the country and across the world who are doing the courses in their local communities. Many of you are asking for the opportunity to take the courses online and we hope to be able to offer that down the road. And you can always check out our website at exploringthebible.org for other news, recommended reading, and to find a course near you.

THE EXPLORING THE BIBLE STUDENTS

The series is designed for two distinct types of students:

The Casual or Informal Students. The first group is made up of those who might know something about the Bible but have gaps in their knowledge or those who just want to test the waters of biblical studies. These students might want simply to take one of the three courses without doing all that is necessary to complete the certificate program. While it's expected that this group will still actively participate in whatever course(s) they select, there is less work expected of them outside the group setting.

The Intentional or "Extra Mile" Students. The second group represents those who have determined that they really want to do some work to build a strong foundation for Bible study. They might be Christians considering seminary, people of faith who don't know their own Scriptures very well, people of other faiths who want a clearer understanding of the Christian text, or even people of no faith who recognize the cultural and geopolitical influence of the Bible and want to understand it better. The common denominator among this group is that they want to do the whole program, including the "Extra Mile" assignments required to earn the Certificate of Biblical Literacy or Continuing Education Units (CEUs).

We hope each study group will consist of both casual and more intentional learners, and our design includes opportunities in class sessions for those engaging the material more deeply to share what they've learned with the others.

THE EXPLORING THE BIBLE SPONSORS

The Benefactor

Exploring the Bible: The Dickinson Series is named in honor of its chief benefactor, Dr. Charles C. Dickinson III, a biblical scholar and long-time trustee of the Massachusetts Bible Society. Dr. Charles Dickinson was born in Charleston, West Virginia, on May 13, 1936; was educated there and at Phillips Academy, Andover, Massachusetts; and graduated cum laude in religion and philosophy from Dartmouth College, Hanover, New Hampshire. After serving three and a half years with the US Marine Corps in the USA and Far East, he studied theology and philosophy in Chicago, Pittsburgh, West and East Germany, at Yale University, and at Union Theological Seminary in New York. He received his B.D. (Bachelor of Divinity) and Ph.D. degrees in Pittsburgh in 1965 and 1973 respectively and did post-doctoral study at Oxford University and Harvard Divinity School. Dr. Dickinson has taught in Richmond, Virginia; Kinshasa, Zaire, Congo; Charleston, West Virginia; Rome, Italy; the People's Republic of China; Andover Newton Theological School; and Beacon Hill Seminars in Boston. He lives with his wife, JoAnne, and their son, John, in Boston.

The Author

This series was conceived and designed by Rev. Anne Robertson, executive director of the Massachusetts Bible Society, who also developed and wrote the three student texts and leader's guides. She is the author of three additional books: *Blowing the Lid Off the God-Box: Opening Up to a Limitless Faith* (Morehouse, 2005); *God's Top 10: Blowing the Lid Off the Commandments* (Morehouse, 2006); and *God with Skin On: Finding God's Love in Human Relationships* (Morehouse, 2009). Rev. Robertson is an elder in the New England Conference of the United Methodist Church, is a winner of the Wilbur C. Ziegler Award for Excellence in Preaching, and is a sought-after speaker and workshop leader. She can be found on the web at www.annerobertson.org.

The Massachusetts Bible Society

Founded on July 6, 1809, the Massachusetts Bible Society is an ecumenical, Christian organization that has historically been a place where those across the theological spectrum of belief could unite for a common purpose. At the beginning of its history, that purpose was simply getting a copy of the Bible into the hands of anyone who wanted one, especially those without the means or opportunity to obtain one themselves. In more recent times, that work has been supplemented by the development of a variety of educational programs highlighting the importance of the Bible for faith, culture, history, and politics, as well as providing a forum for the many different voices of biblical interpretation. Exploring the Bible is a significant addition to those efforts and attempts to continue the historic tradition of being a place where those of many different faith traditions can unite for a common purpose—in this case, biblical literacy. You can find out more about the Massachusetts Bible Society at www.massbible.org.

You

Exploring the Bible: The Dickinson Series is made possible because you have elected to be a part of it. While we believe the course materials are useful in and of themselves, it is the community of students and group leaders who bring those materials to life as you engage with one another in your classes and online. Just by participating, you are helping to raise the level of biblical literacy in our world. You can ensure that this ministry continues by completing the leader and student evaluations for each course, by purchasing the materials, and by telling others about Exploring the Bible. There are also opportunities for you to provide scholarship assistance for future students, to attend training to become a group leader, or simply to offer moral or financial support to the mission of the Massachusetts Bible Society. Our most important sponsor is you. Find out how you can help at exploringthebible.org.

OUR THEOLOGICAL POINT OF VIEW

In the creation of this series there are several obvious biases:

- The Bible is a book that can and should be read by individuals both inside and outside the church.

- Understanding of the Bible is enhanced and deepened in conversation with others.

- The tools of scholarship are not incompatible with a faithful reading of Scripture.

- Diversity of opinion is both a welcome and a necessary part of any education—especially biblical education.

Beyond those points we have tried to give an unbiased theological perspective, describing differences of opinion and scholarship in neutral terms. Although named for and written by Christians, *Exploring the Bible: The Dickinson Series* is designed to be an educational tool, not an evangelistic tool. The Massachusetts Bible Society affirms that the making of Christian disciples is the job of the local church. These materials are designed either to fit into the overall disciple-making effort of a local church or into a secular environment where people of other faiths or of no faith can gain a deeper understanding of the nature and content of the Bible.

COURSE ADMINISTRATION

Obtaining Credit for Certification or CEUs

Those wishing to enroll in the certificate program or obtain CEUs for their work must fill out an application and do the work in an approved small-group setting. Those who simply work their way through the materials on their own are not eligible for credit or certification. To find out more or to obtain an application, go to exploringthebible.org/getting-credit.

The Cost

Costs will vary depending on whether you are a casual student (which has no cost apart from the books) or are taking the course either for CEUs or certification (for which there is a fee). Please check our website at exploringthebible.org/getting-credit for more information, current rates, and information on discounts and scholarships.

Keeping in Touch

Go to exploringthebible.org to learn more or contact the Massachusetts Bible Society at 199 Herrick Road, Newton Centre, MA 02459 or dsadmin@ massbible.org. You may also call us at 617-969-9404.

TO THE STUDENT

Welcome to *Exploring the Bible: The Dickinson Series*. Most people who decide to study the Bible attempt to do so by just diving in. They get a Bible and start reading on page one, often expecting that it will flow in some kind of orderly succession to the end.

While it's not impossible to study the Bible that way, it may not be the most helpful strategy, because the Bible is a different sort of book. In fact, it isn't even really accurate to call the Bible a "book"; it's more like an anthology of texts, collected in one bound volume, that have become sacred to a variety of religious traditions. Without some understanding of what the Bible is and isn't, conflicts about its contents can easily escalate.

Most of the arguments and conflicts over the Bible aren't really about *what* the Bible says, but about how to *interpret* what it says. At their root, the conflicts represent different ways that people approach the book as a whole and which biblical texts are most important or authoritative, as well as what sort of book they believe the Bible to be. We'll examine a number of those differences in these courses.

For example, the debates about creationism versus evolution aren't about what the Bible says per se. They're about whether what the Bible says should be read as religious truth (and therefore full of metaphor and symbol), as scientific fact (and therefore if the text says "seven days," it means precisely seven twenty-four-hour periods), or as a historical document that describes what an ancient people once believed about the creation of the world.

These courses will allow you to dip your toes into some of the more famous stories and passages of the Bible as you read and discuss parts of the text itself.

The broader purpose, however, is to take you up to the balcony that overlooks several thousand years of history and to help you to understand how we got this particular collection of ancient texts into a bound volume called the Bible.

QUESTIONS, PLEASE!

You'll probably finish any one of these courses with more questions than you had at the beginning—or at least with a different set of questions. So it's important to see yourself less as a typical student in a classroom and more as an explorer or investigative reporter. Learning to ask good, incisive questions is more important to the learning process than memorizing answers that have been handed to you.

Don't be afraid of your questions and try not to be frustrated if there doesn't appear to be an easy answer. When dealing in the realm of religion (whether that religion represents your faith or not), people often spend entire lifetimes seeking answers and sometimes the only "answer" available will be a variety of opinions. Even on matters that seem like they should have verifiable, factual answers, like "Who wrote this text?" or "When did this happen?" the response, "No one really knows but there are several schools of thought" is more common than you might expect.

As questions arise for you, write them down. Especially if you plan to go on to other courses in the Exploring the Bible series or even other Bible studies in other places, keeping a journal of your questions and thoughts can be very helpful. You may find that some of your early issues are settled later on. At the very least, be sure your question is raised either in your group or in the online forums. If you have the question, you can bet someone else does also, and if it turns out that a lot of people are asking the very same question, we can revise this text to address it for others down the road.

From the second session onward, there will be an opportunity for each person to ask a question about the material at the very beginning of each class, and there is a section at the end of each session in this text to encourage you to think about your questions ahead of that "check-in" time. These "check-in" questions will be noted by your group leader but not immediately addressed, as many of them may be dealt with during the ensuing class(es). You'll also be learning about the various Bible study tools and resources available to you, so that you can seek out your own answers. See Appendix 8 (page 265) for a list of tools and resources to help you find answers to your questions.

DIVERSITY HELPS YOU LEARN

Exploring the Bible isn't designed solely for people of Christian faith. It is our hope that people of other faiths, or even of no faith, who wish to better understand the Christian Scriptures can engage with this series to learn more about the book that has shaped so much of the world's culture, politics, and even geography. We hope that many groups will have a mix of people with many different perspectives learning about the Bible for a variety of reasons.

We learn very little when we're only exposed to thinking that mirrors our own, and we encourage every person using this book for study to find a way to engage others in dialogue. Ideally that's your small group of eight to fifteen people who get to know one another over the six-week period. But if you're doing the study on your own, try to visit the Exploring the Bible Facebook page, @ExploreBible on Twitter, and exploringthebible.org to see what others who are studying the same text are asking and talking about. This will enhance your learning experience.

PICK YOUR LEVEL OF ENGAGEMENT

Exploring the Bible: The Dickinson Series has two different levels of engagement and you may well have both represented in your group. In fact, class sessions have been designed with the assumption that most groups will have both kinds of students in the same group.

As explained in the Introduction, the series of three courses is designed to culminate in a Certificate of Biblical Literacy and each of the three courses can be taken for Continuing Education Units (CEUs), which might be required by various professional organizations. Students seeking either certification or CEUs are asked to do extra work to earn that recognition. We have called this group the Extra Mile students and at the end of each session in the Student Text, you'll see an additional homework assignment just for them.

We expect, however, that other students will simply engage the courses from a sense of general interest. Some may feel that only one or two of the three courses would be helpful to them or that their current circumstances would not allow for doing the extra work. These "informal" students also have homework, but to a much lesser degree. Of course, any informal student is welcome to do the Extra Mile exercises simply to delve deeper into a topic of interest.

Several class sessions have time set aside for those who have done the Extra Mile work (no matter to which category of student they belong) to share what they've learned with others in the group.

Whichever group you're in, try not to leave the homework until the last minute. Extra Mile students can always count on several hours per session for their homework, but the informal student homework ramps up from about an hour per session for the first course to almost three hours in some sessions of courses two and three. Plan ahead.

As with most everything in life, you'll get out of this course what you put into it or, as the Bible so aptly puts it, "You reap whatever you sow." (Galatians 6:7) If you're an Extra Mile student, not doing the work will waste your money and cost you your certificate or CEUs. If you're an informal student, you simply won't learn as much and the others in the group will be deprived of the insights, questions, and opinions that you might have otherwise contributed. You came here to learn, so don't shortchange yourself. Do the work.

FOR THE CHRISTIAN STUDENT

If you're coming to this class as a Christian seeking to enrich your faith by engaging your own sacred text, you'll almost certainly have different kinds of questions than those who want to learn about the Bible for other reasons. Information in this course and others may challenge some of your basic faith assumptions. Be assured that there are literally millions of Christians with a deep, Spirit-filled, Christ-centered faith who have found their faith grounded and strengthened by some of the very questions that once felt strange or threatening to them.

Hang with it. Keep a journal to record your feelings and your questions. Bring them to your specific faith community, raise them on the Facebook page or in your denominational gatherings. Pray about the issues that arise for you. Christian faith is never static. It is a journey during which we change and grow along the way. Sometimes we take a wrong path and have to cut through the brambles to get back on track, and other times we come out of a hard climb to suddenly see the most splendid view.

The questions you have will be your own and you will be the one sorting through the variety of responses to see what resonates in your spirit. The Bible itself is full of people having their faith challenged by the circumstances they face or the information they obtain, and none of them are struck by lightning for their honest searching. If you find yourself in such a place, remember the words from Joshua 1:9: "Be strong and courageous. Do not be afraid; do not be discouraged, for the LORD your God will be with you wherever you go."

Be sure to recognize, however, that the goal of this series is to make the Bible more understandable and accessible to all people, regardless of their faith perspective. If you have people of other faiths or of no faith in your group, recognize and respect those differences in your questions and discussions. Trust the Bible to speak in its own way to those who choose to study it for their own reasons.

FOR STUDENTS OUTSIDE THE CHRISTIAN TRADITION

While the Bible contains texts that are sacred to other faiths, *Exploring the Bible: The Dickinson Series* examines the text as it is used in Christian communities. It is more than likely that there will be some in your group taking this class for reasons related to their Christian faith, and their questions and comments will often be quite different from yours.

It is difficult to truly understand the Bible apart from hearing the perspectives of those who turn to this set of texts as part of their faith. At the Massachusetts Bible Society, we recognize that the use of the Bible by Christians has at times been harmful, oppressive, and counter to the very faith Christians claim to represent. We also believe, however, that such uses are not the inevitable result of a Bible-based faith.

We have tried in this book and in the class exercises to present the sacred text of Christians in a way that is welcoming of those who want to know more about it for other reasons. Our goal in the Exploring the Bible is educational rather than evangelical. This doesn't mean you won't hear a variety of Christian perspectives and/or debates, but it does mean that you should not feel pressured to adopt the Christian faith or engage those debates on any basis other than their own merits.

GIVE US FEEDBACK!

If the Bible is taught in public schools, it excludes the faith perspective. If it is taught in a religious setting, it often either ignores or attempts to discredit secular issues and perspectives. *Exploring the Bible: The Dickinson Series* seeks to include both perspectives and all kinds of students in mixed groups and with the same study—and that is perhaps our greatest challenge with this material. We welcome your feedback regarding the success of our efforts and encourage you to complete the evaluation at the end of this text. If you don't want to cut it out of your book and didn't receive one in class, you can also download a copy at exploringthebible.org/forms.

R-E-S-P-E-C-T

You are about to engage with others in reading, talking, and learning about the Bible. For some, the Bible is the text that led them to encounter God and so it can have deep and powerful resonance. For some, what seems like a simple question about the Bible can be heard as an attack on everything they know to be true and believe. Others may have experienced the Bible as an instrument of great harm in their personal relationships, or they may have learned about its negative effects in history and politics. For still others, the Bible is a curiosity—a foreign object about which they have no strong feelings.

The conflicts between faith traditions and the conflicts in our culture can easily become evident in your group. You have the chance in this study to model something our culture desperately needs—civil and respectful dialogue about important and meaningful differences.

Don't be a hater. Don't flame the Facebook page or Twitter feed. Don't rant in your group or condemn the perspectives of others. If you find a discussion is raising strong feelings and you don't know how to express them with respect, you can always say, "I'm having a very strong reaction to this and don't know how to express it well." Your group leader can then help move the group forward.

DEFINING THE ERA: NOTATING THE DATE

When it comes to measuring time, Western culture has often adopted the calendar of Christianity, which puts the birth of Jesus at the center of history. In the Christian calendar everything that happened before that time is notated as B.C. (before Christ) and everything afterwards as A.D. (Anno Domini in Latin, meaning "the year of the Lord"). According to Merriam-Webster, the first known use of A.D. in a system of dating was in 1512.

It is no surprise that other faiths and other cultures have retained their own methods of dating the years, which then becomes problematic in a global culture trying to figure out a common way to measure time. This problem has been addressed by an academic compromise of keeping the year zero as it has been on the Christian calendar, but adopting a more neutral system of describing the years before and after. In that compromise system what Christians refer to as Before Christ (B.C.) becomes Before the Christian (or Common) Era (B.C.E.) and what Christians refer to as Anno Domini (A.D.) becomes simply the Christian (or Common) Era (C.E.).

Because we want this course to be a resource for all who want to know about the Bible—regardless of their religious beliefs—we have adopted the more neutral B.C.E. and C.E. system of annotating time.

OLD TESTAMENT VS. HEBREW BIBLE

One of the first things Christians have to acknowledge about the first portion of our holy book is that the Jews know what we call the Old Testament as the Hebrew Bible. As Jews and Christians dialogue about this set of texts, one of the points of discussion is about how Christians should refer to this group of writings. Are we diminishing its importance to Judaism by calling it the Old Testament? Should we use the term "Hebrew Bible" instead?

I have opted to use the term "Old Testament" for the following reasons:

- I once heard a rabbi weigh in on this issue. His comment was that when Christians read the Hebrew Bible, they bring a fundamentally different kind of reading and interpretation to the text than Jews do. In his eyes, the term "Hebrew Bible" should be reserved for those reading the text specifically as a Jewish book. The term "Old Testament," he argued, accurately represents the fundamentally different reading that Christians bring to the text. This rang true for me. Although I hope this course is accessible to people of all faiths or no faith, it is part of a three-part series that deals with the Christian Bible, and so the term "Old Testament" seems the better choice for our purposes.

- There are also differences in the order—and sometimes even the content—of the Hebrew Bible and the Old Testament as it is presented in Christian Bibles. Having different terminology allows for those distinctions to be made more clearly.

The issues can be complex, but I hope this explains why I adopted the terminology that I did. It doesn't mean this is the only right way to do it—others make different choices for equally good reasons. I was just swayed by these particular arguments and circumstances.

WELCOME: OH, HOW I LIKE JESUS

Everybody likes Jesus. People may not like religion, they may hate Christianity, they may not believe for a minute that Jesus was in any sense "divine," but when they read his teaching and examine his life, they like him. Even renowned atheist Richard Dawkins likes Jesus. You can buy "Atheists for Jesus" T-shirts and visit atheistsforJesus.com. Whatever else you might say about Christianity, you have to admit that its adherents picked a darned good central figure.

Jesus is the hub of the New Testament wheel. Different spokes go out from that hub, connecting him to the outer rim of the church, and we'll look at those spokes in time. First, however, let's turn our attention to the center and really look at the person who started it all.

To do that, we'll take three different, but overlapping, approaches. First, we will look at Jesus as a man—the human being who came to be known as Jesus of Nazareth. What does the New Testament tell us of his human life and circumstances? What does scholarship verify and where are there still questions?

The second session will help us take a look at Jesus in his religious context as a Jewish man. "Rabbi" was a title used frequently for Jesus. What did that mean in Palestine in the first century? Who were the scribes, Pharisees, and Sadducees? What were the expectations of a messiah?

In the third session we'll look at how the rabbi, Jesus of Nazareth, became Jesus the Christ—that central figure of Christian faith and practice. We'll look at the miracles, the visions, the resurrection narratives, and the foundations for the claims of Jesus' divinity.

Only with that complete picture of Jesus can we adequately understand the work of the apostles and the movement that eventually became the church. With Jesus firmly in the center, the final three sessions will move out from the hub along the spokes of the apostles and out to the rim of the great wheel of the church.

THE FOUR GOSPELS: A PRIMER

As we look at the life of Jesus, we will be reading sections of the four gospels: Matthew, Mark, Luke, and John. These are the primary sources of information about Jesus so we should know something about the books themselves. The word "gospel" means "good news," and is derived from the Anglo Saxon word "godspell." Yep, just like the musical.

The Greek word that we translate as "gospel" or "good news" is evangelion, meaning either the reward for bringing good news or the good news itself.

Poster for *Godspell* in the Cherry Lane Theatre by artist David Edward Byrd

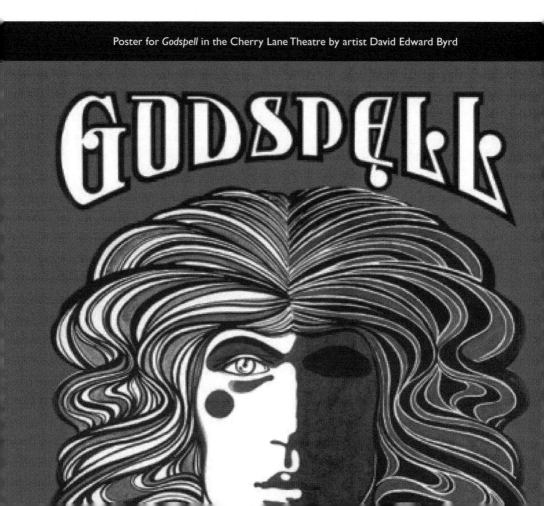

They're Not Objective

So when you pick up a Bible and see that there are four books called "gospels" and that they're the headliners for the entire New Testament, you know right off the bat that you're not dealing with neutral sources. And they don't claim to be. The gospel writers are often called the four evangelists, and with good reason. They are writing to different audiences and sometimes stress different things, but they are all writing to promote belief in Jesus.

John is the most explicit about this. He could have spoken for all the gospel writers when he says in John 20–31:

> Now Jesus did many other signs in the presence of his disciples, which are not written in this book. But these are written so that you may come to believe that Jesus is the Messiah, the Son of God, and that through believing you may have life in his name.

When you pick up the gospels, you are not reading a historian's objective account of the life of Jesus. You are reading passionate accounts of Jesus' life and ministry that are designed to lead the reader or listener toward belief. Two millennia later we would have to say that they have been extremely effective.

There were other gospels written besides these four. I've included an appendix on p. 239 that has a discussion of other writings about the New Testament period that did not make the cut into the canon of Holy Scripture. Also, as an appendix on p. 205 is the chapter from *What Is the Bible?* (the first book in this series) about the New Testament, which describes the process of selection in more detail. But this is a course about the Bible we have, not the Bible that might have been, so let's look more closely at the four gospels that begin the New Testament.

They're the Same, but Different

The first thing we notice is that the first three gospels are very similar. In fact, Matthew, Mark, and Luke are called the "Synoptic Gospels," from the Greek meaning "to see together." These three gospels tell mostly the same stories, frequently in the same order and often with the exact same wording. Scholars call this the "Synoptic Problem," but I prefer to call it the "Synoptic Puzzle."

The problem or puzzle is how to account for both the similarities and the differences together. Only 1 percent of Mark is not included in either Matthew or Luke, but 15 percent of Luke is unique to his gospel. Matthew has a slightly smaller amount of unique material than Luke, but then Matthew and Luke have a bunch of material in common that Mark doesn't have.

Puzzled? Me too. We won't solve that puzzle here, but the majority of scholars have come to believe two basic things about the Synoptic Gospels:

- Mark was written first and Matthew and Luke had Mark in front of them when they wrote their accounts.

- There was at least one other source that all three of these gospel writers had that we don't. This hypothetical source has been nicknamed "Q." (Q stands for the German word *Quelle*, which means "source.")

You can really get down in the weeds with the debate, but we'll leave it at that.

The Gospel of John is a completely different kettle of fish. John does give us some of the same material that we find in the others, but a whopping 92 percent of John's gospel is unique to John.

The content in John's gospel is presented in a more mystical way—multi-layered and very frequently symbolic. Many of those who later became adherents of Gnosticism look to John for inspiration. In John's gospel Jesus is frequently frustrated with people who take his words literally and he talks about himself in metaphors and symbols. All of the "I am" statements that Jesus makes come from John. "I am the vine." (John 15:5) "I am the bread of life." (John 6:35) "I am the light of the world." (John 8:12) "I am the way, and the truth, and the life." (John 14:6) There are seven of them, which is in itself a symbolic number.

When John does recount events found in the Synoptic Gospels, they are often significantly different either in content or order. We'll see examples of that in some of the class exercises for the first three sessions. But these differences don't exist because John couldn't get the facts straight. It could be that in some cases John knew additional information, but it's just as likely that John is working with symbolism or in some other way trying to give us an interpretation in the way he tells the story. John almost never means only what the words say on the surface.

GOSPEL **FACTOIDS**

Mark is the shortest gospel and Luke is the longest.

The author of Luke also wrote the book of Acts. Many scholars believe that Luke/Acts should be considered one account, divided into two books only because each book required an entire scroll.

Matthew has more Old Testament references than any other gospel and was likely written for a Jewish audience.

Luke has the most parables and has more stories about the the poor and powerless in society.

Mark has the most exorcisms.

In early iconography Matthew is pictured as a man, Mark as a lion, Luke as an ox, and John as an eagle.

All four Gospels are anonymous. The names used as their titles come from tradition and not the texts themselves.

Luke is written in the most elegant Greek of the four gospels.

Mark may represent the preaching of Peter.

With that in mind, let's turn our attention back a couple thousand years.

SON OF MAN

Your study Bible

This student text

Materials for taking notes

THE HISTORICAL JESUS

While the phrase "Jesus lives" is a statement of faith and belief, the phrase "Jesus lived" is not. The assertion that there once lived a Jewish man known as Jesus of Nazareth is a historical fact accepted by the vast majority of scholars. You can find naysayers, of course, but the evidence is overwhelmingly weighted toward the actual, physical existence of Jesus.

Scholars of all faiths and of no faith agree that you can take the following to the bank:

- Jesus was born a Jew somewhere between 7 and 2 B.C.E. and was raised in the insignificant Galilean village of Nazareth;

- He surely spoke Aramaic and perhaps also Hebrew and Greek;

- He was baptized by John the Baptist;

- His ministry was limited to the regions of Galilee and Judea;

- He was crucified at the order of Pontius Pilate, the Roman prefect, between 30 and 36 C.E.

However, that's where the scholarly kumbayah moment ends.

If you've ever done any genealogy work, you know that it can be very difficult to verify details, even for someone just a few generations back. Verifying historical information for someone who lived over two thousand years ago is a tricky business, and it is in those details of what, exactly, Jesus said and did that the scholarly consensus breaks up.

Not surprisingly, the breakdown is directly related to how people approach the Bible. Some take a literal view of the Bible and accept that if the Bible says something happened, it did—and in just the way the Bible describes. But even that literal approach is not as clear-cut as it might seem.

For example, what do you do when different gospels tell the same story differently? Matthew, Mark, and Luke tell us that Jesus drove the moneychangers out of the Temple at the end of his ministry—but John puts it at the beginning. Some scholars take differences like that and "harmonize" them. For them it is obvious that Jesus must have cleared out the Temple twice, once at the beginning and again at the end of his ministry. Others take the accounts literally, but

| Read Mark 11:15–19 and John 2:13–16. |

separately, allowing that each gospel writer arranged the material about the life of Jesus to help shape a unique message.

And what about areas of Jesus' life where the Bible is silent? What was he up to between the ages of two and twelve? Is it possible that he had a wife, as some early Christian communities believed? John reports at the very end of his gospel, *"But there are also many other things that Jesus did; if every one of them were written down, I suppose that the world itself could not contain the books that would be written."* (John 21:25) The Bible tells us a lot about the life of Jesus, but by its own admission it doesn't tell us everything.

For those who don't take the Bible literally, there is a dilemma. There is near-universal acceptance of the basic facts about Jesus I have listed above, making it difficult to say that everything in the Bible is pure fiction. Some significant events are, in fact, true. But how many and to what degree?

A man from an unremarkable village, with parents who held no significant places in the religion or politics of the day, gets executed for treason at about the age of thirty. That's not the biography you'd expect from someone who has human history divided into time periods before and after his death (B.C. and A.D.) or whose name is synonymous with a major world religion two thousand years after his execution. That's real staying power and inquiring minds want to know why. What else about the life and teachings of Jesus might account for his influence down through the ages, and can any of that be proven through the rigorous tests of scholarship?

SCHOLARS ON A QUEST

While some see those answers as obvious from the text, many Christians as well as other historical scholars began looking for such answers as early as 1778. Their search marked the first "Quest for the Historical Jesus," a phrase coined by Lutheran theologian and Nobel Peace Prize winner Albert Schweitzer in his book by that name. As the tools of scholarship improved, the question has been engaged again and again across the centuries. It is alive and well today in the form of the Jesus Seminar, a group of about 150 scholars and laypeople founded in 1985.

While any one of these attempts has its questionable practices and assumptions, millions of Christians today belong to denominations whose theological views and approaches to the Bible have been shaped by the general practice of looking at the Bible through the lens of critical scholarship. While not the only way to look at the Bible, an underlying principle of the *Exploring the Bible: The Dickinson Series* is that using the tools of scholarship is both a valid and faithful approach to the Scriptures.

All of that may sound scary, dry, and too focused on proving what should just be accepted on faith by those in the Christian tradition. After all, you might be thinking, there's a reason we call it "faith" rather than "knowledge." Science and religion, after all, are not opposites; they just deal with different realms and forms of knowing. In general, science and religion both need to recognize the limitations of their fields and the boundary between them and move on.

But if you have been using a study Bible for these courses (as is recommended), chances are you have benefitted from some of the efforts of these attempts to find out who the "real" Jesus was and what he actually said and did. For that reason I want to take you through some of the more common questions and assumptions that these scholars use, so you will be a little less puzzled when you run across them. Since most of these terms involve the word "criticism," remember that in academic circles that doesn't mean anything harsh. It just means a kind of evaluation or test—quality control, if you will.

Albert Schweitzer, Print of Etching by Arthur William Heintzelman, 1950

Technical term: *Textual Criticism*

What it means: The practice of looking at ancient manuscripts and sorting out what belongs to the text itself and what might be notes made in the margins by those who hand-copied the material. Wait…what? Notes in the margins?

Why it's important: Remember that even the "New" Testament texts are nearly two thousand years old. We don't have a single scrap of an "original" biblical manuscript that came directly from the pen of the author. Even the very oldest writings we have are copies of copies of copies.

Those who made those copies knew they were dealing with sacred texts, and they were careful. In fact, they were so careful that sometimes they made notes to themselves in the margins, especially if they were looking at a word on parchment that may have been torn, blurred, or otherwise unclear. Hmmm…that word might be "bull," might be "bell." Just about every Bible printed today has notes about such questions, but you find them clearly marked as notes. Ancient scribes just put those comments in the margins.

Enter the next person to copy the manuscript. Now that next person has the same bull/bell problem, but if the first scribe didn't have much room in the margin it might be even harder to tell if those extra words were added by the scribe or were part of the original. By about the fourth or fifth scribe down, there's always a chance that a marginal note has somehow become, very literally, gospel.

While that happened much less frequently than you might think under the circumstances, those who really cared about the integrity of the text needed to go back and be sure. So they called in experts in the language, scholars who had studied the ways in which both the alphabet and forms of writing evolved and had other kinds of textual expertise to try to sort it out. That's textual criticism.

Why some people don't like it: Can there be mistakes in the Bible? Throw out that question on an Internet forum and you'll probably have to change your name and address. People have very strong feelings about this, and there are four main ways that Christians answer it. One group says, "Of course there are errors," end of discussion. The three remaining groups all claim that the Bible is "inerrant," but they don't all mean the same thing.

Group one claims that the texts of the Bible are without error *in their original form*. As we've seen, we don't have any original biblical texts, so this kind of criticism has no effect on that group. They allow that errors can creep in via copying mistakes, translation missteps, and so on. For them it's good to go as far back as you can, to the earliest manuscript you can find, and clean it up.

Group two claims the Bible is inerrant in matters of faith and practice, but not in matters of history, science, and other non-religious matters. Whether this group would have problems with textual criticism depends on which text is being questioned.

Group three believes that God guarded the whole transmission process and would not have allowed for any error of any kind either in the original manuscript or in the process of copying and translating it. Since textual criticism implies that error is possible, the very concept of textual criticism is suspect to this group.

EXAMPLES:

The oldest copies of the Gospel of John do not contain what we know as John 7:53–8:11, the story of Jesus confronting the woman taken in adultery. Of course because it may not have been original to John doesn't mean it wasn't an authentic record of an event in the life of Jesus. But most Bibles have a note indicating that this section might have been added to John's gospel at a later date.

The section of Luke that tells us Jesus sweated blood in the Garden of Gethsemane and was comforted by an angel the night he was arrested (Luke 22:43–44) is also lacking in some of the older manuscripts. So is the entire ending of the Gospel of Mark. Most scholars now think that the Gospel of Mark originally ended with chapter 16, verse 8: "So they went out and fled from the tomb, for terror and amazement had seized them; and they said nothing to anyone, for they were afraid."

Scholar at his Writing Table
by Rembrandt van Rijn, 1641

Technical term: *Biblical Criticism*

What it means: The practice of looking at the context and circumstances in which the Bible was written.

Why it's important: Biblical criticism is part of what most pastors do before crafting a sermon. Using this process, they ask questions like, Who put this part of the Bible down on paper and why? Did the writer have a particular audience in mind? Was the writer trying to address a particular debate or concern? Are there idioms in the language used that might help us understand the meaning? Digging into each of those questions can help a pastor craft a better sermon—and help us better understand what we're reading.

Archaeology, anthropology, and linguistics are just a few of the academic disciplines that help us sort out these questions.

Why some people don't like it: A key part of biblical criticism is interpreting the meaning of a text in light of the culture and historical period in which it was written. Doing that implies that it's possible some teachings or even some commandments were culturally influenced and/or appropriate in that time and place but perhaps not in others.

In practice that could mean, for example, that some of the history recorded in the Old Testament might have been shaped by political agendas. It could also mean that statements and laws about family relationships, the role of women, and sexual practices might have reflected the norms of the day but weren't meant to be mandates for all time.

For many Christians, such change and influence is a given, but for many others that assumption is an assault on God's truth and sovereignty. Biblical critics are caught in the crosshairs.

EXAMPLES:

Biblical critics are the folks who let us know that when Genesis says, "Now the man knew his wife Eve…" (Genesis 4:1), the word "knew" means much more than an intellectual exercise. The result of that "knowing" was the conception of their first child. The biblical critics can tell us that when Jesus says to a Canaanite woman, "It is not fair to take the children's food and throw it to the dogs" (Matthew 15:26, Mark 7:27), he is using a common slur (dogs).

Technical term: Form Criticism

What it means: Trying to determine the original literary type or form of the text.

Why it's important: Form critics know the history of literature and the role of storytelling in human culture. They look for signs that something might have been told orally for a time before it was written down. They look for similarities between biblical accounts and other writings in the same time period.

Form critics who study the Bible tell us, for instance, which of Jesus' sayings can be identified as a parable and what role that literary form played in the culture of the time. Form critics know what made up an "epistle" in the first century, and how and why these epistles were circulated. That can be really important information, and we'll see what a difference it makes when we get to Paul's letters in Session 4.

Why some people don't like it: There are certain words and phrases that can clue us in about the nature of the literature we are reading. If you read, "In 1775 there was unrest in the British Colonies in America," the specifics of your sentence tell you that you are reading history. If you read, "Dear Charlotte…" you know you are reading a letter, and so forth.

It was the form critics who mentioned that the opening of the Old Testament book of Job begins with the Hebrew equivalent of "Once upon a time." Their study tells us that we're reading not history, but fable. The way form critics read some of the very early stories of Genesis tell us we're dealing with myth. Those who want to take every word of the Bible as historical fact are not always fans of form criticism.

EXAMPLES:

It is the form critics who figured out that the first part of Philippians 2 was in fact a hymn of the early church and realized that the song Moses and Miriam sing about the destruction of Pharaoh's army in Exodus 15 was in existence long before the rest of the material. Form critics are the ones who can identify which of the Psalms were likely used in a ritual setting and which were intended for a more private audience.

Form critics working on the New Testament will tell you that the series of statements that comprise what we now call the Sermon on the Mount in Matthew 5–8 is actually an ancient technique called "stringing pearls."

Technical terms: Redaction Criticism, Source Criticism

What it means: To redact means, basically, to edit. This type of study tries to determine to what extent a biblical writer served merely as an editor and compiler of other sources. Working closely with the redaction critic is the source critic, who tries to determine what sources the redactor was using for the editing process.

Redactors compare accounts, look for common themes, and are good at identifying the vocabulary and style of particular writers. If you've plagiarized something, it's a redactor who's going to sniff you out.

Why it's important: Beyond simply trying to identify sources, the ultimate goal of the information that redaction and source critics discover is to determine the underlying theological purpose for the work, which helps us better understand what we read and why some accounts are told multiple times in different ways.

For example, source critics found that the Gospel of Matthew quotes the Old Testament far more than any other gospel. By contrast, the Gospel of Mark often explains Jewish terms and practices. From that information, critics can tell us that it's likely that Matthew was writing to a Jewish audience, while Mark was directed more toward Gentiles who wouldn't have understood Jewish references or terms.

Why some people don't like it: Here's an example. In telling about the birth of Jesus, Matthew 1:22–23 refers to an Old Testament prophecy: "All this took place to fulfill what had been spoken by the LORD through the prophet: 'Look, the virgin shall conceive and bear a son, and they shall name him Emmanuel,' which means, 'God is with us.'"

The source critic asks, "Okay, what prophet? Where?" The answer is Isaiah 7:14. The critic turns to Isaiah and throws a flag. Isaiah was originally written in Hebrew and the Hebrew word there means simply "young woman," with no reference to her sexual status. But when Matthew quotes the passage in Greek, he chooses a word with a different meaning. So is the word "virgin" Matthew's interpretation? Or was he using another source?

For help, the source critic digs deeper and finds the following answer. When Greek became the language of much of the world after the conquests of Alexander the Great, tradition reports that a group of seventy Jewish scholars gathered in Egypt and translated the Old Testament into Greek. This translation, known as the Septuagint (or LXX, after the seventy scholars who worked on it), was widely used in the Jewish community. When those scholars got to Isaiah 7:14, they chose a more particular Greek word that meant "virgin."

The source critic informs the redactor that the writer of the Gospel of Matthew was using the Septuagint instead of the Hebrew Bible as his source for Old Testament quotations. The Greek of Matthew 1:23 is, word for word, the Greek of the LXX.

Does that mean that Mary was not a virgin? No, a young woman could certainly be a virgin. But having that information from source criticism cracks open a door that plenty of people resent redactors for cracking.

EXAMPLES:

Redactors and source critics who tell us that the books of Chronicles and Kings provide different accounts of the same period because Kings was using

The Annunciation (Study 4) by Sorin Dumitrescu

sources written and edited in Babylon and Chronicles was using sources written and edited by the Jewish community in Egypt.

Redactors think stories common to the first three gospels were included because the writers of all three gospels were looking at a common set of stories about Jesus (which the source critics have nicknamed the "Q"). Redactors believe that John probably had Matthew, Mark, and Luke in front of him when he wrote his gospel.

FOR **REFLECTION**

Which of these approaches to Bible study is the most interesting to you?

Do any of them feel uncomfortable? Why or why not?

Do you think the work of biblical criticism is important? Why or why not?

Faith and Scholarship

No scholarly effort can prove or disprove the faith claims of Christianity. Scholars and scientists of various types can help us understand the books, stories, and world of the Bible, and this has enormous value. We often get stuck in our Bible reading because we're trying to find something that the Bible was never meant to give us. But no scholar or scientist in any discipline can prove or disprove the existence of God, the resurrection of Jesus, the work of the Holy Spirit, or anything of the kind. Those are faith matters and are beyond the ken of science. Christians have no need to be afraid of biblical scholarship.

CAN ANYTHING GOOD COME FROM NAZARETH?

Beyond what historians agree on about the life of Jesus, what else does the Bible itself claim about Jesus as a human being? We'll deal with the faith claims in Session 3 and the Jewishness of Jesus in Session 2. But what of Jesus the man? What was his life like?

Read John 1:35–51.

The gospel accounts agree that Jesus was the son of Mary and Joseph, who made their home in Nazareth. Matthew has them settle in Nazareth after Jesus' birth and Luke has them living in Nazareth before the birth of Jesus, but everybody puts the family there when Jesus was very young.

Nazareth was East Podunk. It was a nowhere town in the broader region known as Galilee. In the Gospel of John, when Jesus is calling his disciples, Jesus asks Philip to join him. Philip joins gladly and then runs off to find Nathanael. Philip says to Nathanael in John 1:45, "We have found him about whom Moses in the law and also the prophets wrote, Jesus son of Joseph from Nazareth." Instead of jumping up in amazement, Nathanael sneers, "Can anything good come out of Nazareth?" That was the reputation. It wasn't exactly an up-and-coming town.

Nazareth had no paved roads, no public buildings or inscriptions, and fewer than four hundred residents at the time of Jesus. Archaeologists working there have found some locally made, purely functional pottery, a few underground cisterns for water, grinding stones for grain and vats for wine, but not much

1ST Century Galilee

else. Some of the land was terraced for farming and there was a stone quarry. There were no imported wares, no fancy mosaics—not even any plain ones. There was no glass.

HOME AND SYNAGOGUE

Matthew and Mark both tell us that Jesus went home and preached in the synagogue in Nazareth, and all the artwork of the event puts him in a building. He may well have been indoors somewhere, but it is unlikely that Nazareth had a special building devoted to that purpose—or at least archaeologists haven't found one. Puzzled, we turn to our friends in biblical criticism, the folks who teach us about the customs, history, and practices of the time.

Read Luke 4:14–22.

"What about the synagogue in Nazareth?" we ask. As it turns out, the word "synagogue" in the first century referred to the gathering of the people, whether they gathered in a specially dedicated space or in someone's home. In Sunday School we used to sing the hymn "We Are the Church" by Richard K. Avery and Donald S. Marsh, which includes the line: "The church is not a building, the church is not a steeple, the church is not a resting place, the church is a people." It was the same with the first-century synagogue, which referred to the people, whether or not there was a building dedicated to meeting and worship. So Jesus could well have read from a scroll at a synagogue service in his hometown, even though it appears that Nazareth didn't have a formal building devoted to that purpose.

If they gathered in a home, what might that have looked like? Homes in first-century Nazareth were stone and mud with thatched roofs. Interior walls would have been rubbed with plaster and perhaps decorated with paint. Most homes were a single room, often divided into public and private areas. Some areas of the home were on a raised platform. Those with more than one room would have had a central courtyard for cooking. Outside stairs often led to a rooftop living area partly shaded by matting or a partial tent.

A home in Nazareth might have had a small window or two up toward the roof, but mostly indoor rooms were dark, lit by oil lamps. Work was done either in the courtyard or on the roof. There would not have been furniture, as we know it—no tables, beds, and so on, although there might have been a stool or two or perhaps a chest. Nooks and shelves provided a place to put lamps, utensils, bedrolls, and clothes; there were separate storage areas, some underground, for larger jars. Cushions, pillows, and mats provided comfort for seating and sleeping on the floor.

Of course, much fancier homes existed at the time, but not in the rural back-water of Nazareth.

I LOVE **TRASH**

How can we possibly know these details about ancient places? Well, the short answer is that everything is guesswork when it comes to how ancient people lived. But that guesswork is often based on strong circumstantial evidence, and a lot of that evidence comes from trash.

continued on next page

When an archaeologist digs and discovers old walls or other remnants of a city or village, somewhere on that site are usually one or more trash heaps known to archaeologists as middens. While some things in that trash decayed and disappeared long ago, other things are still present and available for study.

Bones, for example. Are there charred cow bones in the midden? Chances are good that the people who lived there ate beef. And if there are charred pig bones or mollusk shells, chances are good that it's not a Jewish neighborhood or at least not a neighborhood where strict Jewish law was practiced.

Pieces of pottery also have many stories to tell. Finding a pot in one piece is always nice, but even the broken bits—called shards—can reveal much about a people. Pottery shards can show what ancient period a pot comes from and where it originated based on shape, design, and the material used. If archaeologists find Chinese designs on pottery in an ancient Italian village, they know that either the pot or its owner has traveled—the dig site might be on a trade route or it might be the remains of a village of mercenary soldiers, for example.

Middens can tell an archaeologist what people ate, what tools they used, and if the climate and soil conditions are right; preserved clothing can show what people wore and what the ancient weather conditions were like.

IF I HAD A HAMMER

Joseph (and perhaps Jesus early on) was a carpenter by trade. In a town like Nazareth that would have meant basic, rough work—but it didn't mean only working with wood. The Greek term used for "carpenter" is broader and could have referred to any trade involved in building. A carpenter could have made shelves or platforms and put in roof timbers, but he also might have thatched the roof or plastered a wall or worked on some other part of getting a house up and useable.

Workmen used hand tools and got their lumber by cutting down a tree, not by ordering from the lumberyard. A carpenter might have been in the skilled or unskilled labor category, but physical strength would have been necessary to get much work.

Since Nazareth was so small, it's likely that a first-century carpenter traveled to other towns in the region to find work. When Jesus was growing up, the nearby city of Sepphoris was being rebuilt to suit Herod Anitpas (the son of the Herod at Jesus' birth), and a good carpenter could probably have found plenty of employment there.

Probably Joseph's work also included crafting yokes for donkeys and oxen, ploughs, and other agricultural tools. Since there is no indication that Nazareth imported anything, all the citizens of Nazareth were likely farmers in addition to their primary trades.

But this aspect of life was in flux as Jesus grew. Once the rebuilding of Sepphoris was completed, Herod Antipas set about making it a center of wealth, buying up land in neighboring towns and villages and then leasing it back to the one-time owners to produce crops of his choosing. Local economies were devastated and families lost any way of providing for themselves.

MMMM... **FOOD**

Scott Korb's *Life In Year One* (Riverhead Books: NY, 2010) does a good job of describing the food that would have been commonplace in a Jewish village of the first century, so I quote from it here:

What people ate in the first century constituted a fairly typical agrarian diet of the Mediterranean... They ate olives and olive oil, figs, dates, pomegranates, legumes, cheese, and different butters (churned at home), on rare occasion some small amount of beef, veal, lamb, or mutton, fish, if you lived near the coasts, and small roasted fowls. Cow or goat milk would have been drunk fresh or processed into yogurt (also a drink), which would have given them whey, which they would have likewise consumed.

Since fermentation was the best way to preserve grape juice (or even the juice of pomegranates or dates), wine was ubiquitous...beer was a fairly common drink in Palestine...There were some vegetables—onions, garlic, and dandelion greens, to name a few—as well as nuts, other wild greens, and berries...You could count on every meal to begin with some bread, and bread would have made up some 70 percent of the calories a person would have consumed in a given day...the same word used for bread, lehem, was used for food in general... and rather than using plates, most of what was served—from olives to lentils to that rare piece of meat or fish—was scooped out or laid across a piece of pita. (pp. 82-83)

If Joseph did look for work in other cities, the work did not make him rich. Mary and Joseph were poor when Jesus was born. How do we know? Well, apart from settling in lowly Nazareth, the Gospel of Luke tells us that when Joseph and Mary brought Jesus to the Temple to satisfy the Law of Moses, they brought the offering specified for poor people.

> **Read Luke 2:21–40.**

Leviticus 12 specified that after bearing a male child, the mother had to wait forty days before she could go to the Temple to be ritually purified and an offering was required. The preferred offering was a lamb, but Leviticus 12:8 gives an option of two turtledoves or two young pigeons for those who can't afford a lamb. Luke 2:24 tells us that it was this poorer offering that Mary brought.

There are very few stories about Joseph, and those center on Jesus' birth and early years. So although it's not actually stated in the texts, it's assumed that Joseph died before the start of Jesus' ministry.

All the information discovered about life in first-century Palestine gives us some sense of the world in which Jesus lived. Understanding that life gives us a basis for understanding many of the metaphors Jesus uses in his parables and teaching. We can now read a phrase like "bread of life" through the eyes of someone who got 70 percent of his calories each day from bread instead of through the lens of a low-carb diet. But the Bible also gives us a more intimate portrait of Jesus as a man. Let's turn to that now.

THE HUMAN JESUS

FAMILY

Like all of us, Jesus was born as a baby into a family: a mother named Mary and a father named Joseph who worked as a carpenter. As we've noted earlier, they were not a wealthy couple, and they settled in the unremarkable village of Nazareth in the broader geographic area known as Galilee.

The Bible speaks of Jesus having brothers and sisters. When Jesus is teaching in his hometown, the people say in Matthew 13:55–56, "Is not this the carpenter's son? Is not his mother called Mary? And are not his brothers James and Joseph and Simon and Judas? And are not all his sisters with us?" Mark 6:3 records basically the same conversation. St. Paul in Galatians 1:19 reports, "I did not see any other apostle except James the Lord's brother." Matthew 12:46, Luke 8:19, Mark 3:31 all say that Jesus' mother and brothers are waiting to speak to him. John 7:5 reports that his brothers did not believe in him. Mark 3:21 goes even further and talks of his family actually coming to restrain him, thinking he had lost his mind!

You can find people arguing about Jesus' family online, which may seem odd until you realize that church traditions differ in their teachings about Mary.

Almost universally, Christian traditions view the conception of Jesus as miraculous—"born of the Virgin Mary." However, a large group of Christians come from traditions that teach that Mary remained a virgin throughout her life and that Jesus, conceived by the Holy Spirit, was her only child. Thus Jesus' family becomes one more thing that Christians fight about. The bickering is, however, unnecessary.

Holy Family by Marc Chagall, 1976

The Bible tells us next to nothing about Joseph. Most scholars think he died early in Jesus' life, since he is not mentioned in any of the stories of Jesus' adulthood. Was he older when he married Mary? Was he a widower with children from another marriage? We have no way of knowing any of that. The Bible tells us that Jesus had siblings, but not if those siblings had the same mother.

What we believe about Mary's virginity cannot be proven or disproven. It is a matter of faith. For some it matters greatly, for others it matters little. What

---

OH, **MARY**

The name Mary, or Miriam in the Hebrew, was very common in Jesus' day, just as it is today. The life of Jesus is full of Marys and we can get very mixed up if we don't pay attention to which Mary is being discussed in a certain passage. Here are the most important four.

Best known is **Mary, the mother of Jesus**. She is the first Mary we meet in the gospels, and once Jesus is born, Mary's role as mother is almost always used as an identifier. We will learn more about her in Session 2.

Next on the list of famous Marys is **Mary of Magdala, better known as Mary Magdalene**. There is not a shred of evidence, circumstantial or otherwise, that she was ever a prostitute. The gospel accounts don't tell us when she first met Jesus, but Luke 8:1–3 tells us that Jesus once drove seven demons out of her and that she was one of several women who traveled with Jesus and helped finance his mission. She is at the cross when Jesus dies and is at least one of the first, if not the first witness to the resurrection. See her entry in Appendix 2 on p. 228 for more.

continued on next page

OH, **MARY** Cont.

We also have **Mary of Bethany**, sister of Martha and Lazarus—we'll learn about her in this chapter as one of Jesus' friends. Although she was frequently confused with Mary Magdalene in various medieval accounts, most scholars believe Mary of Bethany and Mary Magdalene were two separate people.

John's gospel gives us a Mary puzzle. In John 19:25 he says, "Standing near the cross of Jesus were his mother, and his mother's sister, **Mary the wife of Clopas**, and Mary Magdalene." Tradition names Clopas as the brother of Joseph and thus the sister-in-law of Mary the mother of Jesus.

The text, however, could be referencing either three or four women, depending on whether "his mother's sister" was meant to define "Mary the wife of Clopas." Since there was no punctuation in Greek documents, it's only guesswork. It could have been that both Mary's sister (possibly Salome—see the entry for James, the Elder, in Appendix 2 on p. 222) and Mary's sister-in-law (Mary the wife of Clopas) were there along with Jesus' mother and Mary Magdalene.

we do know from the biblical text is that Jesus knew what it was like to have a mother, brothers, and sisters in his home. He perhaps experienced the loss of a father at an early age. Jesus' mother and siblings were sometimes there for him and sometimes thought he was in a bit over his head. Some siblings doubted him, some apparently became church leaders. Some may even have been among his closest disciples, although the names of his brothers were common ones throughout the region. His mother was with him when he died.

FRIENDS

We know that Jesus had disciples. The word "disciple" means one who studies to become like a master, and there were multitudes who could be considered "disciples" of Jesus. Of those multitudes, Jesus hand-picked twelve to receive special teaching and who were given special access to Jesus. Of those twelve, there were three—Peter, James, and John—who were singled out from the twelve as Jesus' most trusted inner circle. Undoubtedly all of those twelve disciples (sometimes referred to in the Bible as "The Twelve") were friends of Jesus to some extent or other, with the closest being Peter, James, and John. You can read the biographies of the twelve disciples on p. 217.

Any pastor can tell you, however, that friendships in a local congregation have boundaries that other friendships don't have. The same is true for teachers and students. Did Jesus have any friends who didn't expect things from him apart from the love and kindness born of the friendship itself? Were there people who would welcome him if he wasn't in the mood for teaching, healing, or doing anything particularly remarkable?

It seems that there were: Lazarus, Martha, and Mary—a family of siblings who lived in Bethany, a small town just outside of Jerusalem.

Jesus' home away from home seems to have been the home of Lazarus, Mary (this is *not* Mary Magdalene), and Martha. When he travels to Jerusalem, he seems to always stop by, perhaps even staying there.

There are three stories in the gospels about members of this family.

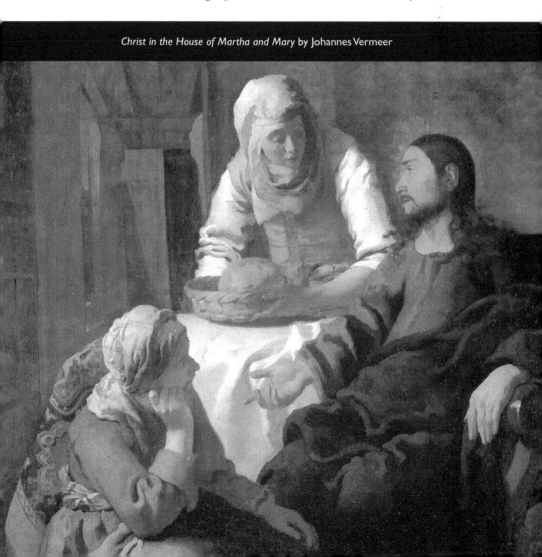

Christ in the House of Martha and Mary by Johannes Vermeer

Luke paints a portrait of the two sisters in Luke 10:38–42. He writes that Martha invited Jesus into her home, but then gets annoyed when her sister, Mary, sits at Jesus' feet and listens to him while Martha does all the work. Martha complains to Jesus that Mary isn't helping and Jesus famously responds, *"Martha, Martha, you are worried and distracted by many things; there is need of only one thing. Mary has chosen the better part, which will not be taken away from her."*

We should note that when the Bible describes Mary as sitting at the Lord's feet and listening, this is the language and the posture used for the relationship between a master and a disciple of the day (thank you, biblical criticism). While all twelve disciples were men, there were clearly women who fit into that category too, and in this passage this honor seems to be bestowed on Mary of Bethany.

The next time we see Mary and Martha is in the Gospel of John, chapter 11. They're distressed because their brother Lazarus is seriously ill. When your brother is at death's door and one of your best friends is known for healing miracles, you know whom to call. Mary and Martha send for Jesus with the words, "Lord, he whom you love is ill."

The Raising of Lazarus after Rembrandt by Vincent Van Gogh, 1890

This is a long and famous story for a number of reasons. If you've ever been to a Christian funeral, chances are you've heard passages from it. It is a miracle story—Jesus raises Lazarus from the dead—but I include it here because of the human side of Jesus that it reveals.

> **Read John 11:1–57.**
> Raising of Lazarus.

The first thing we see is that these four people—Jesus, Lazarus, Mary, and Martha—love each other deeply. You can see it in the actions, but it is also stated plainly in the text. We also see a very emotional Jesus, which is puzzling at first. Jesus knows he has come to raise Lazarus from the dead—in fact he doesn't come at the first word of illness for that very reason. The outcome of the story is not something Jesus questions. (John 11:11–15)

Yet when he gets to the tomb of his friend and sees Mary, Martha, and the others in such distress, Jesus himself weeps. It's actually the shortest verse in the entire Bible—John 11:35—"Jesus wept." (NIV) Why weep when he knows what he has come to do? It is a human moment.

In another human moment, those who see Jesus crying ask what people have been asking in times of tragedy every since, "Could not he who opened the eyes of the blind man have kept this man from dying?" (John 11:37).

> **FOR REFLECTION**
>
> Why do you think Jesus wept upon arriving at Lazarus' tomb?
>
> Have you ever shed tears in sympathy for the grief of others?

THE LAZARUS **TRADITION**

The Bible tells us that after Jesus raised Lazarus from the dead, those in power sought to kill not only Jesus, but Lazarus as well (John 12:9–11). Eastern Orthodox tradition claims that Lazarus fled Judea and went to Cyprus, where Paul and Barnabas made him the first Bishop of Kition (present-day Larnaka on the south coast of Cyprus). In 890 C.E. a tomb was found in Larnaka bearing the inscription "Lazarus the friend of Christ." Those remains were transferred to Constantinople in 898 on the order of Emperor Leo VI of Byzantium. When Constantinople was sacked in 1204, the remains were taken by Crusaders to Marseilles, France, and were promptly lost.

continued on next page

This story has everything in it. We see complex family and friend relationships. We see Jesus the miracle worker and Jesus the human mingled together. We see friends and disciples struggling to understand just who this person was, and we see the event that, in the Gospel of John at least, was the catalyst for Jesus' arrest and execution.

The raising of Lazarus also helps to explain the third appearance of Mary of Bethany, which comes in John 12. Jesus is again visiting Mary, Martha, and Lazarus just six days before his last meal on earth. Martha again serves dinner, and during the evening Mary takes a very expensive perfume and uses it to anoint Jesus' feet, wiping his feet dry with her hair.

Apparently Jesus has at least some of his twelve disciples in tow, since Judas Iscariot objects loudly to this, saying that there were better ways to use money than spending it on costly perfume. Jesus responds, "Leave her alone. She bought it so that she might keep it for the day of my burial. You always have the poor with you, but you do not always have me." (John 12:7–8)

This story also appears in Matthew 26:6–13 and Mark 14:3–9 but with some variation. In those versions the meal and anointing also take place in Bethany, but the woman is not identified and it's the disciples in general rather than Judas specifically who object. And in Matthew's and Mark's versions, the story takes place not in the home of Lazarus but that of Simon the Leper. Jesus' response in all three accounts, however, is the same; Matthew and Mark add that the woman's actions should be told throughout the world in remembrance of her.

We can't know whether this gesture—at once both humble and grand—was made by Mary of Bethany or some other woman in the town. But given what we've seen of the relationship in the other two stories, it's easy to imagine that it's Mary of Bethany, surely grateful to the friend who brought her brother back from the dead.

The perfume used, nard, was chiefly a burial perfume, which Mary and Martha would have recently purchased for their brother. But why would they get some for Jesus? Consider this. The average life expectancy for a first-century man in Palestine was twenty-nine years. Jesus is past that age, his mother is presumably a widow, and Mary, Martha, and Lazarus have the means to host dinners for not only Jesus but at least several of his disciples as well. It's easy to see why this gesture might have been a gift of overwhelming gratitude to a beloved friend.

FULLY HUMAN

Although our focus naturally shifts to the stories about miracles, power, and wisdom, many places in the Bible show us a Jesus who simply knew what it was like to be human. He grew up in a family in a small village with not much going for it. He went hungry at times; he got tired enough to fall asleep in the bottom of a boat in a storm. He got frustrated with his disciples and called them dense. He got angry and cursed a fig tree for not having figs when he was hungry, even though it wasn't the season for figs. He felt compassion; he grieved the loss of his friend Lazarus with real tears. He went to weddings with his mother. In his fatigue, Jesus even used an insult (dog) for a Canaanite woman. He was homeless and depended on others for support.

Jesus felt righteous indignation at the Temple economic system, made a whip, and drove the merchants and moneychangers out. He called religious leaders nasty names. He worked from dawn until dark. He was anxious enough to sweat drops of blood. He said important prayers that were answered with a "No." He was strong enough to carry his own cross for a time, even after being severely beaten. He knew what it was like both to be revered and to be mocked. He knew torture and death.

It is faith in the signs of Jesus' authority and divinity that leads people to worship Jesus. It is the wisdom of Jesus' teaching and example that leads people to respect Jesus. But I think it is fair to say that it is the Jesus who lived and laughed, suffered and died as we all do—the fully human Jesus—who leads people to love Jesus.

While the Jesus of the Bible does amazing things that we can hardly imagine happening, his mass appeal comes from the fact that he is a teacher who is fully accessible to his students as a human being. We don't just see a triumphant resurrection. We see a man pleading with God for a less painful road, and a brave man bearing up under brutal injustice. We don't just see a superhero casting out demons, we see a man wrestling with his own demonic temptations to fame, power, and glory.

For the Christian, knowing that Jesus lived a human life, starting from scratch as a baby without any human advantage, can sometimes be all we need to get up in the morning and keep going. For us, it can sometimes seem that to disbelieve in Jesus would be to disbelieve in ourselves. The humanity of Jesus allows us to remain hopeful for our own humanity. And for that we love him.

PREPARATION FOR CHECK-IN

(Prepare for the next group session by thinking about and writing a brief response to these two questions.)

What is one thing that was new to me in this material?

What is one question that this week's topic raises for me?

HOMEWORK

(ALL STUDENTS)

☐ Read all of Sessions 1 and 2 in your Student Text, including the Bible passages in the clear boxes. Think about the reflection questions you find along the way.

☐ Begin reading the Gospel of Luke with a goal of finishing the entire gospel by the end of Session 3. There are twenty-four chapters in Luke so you'll need to do approximately twelve chapters per week to finish by Session 3. If you want to keep going, just jump into Acts. That's what you'll be reading in Sessions 4 through 6.

EXTRA MILE

(CEU AND CERTIFICATE STUDENTS)

☐ Read the section on p. 6 of the Student Text about the various types of criticism carefully. Research the "Q" source and write five hundred to seven hundred words reflecting on its importance to the gospels.

☐ Begin reading the gospels with the goal of finishing all four gospels by the end of Session 3.

SON OF DAVID

JESUS, THE JEW

Jesus was a Jewish man. He was born a Jew, he lived as a Jew, and he died as a Jew. The vast majority of scholars—of all faiths and of no faith—accept this as fact.

JOSEPHUS

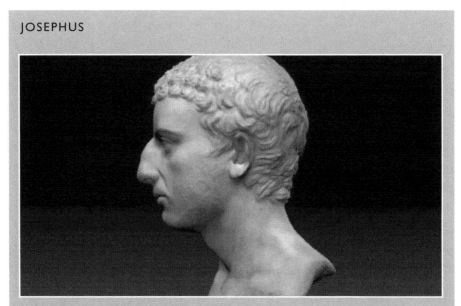

Bust of Titus Flavius Josephus

The lion's share of what we know about Judaism in the first century comes from the ancient historian Titus Flavius Josephus. You have already heard his name and you will hear it plenty more, so it pays to know a bit about him.

He was born in Jerusalem in 37 B.C.E. with the name Joseph ben Matityahu. His father was from the priestly line and his mother claimed descent from the Hasmonean kings. It was the Hasmoneans who ruled during the brief period of Jewish independence from roughly 140–37 B.C.E. Josephus was a scholar from a wealthy family, but he was also a soldier, leading the forces in Galilee against the Romans in 66 C.E.

In the year 67, however, Josephus decided he was on the losing side and surrendered to the Roman commander, Vespasian. During that surrender, Josephus mentioned that he thought Jewish messianic prophecies pointed to Vespasian being that long-awaited messiah. Vespasian had no quarrel with that and decided that Josephus would be handy to have around, so he took Josephus on as a high-ranking slave and interpreter.

continued on next page

In the final session we'll look at how Christianity came to separate from its Jewish origins, but that happened at least decades if not centuries after the death of Jesus. As you read the gospels, unless someone is specifically named as a Gentile, Canaanite, Samaritan, or other nationality, you're meeting people who considered themselves to be Jews and who practiced Jewish faith to one degree or another.

In this chapter, I want to take a little bit of time to lay out the information we have in the Bible about the heritage and practices of Jesus and the specifically Jewish context in which he lived. Along the way we'll look at the political climate and all the various groups we'll encounter in the pages of the gospels.

GENEALOGY

If you've read through the Old Testament, you know that quite a bit of ink was spent on long genealogies. You may not have found them particularly engaging, but establishing someone's lineage was important for the biblical writers. Why?

Judaism was and still is a complex combination of ethnic, national, and religious factors. Someone born to a Jewish mother is automatically considered a Jew, even if he or she doesn't actively practice Jewish faith. Sometimes even if you convert to another faith you are still considered a Jew. People with no Jewish relatives in their lineage can also convert to the Jewish faith and be considered a Jew. The situation is complex enough to require an entire Wikipedia article called "Who Is a Jew?" Look there if you want to know more.

For our purposes, we need only know that if you wanted to be a leader of any type in the Judaism of the first century, it was helpful to your cause to show that you were biologically as well as religiously descended from Abraham. Two of the four gospels take pains to show this connection for Jesus as they seek to convince their readers to become his followers.

Son of David

The first line of the New Testament begins, "An account of the genealogy of Jesus the Messiah, the son of David, the son of Abraham." (Matthew 1:1). If you were paying attention in the previous course in this series, you'll remember that David isn't technically the son of Abraham—at least a thousand years separated them. Likewise, Jesus is not biologically the son of David. A thousand years, give or take, separated them as well. The word "son" in the Bible can mean the immediate biological child of a person, or it can be used to reflect someone's biological, cultural, or spiritual heritage.

King David (Le roi David)
by Marc Chagall, 1963

What Matthew is trying to say with his genealogy is that Jesus is descended from Abraham (the patriarch of Judaism) and from David (the kingly line). Matthew is writing to a primarily Jewish audience, so he seeks to establish the ethnic Jewish bona fides of Jesus early on. Luke also includes the genealogy of Jesus in Luke 3:23–38. Luke's audience is a bit different and so Luke takes pains to trace the line of Jesus not only to Abraham but all the way back to Adam, perhaps to help stress Paul's point that Jesus was the "last Adam." (1 Corinthians 15:45)

Matthew's genealogy is that of Joseph. But wait, if Jesus was born of a virgin, why would Joseph matter? The answer is that you only had to be a legal heir to inherit the throne. A little later in this chapter we'll look at what being "the Messiah" meant to various people and groups. Matthew's opening claim and subsequent genealogy of Joseph show us that part of the equation for him was to show that Jesus was a legitimate heir to the throne of David.

Debate swirls about whether Luke's genealogy is that of Mary or Joseph, since there are some differences in detail. Whichever

He Is Born. Only Matthew and Luke have accounts of Jesus' birth. Read the first two chapters of both gospels.

it is, it is clear from references outside these genealogies that Jesus also had a Jewish mother. Luke tells us that Mary is kin to Elizabeth (the mother of John the Baptist), and that Elizabeth is a descendant of Moses' brother, Aaron. Remember that Aaron was the first Jewish priest, and his descendants laid claim to the priesthood ever after. Christians reading these genealogies often see significance in Jesus being an heir to both the kingly (Joseph) and priestly (Mary) lines of Judaism.

Mary and Elizabeth by Kathe Kollwitz (1867-1945)

Of course the genealogy of Jesus is not the only indication of the Jewishness of Jesus. When Jesus is eight days old, his parents take him to be circumcised and named according to Jewish law (Leviticus 12:1–8). We saw back on p. 17 that they also followed the instruction for the purification of a mother after giving birth.

Luke 2:21–24 tells us that all these laws were followed. The gospels tell us that Mary and Joseph were faithful in taking their family to Jerusalem every year for Passover, and we get a lot of detail about one year's visit when Jesus was twelve.

Because going to Jerusalem for Passover was required and because travel was difficult and dangerous, people traveled in groups of family and friends. Travel between Jerusalem and Nazareth by car takes an hour and forty-three minutes—two hours and twenty minutes in traffic. It's a little over 63 miles (102 km). But that's a direct route and requires passing through Samaria, which wasn't done in Jesus' day—Jesus and his family would have skirted around it. And it's hot (or, alternatively, rainy), and this group of pilgrims

FROM NAZARETH TO JUDAH   LUKE 1:26–29, 39–

from Nazareth had pack animals with supplies, as well as children. So for them, it took the better part of a week to make the trip one way.

Jesus and his family made that trip every year and the gospel tells us a story about what happened when Jesus was twelve. A day or so into the journey, Mary and Joseph notice that Jesus doesn't seem to be anywhere in their large group—not with his best buddies, not with aunts, uncles, or cousins. So they turn back. It takes them three days to find their son. Where do they find him? In the Temple with the teachers, asking questions and listening.

Mary and Joseph are none too pleased. Joseph is already losing about three week's work to attend the festival and now it's going to be a month and their safe, family group has gone on without them. "Child, why have you treated us like this? Look, your father and I have been searching for you in great anxiety." Jesus famously responds, "Why were you searching for me? Did you not know that I must be in my Father's house?" (Luke 2:48–49) (This may be the real reason that Mary and Joseph were made saints.)

The story tells us that Jesus lived a Jewish life and continued to do so as an adult. In the gospel accounts he attends synagogue and also teaches there. He is called "rabbi." He and his disciples are questioned when they violate Jewish Sabbath laws; he travels to Jerusalem for Passover. Jesus is a Jewish man with Jewish disciples living in a Jewish nation under Roman rule. He actively resists the expansion of his ministry to other peoples and areas, although he relents for a few individual circumstances.

It is decades after Jesus' death before anyone is called a Christian, and at least many decades if not centuries after his death that Christianity definitively splits from Judaism to become a distinct religion. What we read in the gospels are the stories about the origins of one particular branch of Judaism that later split from its Jewish origins to become a distinct and different faith.

But the conflicts we read about here aren't conflicts between Christians and Jews—after all, there are no Christians to be in conflict with. There are conflicts between Romans and Jews, Samaritans and Jews, and between a number of different Jewish factions, some religious and some political, vying for power and authority in an unsettled age. Let's look at some of those factions next.

THE SETTING

Jesus was born during a fractured and distressed period in Jewish history. The broad period in which he lived is known in religious studies as the "Second Temple" period. If you remember from the last course, King Solomon built the First Temple in Jerusalem during the tenth century B.C.E. Babylon razed it to the ground in 586 B.C.E. and carted the people off to Babylon. When Cyrus the Great led the Persians to victory over Babylon, he let the Jewish captives go home to rebuild the temple and the story of that effort is told in the Old Testament books of Ezra and Nehemiah. That was in 538 B.C.E.

The efforts of Ezra and Nehemiah built the Second Temple, although we are told in Ezra 3:12 that those old enough to remember Solomon's Temple wept in grief at the sight of the new one. The second was not nearly as glorious as the first. In the decades right before Jesus' birth, King Herod the Great apparently agreed with that assessment and began massive renovations and upgrades to that second temple. Those renovations were still going on during Jesus' day and still were incomplete when Rome sacked the whole

Model of Herod's Second Temple in Jerusalem

thing again in 70 C.E. That whole era—from Ezra/Nehemiah to the Roman destruction—is known as the Second Temple period.

It was a difficult period from start to finish. Empires came and went. The Jews rose up in revolt against repressive regimes, took over for a while (courtesy of the Maccabean revolt), and then were squashed again. In the midst of the political upheaval and intrigues, there were religious debates and divisions. People were conflicted over how much religious leaders like the high priest should be involved in governing the nation as well as theological questions about the nature of God, human freedom, and how strictly religious law should be applied.

In a more stable society, most people would probably ignore most of those debates. And probably the majority of folks were just trying to get by and keep themselves out of the notice of the Romans. But in the absence of a single established form of Jewish law and practice, more people than usual were exposed to the various ideas being debated. Different Jewish groups sprang up in the vacuum. They were all Jews, but they held some competing beliefs about God and the world, which led them to establish different groups with different practices. As with the various Christian denominations today, sometimes they got along, and sometimes they didn't.

Into this swirling vortex of empires, theologies, wars, and intrigues walks Jesus.

WHO'S WHO

During the years of Jesus' ministry, there were three or four major groups that played a role in Jewish thought and practice. But in our Bible reading we also encounter other groups that represent professional, political, and foreign influence in first-century Palestine. Remember that this land borders the Mediterranean and, with desert to the east, this little strip of earth has always been a key holding for those who want access to the bustling trade prospects in the west. Jesus encounters people from all sorts of groups at all levels of society, so let's take some time to understand who they all are.

Pharisees

The group getting the most ink in the gospels is the Pharisees. St. Paul identifies himself as a Pharisee. Nicodemus (of "you must be born again" fame in John 3) is a Pharisee. Jesus eats with Pharisees (Luke 7:36), cleverly avoids their legal traps (Mark 12:13–17), debates with them (Matthew 15:1–20), and both acknowledges their authority and lashes out against their hypocrisy (Matthew 23:1–36). The writings of Paul actually provide one of the few surviving examples of the writings of a Pharisee, giving us a unique glimpse into their methods and beliefs. So who were they?

The Pharisees first show up as a named group in 150 B.C.E. during the period of Jewish self-rule known as the Hasmonean Dynasty. During this period they operate largely as a political party, pushing the nation's rulers to keep to their Jewish roots and to avoid as much Greek influence as possible. We covered this period at the end of Course 2, and you can read about it in the books of the Maccabees found in the Apocrypha.

You wouldn't necessarily know it from the gospel accounts, but the Pharisees were very popular with the middle and lower classes. Although we know that Jesus considered them to be too bound to the letter of the Law, they actually allowed for more flexibility in interpretation than the other groups we'll look at. Most of them were probably laity, although some may well have been priests. They sought political power and influence, but rarely achieved it.

> **Read Matthew 15:1–20.**
> Tradition.

When it came to the Law of Moses, or Torah, the Pharisees believed there were two parts: the written law (what we have in the first five books of the Bible) and the traditions of the elders (later known as the oral law). They believed that God gave some laws to Moses in writing but also gave a lot of spoken instruction to help Moses interpret the written law and adapt it to future situations. This oral law, or tradition, was just as important to them and, over time, became the larger body of laws in later Judaism. It is this oral law that is at the root of the debate about "traditions" in Matthew 15.

The flexibility that came from using this oral tradition to interpret biblical texts allowed Judaism to bend and stretch during all the political upheavals of the Second Temple period and beyond. The Pharisees could hold on when

The Pharisees and the Sadduccees Come to Tempt Jesus (Les pharisiens et les saduceens viennent pour tenter Jesus) by James Tissot, 1886-1894

others could not and therefore became the root from which Rabbinic Judaism and all subsequent forms of Jewish life and faith sprang.

But following the traditions was not the only thing that distinguished the Pharisees. They believed a person would be resurrected to either reward or punishment after death. They believed in angels. When it came to free will, the Pharisees took a middle road. They believed that God did intervene in human affairs (hello, angels), but rejected any notion of predestination. God allowed for real human freedom and then occasionally stepped in to help people from whatever messes they had gotten themselves into.

The Pharisees themselves had divisions, however, when it came to the nature and role of government. Some believed that a secular government was completely fine as long as they were free to practice their faith as they saw fit. Other Pharisees believed that the government needed to be a theocracy, run by observant Jews with Jewish law as the national law. That same debate is still playing out across the world today.

Sadducees

Frequently mentioned along with the Pharisees in the gospels are the Sadducees. They had their own sets of tests and debates for Jesus but from their own particular angle. Like the Pharisees, the Sadducees were deeply involved in national politics, although, unlike the Pharisees, they came out on top more often. But they had significant differences from the Pharisees in theology and appeal.

While the Pharisees were mostly laypeople popular with the masses, the Sadducees were chiefly priests and represented the aristocratic classes. The high priest was almost always a Sadducee, and thus often led the ruling political council called the Sanhedrin (see p. 48). They arose as a distinct group about the same time as the Pharisees, in about 150 B.C.E.

The Sadducees rejected the "traditions" claimed by the Pharisees, accepting only the written law as binding.

Some have argued that the Pharisees saw each home, and perhaps even each person, as a mini-Temple, seeing no real division between the sacred and secular. If it was a good rule for the Temple and priests, why should the home of a faithful Jew be any different? We may see some clue to this interpretation in Paul's letter to the Corinthians, when he writes, "Or do you not know that your body is a temple of the Holy Spirit within you, which you have from God, and that you are not your own?" (1 Corinthians 6:19)

Unlike the Pharisees, the Sadducees did not believe in any sort of life after death, and certainly not with any reward or punishment. This is the root of their debate with Jesus in Matthew 22:23–33. And it was the division Paul uses to his advantage in Acts 23 when he appeared before the Sanhedrin. Luke (the author of Acts) describes the scene:

> When Paul noticed that some were Sadducees and others were Pharisees, he called out in the council, "Brothers, I am a Pharisee, a son of Pharisees. I am on trial concerning the hope of the resurrection of the dead." When he said this, a dissension began between the Pharisees and the Sadducees, and the assembly was divided. (The Sadducees say that there is no resurrection, or angel, or spirit; but the Pharisees acknowledge all three.) Then a great clamor arose, and certain scribes of the Pharisees' group stood up and contended. "We find nothing wrong with this man. What if a spirit or an angel has spoken to him?" When the dissension became violent, the tribune, fearing that they would tear Paul to pieces, ordered the soldiers to go down, take him by force, and bring him into the barracks. (Acts 23:6–10)

As mentioned in that passage in Acts, the Sadducees did not believe in angels as supernatural beings and questioned the degree to which God actually intervened in human affairs.

Because the Sadducees were primarily priests whose work centered on Temple law and Temple worship, when the Temple was

Read Matthew 22:15–46.

destroyed by the Romans, the Sadducees disappeared almost overnight and played no discernable role in the formation of later Judaism.

The Pharisees and the Sadducees had strong differences, and we can see from Acts 23:6–10 that St. Paul, a Pharisee, used those differences to his advantage during his trial. But both Pharisees and Sadducees were intimately involved in political as well as religious leadership. This was not true of the third major group of the period, the Essenes.

The Essenes/Qumran Sect

The Essenes numbered about four thousand men, living in communities throughout the more rural areas of Palestine. Like the other groups, they are first mentioned by name during the Hasmonean period, but unlike the Pharisees and Sadducees, they are not mentioned by name in the Bible.

As you look at their beliefs and practices, however, it's hard to imagine that they didn't have a significant influence on the development and expectations of the earliest Christians, so we mention them here. Our information about

Excavation of a Ritual Bath at Qumran

them comes primarily from the ancient Jewish historian Josephus and perhaps, as we'll see, from the Dead Sea Scrolls.

The Essenes were similar to later monastic communities in that they lived together, shared all possessions and assets, and lived a simple, celibate life. There was a process of initiation that lasted several years. They seem to have had an ambivalent attitude toward the Temple and its practices. They sent in voluntary offerings (and were generally known for being quite charitable), but didn't participate in the sacrificial system. They were strict in other observances, however, especially the purity laws and the Sabbath laws. They were known to be experts in the use of plants and stones for healing.

Theologically, they believed in angels and the immortality of the soul (although not the body) but rejected the notion of human free will. The Essenes were the ultimate "everything happens for a reason" people. God had everything planned out and no human action could either thwart that plan or cause God to move to Plan B.

When the Dead Sea Scrolls were discovered in 1947, we began to learn a lot about a Jewish sect that lived in the caves around Qumran during the Second Temple period. Were they Essenes? It's hard to say. The word "Essene" doesn't appear anywhere in the Qumran scrolls and some of the practices and beliefs of the Qumran sect are at odds with Essene habits described in other places.

The sect in the Qumran caves appears to have started with priests who saw the Judaism in Jerusalem as corrupt and separated themselves from it. They shared the belief in predestination with the Essenes but the Qumran sect also had a strong apocalyptic bent (a focus on the end times). They thought the end of the world would occur at any moment, that angels would defeat the nations, and that a messiah would come (two messiahs in fact—one kingly and one priestly) and preside over a great banquet.

Both the Essenes and the Qumran group were composed of adult males, but they did teach and train children in their ways. Some have speculated that perhaps John the Baptist was one such child, since he appears to have led an ascetic life and was from a priestly family. His practice of baptism was similar to initiation practices in the Qumran group, and he clearly expected the end of days to come soon. Of course there is no way to know for sure whether John the Baptist was raised in this community or not.

Some think the Qumran sect was a splinter group of Essenes and some see them as distinct groups. What is clear is that there were many groups and schools of thought, with debates raging over how to interpret the Law (or even what was considered Law), immortality, angels, free will, and the end of all things. The religious groups we've talked about were the major ones, but they weren't all of them by any means.

Read Matthew 3:1–17, Luke 3:1–22, Matthew 14:1–12. John the Baptist.

Priests and Levites

While it appears that the high priest was always a Sadducee and most Sadducees were priests, not all priests were Sadducees. Plus, not all who performed duties at the Temple were priests. Confused?

According to the Law of Moses, the tribe of Levi was set apart to tend to the religious life of the Israelites. Moses' brother Aaron was the first real priest of Israel, and Aaron (as well as Moses) came from the ancestral tribe of Levi. So records talk about both the Levites and the Sons of Aaron. In general, talk of the Sons of Aaron refers specifically to priests, while the term "Levite" is broader and includes everyone from the Temple maintenance staff to the musicians and on up to the high priest.

St. John the Baptist by El Greco, 1579

The appointment of an entire tribe of people to be set apart as priests and religious workers was helpful when worship was mostly local. There were lots of local areas so lots of people were needed. But when worship became centralized in the Temple in Jerusalem, suddenly there were far more priests and religious workers than were actually needed to perform the duties. Imagine if every local church in your state suddenly merged into one giant church. Even though that one big church would need a large staff, you'd still have piles of pastors, priests, organists, educators, and so on out of a job. So what did they do?

Levite Musicians

As early as the book of Chronicles (probably fourth century B.C.E.), this problem was addressed by dividing the priests into twenty-four shifts, each of which served for a week twice a year, with a few getting a third shift before the year began again (1 Chronicles 24:1–17). It seems that this system remained in place until the destruction of the Temple in 70 C.E.

What this meant in practice was that priests and Levites only worked two, maybe three weeks out of the year. Since the Law of Moses invented the system of tithing (bringing one-tenth of your crops, flocks, or other income as an offering) to support the Levites, they did not have to farm or perform other labor in their off weeks. Good work, if you can get it. So what did they do in the fifty or so weeks each year that they weren't working? They got an education.

In other cultures it was only the aristocracy who had the leisure to get an education. In Israel, however, there was this additional large group of priests and Temple workers who were able to enjoy that advantage. Because of this, it is assumed that most scribes were Levites.

THE SAMARITANS

Course 2 in this series, *Introducing the Old Testament*, looked in depth at the origins of the people known as the Samaritans, so I won't repeat that here. What is important to know is that the Samaritans had Jewish roots and practiced many Jewish customs.

The Samaritans first became separated from those roots and known as a distinct group during the march of empires from the eighth to the sixth centuries B.C.E. Although they tried, they were never able to reconcile with those on the opposite side of the political divisions that ensued from the various wars, deportations, and settlements.

The Jews of Judea went through two distinct periods of insistence on ethnic and/or ritual purity of the Jewish faith—once during the time of Ezra and the rebuilding of the Second Temple, and once during the Hasmonean period. Although stories like Ruth and Esther show us that such severity was not always the norm, each one of the harsher purges deepened the gulf between the Jews and Samaritans in some way.

The Good Samaritan by Stephen Sawyer

By the first century, it's fair to say, Jews and Samaritans shared a mutual hatred, with both the Jews of Judea and the Samaritans considering themselves to be the "true" Israelites. The trouble was that the Jews and the Samaritans were not just geographical neighbors; the Samaritan territory actually divided Jewish territory, mostly occupying the space that is today known as the West Bank.

Jews wanting to travel from north to south were faced with a dilemma: the most direct route went through Samaria. The animosity between the two groups was so fierce that most Jews would not set foot on Samaritan soil. Instead they crossed over the Jordan River and went through the desert to get around, adding days—and danger—to their journey.

Jesus stands all these conventions and the hatred overall on its head. He crosses into Samaria in his travels and shares in their hospitality. The longest conversation Jesus has with anyone in the entire New Testament is with a Samaritan woman in Samaria (John 4:1–42). One of Jesus' most famous

> **Read the parable of the Good Samaritan in Luke 10:25–37.**
> The Good Samaritan.

parables makes a Samaritan into a hero, while subtly condemning the priests of Judea (Luke 10:25–37). Jesus heals ten lepers and comments that the only one thanking him for his trouble was a Samaritan (Luke 17:11–19).

Jesus does not interact with and praise Samaritans as a Christian. He does so as a Jew, which was a very powerful statement in his day.

POLITICS

As we've mentioned already, the area known as Palestine in the first century was a Roman colony. Generally, the Romans continued the practices of other successful empires before them (notably the Persians and the Greeks), allowing their far-flung colonies some degree of self-governance.

Empires made their colonies pay taxes and acknowledge the supreme power of the ruling nation, but the successful empires realized that micromanaging the day-to-day activities of all these places wasn't good business practice. Every colony had its own customs, religions, and social structures and to impose something different only resulted in ugly riots and discontent, which would have a negative effect on the empire's bottom line. So local regions under Roman rule generally were allowed to keep some form of their own governing structure.

But it wasn't easy. The lines of who was in charge of what weren't always clean and clear in practice. The question of whether Palestine would be ruled by a local (Roman appointed) king, a governor, a Roman prefect, or something else was in constant flux. In fact, we see all three of those systems in Palestine just in the few short decades of the New Testament period. Plus, the farther a colony was from the empire's capital, the easier it was to skirt or abuse the system, and it's a good 1,434 miles (2,307.8 km) from Rome to Jerusalem.

Roman soldiers made unfair demands on the people; tax collectors demanded as much as they wanted to line their own pockets. Brothers rose to battle each other for power, religious leaders sought political influence through councils, and Herod the Great brutalized his subjects, had his own wife executed out of paranoia, and then went mad with guilt. It all plays out in the pages of the New Testament.

Kings

WE THREE KING HERODS

One of the first governing systems Rome tried for Palestine was appointing a king. Most of them were named Herod, so we need to sort them out.

The first Herod we meet in the Bible is the Roman-appointed "King of the Jews" when Jesus is born. Called Herod the Great for his massive building projects (including the vast expansion of the Second Temple, the port at

Caesarea, and the fortress at Masada), he might well have been called Herod the Monster or Herod the Madman, for he was all that and more.

This is the Herod who, according to Matthew 2:16–18, ordered the slaughter of all children under two years old in the town of Bethlehem. No sources outside of the Bible mention this massacre, but ancient historians like Josephus tell us enough about him that it would not be a surprising addition to his biography. He was cruel, he was power hungry, he was shrewd, he was increasingly paranoid, and he was king.

The Massacre of the Innocents (La Strage degli Innocenti) by Giotto, ca.1320

Herod the Great died at age seventy in the year 4 B.C.E. The documentation of his death combined with the biblical report that he was king at the time of Jesus' birth is largely responsible for dating the birth of Jesus no later than 4 B.C.E. and perhaps a year or two before.

Herod had several sons and, after his death, Caesar Augustus divided Palestine among them. His son Herod Antipas was given the region of Galilee to govern (the region containing Jesus' hometown of Nazareth), and it is this second Herod who is responsible for the execution of John the Baptist and to whom Jesus is sent for judgment after his arrest.

In 39 C.E., Herod Antipas was accused of conspiring against the Roman emperor Caligula (a real sweetheart himself), and Herod Antipas was exiled to Gaul. The person who accused Herod was his nephew, Agrippa (sometimes called Herod Agrippa), who conveniently was appointed king in Galilee upon Herod's hasty departure. You will read about Herod Agrippa later when St. Paul pays a visit to his dungeon in Acts 25–26.

The Sanhedrin

The Jews seem to have had some kind of ruling council of elders for at least two to three centuries before Jesus' birth. During the third century B.C.E., a Greek king visited and was greeted by what he termed the "senate," although we don't know who or what types of people comprised that group. From that point forward there are multiple references to some form of ruling council structure in Jerusalem.

It is during Roman times that we first see the word "Sanhedrin" used to name this council. The word comes from the Greek word *synedrion*, which means "sitting together," and can describe any kind of council—political, legal, or religious; local or national.

During Jesus' lifetime, there was a Sanhedrin in Jerusalem that appears to have served a national function, especially for legal matters. Those charged with the most important crimes were brought to the Sanhedrin in Jerusalem for judgment, although they operated under Roman supervision and were somewhat limited in the verdicts they could render. While no source known to us defines the council's membership during this period, we do know a few things about the group's composition.

Whenever the Sanhedrin is mentioned, both inside and outside the Bible, the high priest was there and was likely in charge of the group. Pharisees and Sadducees are both mentioned and some scribes, as well. Some members are described as "chief priests" and "elders" and may or may not have been Pharisees, Sadducees, or scribes. So it was a diverse group, representing most segments of Jewish society at the time.

In the New Testament we meet the Sanhedrin in their role as judge and jury for high crimes and investigations. Most famously, Jesus stands trial before them, which gives us a clue as to how the Roman and Jewish systems were intertwined, although the accounts differ across the four gospels. After questioning him, Jesus is sent to Pilate with the charge of "perverting our nation, forbidding us to pay taxes to the emperor, and saying that he himself is the Messiah, a king." (Luke 23:2) It was basically a charge of treason.

PONTIUS **PILATE**

Little is known of Pilate's early life. I visited a tiny hamlet in Scotland that claimed to be his birthplace and towns in Italy, Spain, and Germany also claim him. What we do know is that in 26 B.C.E. he was appointed as prefect of Judea, a role that had both civil and military authority. The American equivalent would be similar to a governor, except the Roman governor would have been accountable to Rome and not to the particular region where he was appointed. Pilate was a Gentile and a Roman.

The first physical evidence of Pilate's existence was found in 1961 on a limestone block in the ruins of Caesarea Maritima (the port built by Herod the Great) that inscribes his name and his title as prefect of Judea. Tradition has it that Pilate committed suicide in Gaul about 37/38 C.E.

What is Truth. Christ and Pilate by Nikolai Ge, 1890

Pilate isn't sure what to do with Jesus and decides to punt (in Luke's account) and send him to Herod Antipas for a verdict, since Herod rules Jesus' hometown of Nazareth. Luke reports

> **Read Matthew 27:1–26, Mark 14:53–15:15, Luke 22:66–25, John 18:19–19:16.**
> Trial of Jesus.

that Herod is quite pleased to see this prisoner, hoping to witness some of the miracles for which Jesus has become famous. But when he gets no such show, he makes fun of Jesus, puts a mock royal robe on him, and sends him back to Pilate, who then debates with the Sanhedrin about the whole matter. We know how it ended up.

But the trial of Jesus is not the only place the Sanhedrin turns up. In Acts we see a number of the apostles brought before that council; Josephus tells us that even King Herod the Great was tried before the Sanhedrin. For what it's worth, Herod later killed all the members of the Sanhedrin who summoned him, making it clear that he wasn't into the power-sharing thing.

EDUCATION

The Scribes

The gospels portray another group that frequently stood in opposition to Jesus, the scribes. Josephus doesn't name the scribes as a distinct group, but they seem to have had power and influence in first-century Judaism. Rather than a specific religious group, they appear to have been a particular professional class. As the name implies, they were copyists and recorders—a type of secretary, if you will. They created new or multiple copies of texts written or spoken by others. In the world before the printing press, that's what you had to do.

Of course any place that had documents to distribute or sages to record needed scribes, and the more important the place and its sources, the better the scribe needed to be. The best of the best came to serve kings and councils and, in a religion heavily invested in ancient and sacred texts, they came to serve the Temple. Many were priests or aristocrats, since these would be the groups with enough leisure to pursue an education. But some were laity and a few came from more common stock. But if they were good and exacting enough to become scribes for either the Sanhedrin or the Temple, they had power and influence.

It goes without saying that a scribe had to be literate, which also gave them a lot of power and authority in a largely illiterate age, even in a relatively minor post. There were actually two levels of literacy at the time. The most basic sense of the term was someone who could read. Scribes went the extra mile and were also people who could write with fluency and precision.

Scribes became known not just as copyists, but also as teachers and sages in their own right. They could almost always be found traveling with the Pharisees and Sadducees because their jobs required it, but it's clear from the interactions in the New Testament that the scribes were seen by those other groups as equals in many respects. Many may have become rabbis.

Rabbis and Disciples

Jesus is called a rabbi in the New Testament, although that role was in flux at the time. The word "rabbi"(literally, "My great one") generally means teacher, and while teachers frequently taught in the synagogues during the first century, not every rabbi presided over a synagogue.

The title of rabbi for Jesus indicates that many saw him as an influential teacher. On more than one occasion the New Testament shows Jesus teaching in a synagogue. (The rabbi often sat down to teach, unlike modern clergy who

> **Read Matthew 4:18–22, John 1:35–51, Mark 3:13–19.** Calling the Disciples.

stand before a congregation.) The fact that both the Pharisees and Sadducees sought him out for debate indicates that Jesus received a significant level of respect and bore some amount of influence. That Jesus accepts this teaching role for himself is evident from the beginning of his ministry when he calls his first disciples.

Becoming a disciple has always been a conscious choice to place oneself under the authority of another. That's hard, which we feel in our gut whenever we use the related word, discipline. In first-century Palestine, it was a common Jewish practice for rabbis to take on a group of disciples. In these groups (at some later point to be called "yeshivas"), the disciples would study the Scriptures as seen through the eyes of their rabbi, with a particular eye toward the practical behaviors either mandated or encouraged by the text.

While in Greek society the disciples of philosophers and sages focused on theories about the nature of the universe, the Jewish disciple was looking for more practical guidance. *What specific behaviors are pleasing to God? How can I live in harmony with those around me? What should I do when a difficult situation arises?*

This is an important distinction as we try to understand the teachings of Jesus. First-century Judaism wasn't asking, "What should I believe?" although Jews certainly had their opinions, as we've seen. The purpose of studying God's word was to answer the question, "How should I live?" It was about action, not intellectual exercise or dogma. It was about how to live, not how to think. The teaching form that was most effective for this effort was the parable.

Parables

Jesus frequently teaches the crowds through the literary form known as the parable. Parables are fictional stories designed to teach a moral lesson, and in that sense are like fables or other forms of allegory. The thing that distinguishes a parable from those other forms is its realism. Although a parable is still fiction, most parables could have really happened.

"Have you ever heard the parable of the lawn left unmowed?"

Fables, fairy tales, and other allegories present us with talking animals, fantastical situations, the wind and the sun in conversation, and other characters and events that defy our experience of real life. For example, the famous story of the race between the tortoise and the hare by the ancient Greek storyteller Aesop (ca. 620–564 B.C.E.) is a wonderful fable about persistence. But when we read it we don't really believe that turtles and rabbits have their own secret Olympic Games going on in our backyards.

Parables, on the other hand, are stories with human characters that stick to the laws of physics and behave in ways that the intended audience would understand. The setting is usually contemporary to the listeners, the character types would have been familiar, and the dilemma described would have been something commonly faced in such a situation.

Again we see the difference with the Greeks. Aesop's fables were mainly about more abstract moral virtues: persistence, temperance, modesty, and so on. The parables of Jesus are predominantly about family life, money, helping others, ethical business

> **Read Luke 12–16,**
> **Matthew 13,**
> **Matthew 25.**
> Parables.

practices, and the like. They are trying to teach people how to live in a way that is pleasing to God and conducive to social harmony.

Some parables seem to contradict all of this. A number of parables use an earthly setting to describe the nature of the Kingdom of God or the Day of Judgment. We'll talk about the expectations of the time about these things in a bit. For our purposes here, however, simply note that even these contain advice about behavior. The parables about trees, fruit, grain, harvest, and vineyards all imply that while waiting for the Day of the Lord, there is work to be done. The parables in Matthew 13 are mostly of this type.

The blending of both these types of parables is best seen in Matthew, chapter 25. The first parable (the Ten Bridesmaids) reminds people not to slack off while waiting for God's kingdom to arrive. The second parable, the Parable of the Talents, elaborates by letting people know that God doesn't want everyone holed up in a cave just waiting for God to show up. The message? Live. Take risks. Bear fruit. Show that you have put the gifts God gave you to good use when you had the chance.

All of this culminates in Matthew 25:31–46, as Jesus insists that when that long-awaited Judgment Day finally arrives, nobody is going to be asking whether or not anyone followed Temple procedure or had the correct

interpretation of immortality. Jesus teaches that the final judgment of humanity will be based on our charitable actions. Did we feed the hungry, clothe the naked, visit the sick and imprisoned? He even goes as far as to identify God with those marginalized populations. The "king" in the story tells the people, "Truly I tell you, just as you did it to one of the least of these who are members of my family, you did it to me." (Matthew 25:40)

Of all the gospels, Luke records the greatest number of Jesus' parables. You should be working your way through reading Luke's entire gospel during these first three sessions. For this session, pay special attention to Luke 12–16, a treasure trove of parables. Luke 15 is actually known as the "lost" chapter in Luke because it has three parables about things that are lost and then found: the Lost Sheep, the Lost Coin, and the Lost Son, more commonly known as the Prodigal Son.

Jesus clearly sides with the Pharisees over the Sadducees in terms of the belief that there is a life after death, with a division between a state of favor and a state of condemnation—heaven and hell. But he parts ways with the Pharisees about what types of actions land a person in one state or the other. Both Jesus and the Pharisees go to the Law of Moses for their requirements, and Jesus singles out two that he believed were the most important. In Matthew 22:34-40 this becomes known as the "Great Commandment." The same incident in Luke, leads to one of Jesus' most famous parables.

The Parable of the Good Samaritan (Luke 10:25–37) is told in response to a legal expert who asks, "What must I do to inherit eternal life?" Jesus asks the man to answer his own question by looking at the Law of Moses. This unnamed lawyer answers, "You shall love the Lord your God with all your heart, and with all your soul, and with all your strength, and with all your mind; and your neighbor as yourself."

> ### PRIESTS AND **LEVITES**
>
> The Parable of the Good Samaritan makes a distinction between a priest and a Levite. As we've seen, while priests were taken from the tribe of Levi, not all Levites were priests. Some Levites were assigned to other kinds of duties related to the Temple and its upkeep.

The man's response combines two Old Testament passages, Deuteronomy 6:4–5 and Leviticus 19:18, both part of the Law of Moses—the same passages Jesus himself picks when he's asked, in Matthew 22 and Mark 12, what the greatest commandment is. Jesus tells the lawyer, "You have given the right answer; do this, and you will live." (Luke 10:28)

But the man wanted a bit more nuance. So he pressed Jesus further: "And who is my neighbor?" he demands. That's the question that generates the Parable of the Good Samaritan.

There is a larger Christian theological debate about whether people are saved by their own good works or by God's

> ### FOR **REFLECTION**
>
> Is there a particular parable that speaks to you? Why or why not?
>
> Do you find it easier to learn with stories than with other methods?
>
> What do you think is the best way to teach moral behavior?

grace or by some combination of the two. For our purposes here it is enough to note that Jesus' teaching is centered on how a person should behave. For Jesus, what a person believes intellectually is only important to the extent that it produces loving action.

WHO KILLED JESUS?

The question of who bears the responsibility for Jesus' execution is so fraught with peril that I really didn't want to write this section. I would gladly be a coward and avoid the subject altogether if it weren't for the fact that the words of the Bible about this have been used to fan the flames of anti-Semitism. Too many people have died because of this question, in both ancient and modern times. Friends of mine were taunted as "Jesus killers" as children—here, now, in contemporary America.

"The Jews killed Jesus!" has been a consistent rallying cry to justify horrors visited on Jews. While Christians flock to passion plays to remember the central event of Christian history, Jews often back off trembling, knowing that their portrayal in passion plays across history has meant torment and even death to them.

There are not words strong enough to condemn that leap of interpretation and the blatant anti-Semitism it generates. The Vatican has forsworn the assertion that "the Jews killed Jesus," as have countless other Christian denominations and leaders. Yet many Christians persist in using the Bible to hold the Jewish people responsible.

Since the words of the New Testament have contributed to these horrors, we need to hold them up to the light. But the issues around this question are so complex and volatile that I wanted them to have their own section. So rather than double the length of this session, or try to abbreviate a complicated issue, I have provided a full treatment in Appendix 4 on p. 247.

PREPARATION FOR CHECK-IN

(Prepare for the next group session by thinking about and writing a brief response to these two questions.)

What is one thing that was new to me in this material?

What is one question that this week's topic raises for me?

HOMEWORK

(ALL STUDENTS)

☐ Read Session 3 in the Student Text, along with each of the Bible readings listed.

☐ Think about the Reflection Questions.

☐ Complete your reading of the Gospel of Luke. To finish the story, read Acts 1:1–11, which was also written by Luke. You'll be reading the book of Acts for the next three sessions anyway, so that will put you eleven verses ahead!

EXTRA MILE

(CEU AND CERTIFICATE STUDENTS)

☐ After reading the Student Text for Session 3, you will have seen Jesus in three distinct ways. In five hundred to seven hundred words, write an essay describing how you see Jesus. Who is he to you? What questions do you still have about him? You will not be asked to share this with others.

SON OF GOD

THE COMPLEX MESSIAH

"Christ" is not Jesus' last name; it is a title. If you wanted to refer to Jesus in the way we'd use a last name today, you'd have said "Jesus of Nazareth." The word Christ comes from the Greek *christos* and means "anointed." Christos is a translation of a Hebrew word that is frequently translated as "messiah." We'll look at that more closely in a minute. Those wanting to make a claim about the nature of Jesus' life and ministry call him Jesus (the) Christ or, as Handel put it at the front of his most famous choral work, the Messiah.

In this session we'll look at the particular claims and interpretations about Jesus that eventually led believers to separate themselves from their Jewish roots and become a distinct faith called Christianity.

GREAT EXPECTATIONS
(OR, EVERYTHING YOU ALWAYS WANTED TO KNOW ABOUT ESCHATALOGICAL MESSIANISM IN SECOND TEMPLE JUDAISM BUT WERE AFRAID TO ASK)

Two thousand years of Christians referring to Jesus as either Christ or Messiah has led many to believe that there was one central figure known as the Messiah that was expected by the Jews. Jews who believed Jesus fit the bill ultimately became Christians; those who didn't remained Jews. But it wasn't that simple.

I'm Only Human

Like the Greek word *christos* (Christ), the Hebrew word *meshiach* (messiah) has a very basic meaning. It refers to a human being—traditionally either a king or a high priest—who has been anointed with oil for a special purpose. The term is used thirty-nine times in the Old Testament to refer to the kings and priests of Israel—it's even used to describe the Persian king Cyrus the Great. The Greek version of the Old Testament known as the Septuagint translates every instance of the word *meshiach* as *christos*.

So the first thing to keep in mind is that there is no faith tradition before Christianity (or after) that equated either the word *meshiach* or the word *christos* with a divine figure. Those with such a title were seen as people who had divine favor, but the words do not imply that the person so anointed was divine in himself.

That is not to say that the Christian interpretation is wrong, just that it's different than what came before and isn't part of the general meaning of the word. We should not assume that when we see the word "Messiah" or "Christ" used for Jesus in the New Testament that those speaking meant what Christians who use the words mean today. Given the variety of religious beliefs that we looked at in the last session, the meaning probably varied from person to person.

Signs and Wonders

Christians can also mistakenly assume that the miracles of Jesus would have been instant proof of divinity to the people of his day. But there are huge portions of the Old Testament that make miraculous claims for many of Israel's human leaders and prophets. Joshua gets God to make the sun stand still and keep time from advancing until his army can win a battle (Joshua 10:12). In Exodus 14, Moses parts the Red Sea and performs wonders for Pharaoh—many of which Pharaoh's own magicians can duplicate. Elijah not only heals people but also raises the dead (1 Kings 17:17–22). And Elisha

Moses Speaks to Pharaoh by James Tissot, 1896

didn't even have to be alive to work wonders. The book of 2 Kings 13:21 claims that a dead man mistakenly thrown into Elisha's grave came to life just by touching the prophet's bones!

Our post-enlightenment world might be skeptical about miracles (we'll turn our attention to them later in this session), but the Jews of first-century Palestine had a long tradition of anointed prophets and kings who could do just about anything. And they were all simply human vessels acting as channels for God's work.

When you look at the Old Testament miracle stories, human beings even outperform the angels. The word "angel" literally means messenger, and their primary role is to bring messages from God to earth. And that's what they do—from the ones that tell Abraham about the imminent destruction of Sodom and Gomorrah to the one who shows up with some news for Mary. Angels *bring* news. They don't make news.

For the Israelite, miracles signaled that God was *with* that person, not that God was that person. The miracles of Jesus would've been seen as a clear indication that Jesus was tapped into God's power and had God's favor. But they wouldn't necessarily have concluded that Jesus was divine, even when he raised Lazarus from the grave.

So while there were many different kinds of expectations for a person with God's anointing to show up and help Israel (a messiah), nobody was expecting God to show up in person. That said, however, the Jews had some specific expectations.

Moses and Elijah

The first kind of expectation was for the physical return of a key Old Testament figure or someone like him. In Deuteronomy 18:18 God says to Moses, "*I will raise up for them a prophet like you from among their own people; I will put my words in the mouth of the prophet, who shall speak to them everything that I command.*" So in some quarters, Jews awaited the fulfillment of that prophecy: not Moses himself, but a prophet like him.

More broadly expected was the actual return of the great prophet Elijah. Second Kings 2:11–12 shows Elijah being taken up into heaven in a whirlwind (frequently depicted in art as a fiery, horse-drawn chariot). Since Elijah didn't experience a physical death, it became tradition that he would return. To this day a chair is left empty at the Passover meal, and at every

The Transfiguration (after the fresco by Fra Giovanni da Fiesole)

circumcision, in case Elijah should come back. The expectation of Elijah's return is directly referenced in the gospels—many people think that either John the Baptist or Jesus might be Elijah.

To show how messy it gets, Jesus himself says that John the Baptist is Elijah in Matthew 11:14, while John the Baptist announces

> **Read Matthew 17:1–13.**
> Transfiguration.

in John 1:2–21 that he's neither Elijah nor the messiah. In the story of the Transfiguration, which appears in the gospels of Matthew, Mark, and Luke, the disciples Peter, James, and John experience a mountaintop vision of Jesus standing with Moses and Elijah. In Matthew and Mark, the story ends with Jesus again confirming that John the Baptist was the long-awaited Elijah.

Melchizedek icon in Libotin wooden church, Maramures, Romania

Other Candidates

Some of the Qumran texts also give us a picture of messiah figures related to more obscure Old Testament figures. One is Melchizedek, who is described in Genesis 14:18–20 when he comes to meet Abraham:

> And King Melchizedek of Salem brought out bread and wine; he was priest of God Most High. He blessed him and said, "Blessed be Abram by God Most High, maker of heaven and earth; and blessed be God Most High, who has delivered your enemies into your hand!" And Abram gave him one-tenth of everything.

This ancient king-priest is only mentioned one other time in the Old Testament. We find him in Psalm 110:4, which reads, "The LORD has sworn and will not change his mind, 'You are a priest forever according to the order of Melchizedek.'" The Psalm is a confusing one, but it's the most frequently quoted Psalm in the New Testament. It's used by Jesus in Matthew 22:41–46 to mess with the heads of the Pharisees about the nature of the Messiah. And Melchizedek also appears in the book of Hebrews, chapters 5–7, in references to Psalm 110. The writer of Hebrews claims a priestly role for Jesus as the "priest forever according to the order of Melchizedek."

That's all there is in the Bible, yet somehow we have an entire Qumran scroll, filled with messianic leanings, named for him. It's likely that over time the character of Melchizedek was filled out and interpreted outside of the biblical text, while the Bible itself gives us just brief glimpses of what was obviously a much larger body of tradition about him.

The same is true of Enoch, who we know even less about from the Bible than Melchizedek. Enoch was the great-great-great-great grandson of Adam. He gets noticed because of a deviation in a long and otherwise boring genealogy. The list goes on according to a standard formula: *When so and so had lived x number of years he became the father of so and so. He lived after the birth x years and had other sons and daughters. Thus all the days of so and so were (a huge number) years and he died.*

That's the way every listing goes—until we get to Enoch:

> *When Enoch had lived sixty-five years, he became the father of Methuselah. Enoch walked with God after the birth of Methuselah three hundred years, and had other sons and daughters. Thus all the days of Enoch were three hundred sixty-five years. Enoch walked with God; then he was no more, because God took him.* (Genesis 5:21–24)

All that walking-with-God stuff isn't in the other genealogies and Enoch is the only one whose entry doesn't conclude with "and he died." From just that little bit of genealogy, the story of Enoch grew. By the first century B.C.E. Enoch was a towering figure in Jewish mysticism. Between the first century B.C.E. and the fifth century C.E. three entire books about Enoch were written, so it's not surprising that he surfaces in the New Testament.

Enoch shows up first in Luke's genealogy of Jesus. In the book of Hebrews he's listed as an example

Icon of Elijah and Enoch, Polish, 17th Century

of faith. Finally Enoch appears in the letter to Jude—the single-chapter book of the Bible that appears next to last in the New Testament. Jude tells about a prophecy given by Enoch, but that prophecy isn't found anywhere in the Old Testament. Some believe the source of the prophecy is one of those other books about Enoch, which Ethiopian Orthodox Christians accepted as part of their canon of Scripture.

Some later Jewish traditions came to believe that Enoch was the one responsible for giving God's law to Moses. Mormons and Muslims both revere Enoch as an exceptional prophet of God, and he is a saint in the Armenian Apostolic Church. Some popular Protestant televangelists believe Enoch is one of the two witnesses spoken of in the book of Revelation. Clearly, not everybody skims the genealogies.

Let My People Go

The specific hope for the return of a prophet like Moses was probably mixed with hope for a physical liberator who would rescue Israel from Roman oppression the way Moses rescued the Hebrew slaves from Egypt. This type of hope is most clearly seen in those looking for a more practical and political messiah to come from the lineage of King David. David, a military king, ruled Israel about 1000 B.C.E., consolidating the kingdoms and uniting the nation and establishing a time of peace.

Despite some significant personal flaws, David became the gold standard for Israelite kings, and some strains of Jewish belief continued to look for someone who could trace their lineage back to him to step forward and bring back the good old days. Matthew clearly wants to make this kind of connection for Jesus by beginning his gospel with a genealogy tracing Jesus to David.

While the hope of re-establishing the throne of David had always been present, the desire for such a military leader-king was more pronounced in the first century C.E., during the Hasmonean dynasty, a period of Jewish independence that lasted from 140 to 37 B.C.E.

Under the leadership of Judas Maccabeus, the Jews successfully (and unexpectedly) defeated the Greek army when one of the Greek kings (Antiochus IV Epiphanes) made the mistake of setting up his own image in the Temple. Judas died on the battlefield, but his brother Simon finished the work and established the Hasmonean dynasty. The Jewish festival of

Hanukkah celebrates the purification and rededication of the Temple after this revolt.

Remember the history we covered in the Old Testament course? The Jews had experienced foreign rule by many empires for a long time. Sometimes the periods of domination were relatively peaceful; sometimes they were fraught with horror and destruction. But the desire to be in control of our own destiny is part of human nature, and submission to foreign power is never welcomed. So when Judas Maccabeus rose up and secured Israel's independence, despite overwhelming odds, that was a very big deal.

Menorah by Georg Humann, German, 1904

With the memory of freedom fresh in their minds, losing independence to the Romans in 37 B.C.E., less than a generation before Jesus' birth, was a harder setback for the Jews than it would have been had they just been going from one foreign overlord to another. Jesus' father, Joseph, might well have known those days of self-rule.

Revolutionaries of various types were woven into the fabric of life in first-century Palestine. Roman soldiers were wary and often controlling. In Matthew 5:41 Jesus instructs: "If anyone forces you to go one mile, go also the second mile." That wasn't a random example. Roman soldiers both could and did ask people to stop whatever they were doing and carry their pack for a mile. Imagine walking to work in your hometown and having a soldier legally demand that you carry his stuff for a mile. You then have to walk the mile back, are late to work and perhaps suffer the consequences, and on it goes.

The people responded in predictable ways to such offenses, forming groups both large and small to try to combat or disrupt the Roman forces, or at least make life difficult for them. One of Jesus' disciples is named Simon the Zealot, perhaps an indicator of participation in one of those revolutionary groups. It would have been likely that at least some of Jesus' disciples had revolutionary leanings.

Although not suggested in the text itself, some have suggested that the disciple Judas, famous for having betrayed Jesus, may have been one of those revolutionaries as well. In Jesus' day, after all, Judas was an honored name.

Judas by Fyodor Bronnikov, 1874

Even if it had been passed down in a family (as was frequently the case), no one at that time would have heard the name Judas without thinking of the man who had fought the brave battle that won Jewish independence.

It's interesting to ponder what Judas the disciple may have been thinking when he betrayed Jesus. Was he disillusioned because he wanted a military messiah like Judas Maccabeus? Was he trying to force Jesus into a military confrontation by having him arrested? Or was he just a low-life making a grab for the thirty pieces of silver he was promised for the betrayal? We'll never know. But we do know he wasn't happy with the outcome. Matthew 27:3–10 tells us that Judas returned the money and then hanged himself.

The hope for a political/military messiah could also explain how the crowds that cried Hosanna and waved palm branches when Jesus rode into Jerusalem could, within a week, turn on him and ask Pilate to release

> **Read Matthew 27:1–66.**

the revolutionary Barabbas and crucify Jesus. The Bible calls Barabbas a "notorious prisoner," but one man's murderer is another man's freedom fighter. The Greek that the NRSV translates as "notorious" can also mean "illustrious." It's all a matter of perspective. Is the preference for Barabbas over Jesus an indication that the crowd wanted action?

When people called to Jesus as "Son of David," were they expressing the wish for a new Davidic king? Perhaps when he was arrested without fighting back they thought they had backed the wrong horse. Jesus himself warned in Matthew 24:23–24 that there would be plenty of false messiahs. Maybe they thought he was one of them.

The many and often conflicting ideas about an expected messiah could also explain why Jesus so frequently tells people to keep quiet about what they've seen and heard, most frequently in the Gospel of Mark. In Matthew 16:13–20, Jesus asks his disciples who people think he is. They answer with a variety of possibilities. Then Jesus asks them what they themselves think. Peter famously answers, "You are the Messiah, the Son of the living God."

Jesus' response is to name Peter as the "rock" (Peter's name means "rock" in Greek) on which the church would be built (this is the biblical foundation for the papacy as Peter went on to found the church

> **Read Matthew 16:13–28.**

in Rome), a response that is unique to Matthew. However, Jesus concludes the section with a command that is common to this story in all three Synoptic Gospels: "Then he sternly ordered the disciples not to tell anyone that he was the Messiah."

Somebody…Anybody…Help!

There's no end to the speculation because there was almost no end to the peoples' expectations of what a messiah would be and do—if they expected a messiah at all. I would bet that most people rarely thought about it in any detail. Daily life was too hard for the vast majority of people to sit back and contemplate such matters. They didn't have talk radio going while they worked the fields, threshed the wheat, or made the soap. Nobody was polling them on their messianic options.

But the average person did know that a long, hard day could be made even harder if a Roman soldier decided on a whim to make them carry the soldier's pack for a mile. They did know that the tax collectors lined their own pockets with money that Jews could ill afford to lose. And they did remember that not so long ago they had known what independence was like.

Jewish farmers knew too well that the field they toiled in for a Roman master today had been their own field just a few years before. They knew that the harvest they gathered under the harsh sun used to be brought into their own pantries instead of providing feasts for the wealthy. They were ready to follow someone, anyone, who would lead them to a different life. Many volunteered for that job.

Read Matthew 5–8.
This section of Scripture is known as the Sermon on the Mount and begins with what are commonly called the Beatitudes (Matthew 5:1–12). The Sermon on the Mount.

While most people didn't pay much attention to the religious debates of the Pharisees, Sadducees, and other groups, it was hard to ignore a guy who was really helping the down and out. While Jesus didn't ignore the wealthy or powerful, he was also surprisingly willing to associate with, and even share meals with, those the more esteemed classes deemed to be unfit.

Jesus healed both beggars and the children of Roman centurions. He ate with the Pharisees and also with tax collectors and sinners. And he stood out in the open air and proclaimed that those who were poor, hungry, and persecuted were especially blessed in God's eyes. When the crowds came and listened to him for hours, he worked miracles to be sure they were physically as well as spiritually fed.

The words of Jesus were a balm to the oppressed, but they probably wouldn't have paid much attention to those words if it hadn't been for the miracles. The miracles take up a lot of ink in the gospels, so let's look at them for a bit.

IT'S A MIRACLE!

So what, exactly, is a miracle? Many people define a miracle as something supernatural—something that happens that seems to go against the laws of nature, usually getting a person out of a predicament. The hungry lion refuses to eat Daniel when he's thrown into the den (Daniel 6:10–28), Jesus walks on water (Matthew 14:22–33), and so forth.

Yet we often feel that a miracle has occurred when something completely natural happens at an unexpected time. Someone is poised with a razor to her wrist and suddenly a long-lost friend shows up at the door for a visit. You don't know how you can possibly meet a work deadline and, just as you're preparing to be fired, your boss says, "Hold off on that for a couple of weeks."

Then there are completely natural and planned events that can cause us to feel like we have witnessed a miracle. The birth of a child. Celebrating the deep love of a spouse over time. Watching the sunrise over the mountains. Realizing that another species of creature is content to sit on your lap. Watching a plant grow from a seed. Observing your body heal itself of a cut on your finger. All those things can be explained by science. They're neither supernatural nor unexpected. Yet they can produce such a sense of wonder and awe that "miracle" sometimes seems like the only appropriate word.

The Disciples See Christ Walking on the Water
by Henry Ossawa Tanner, 1907

Some assume that if a miracle story in the Bible can be shown to have a scientific cause, it's no longer a miracle. Others spend a lifetime thinking that if they can prove that a biblical miracle can be explained by science that the Bible is proven "true." But if your definition of miracle is broader, the fact that Jesus—or anyone else—may have been operating within natural laws of science becomes irrelevant.

Let's take the star of Bethlehem as an example. The Gospel of Matthew (but none of the other gospels) tells us that wise men from the East observed a star they believed to portend the birth of a great king. They followed it until they came to Bethlehem and found the baby Jesus (Matthew 2:1–12). There are entire websites devoted to analyzing this star and trying to prove that there are astronomical bodies that behave in exactly the way the Bible describes that were active at exactly that point in history at exactly that spot on the map. For them, the truth of the event is completely linked to whether or not the account of the wise men can be taken at face value. These sites want to prove the Bible through science.

In an opposite kind of attempt, let's look at Jesus feeding five thousand people. This is a miracle recorded with some slight differences in all four gospels: Matthew 14:13–21; Mark 6:30–44; Luke 9:10–17; John 6:1–15.

In each account, Jesus blesses five loaves of bread and two fish and is able to feed five thousand people, with baskets of food left over.

Some biblical detractors like to say that this isn't a miracle, it's just a story about sharing. They suggest that when a huge crowd sees someone offering others the little bit of food they have, everybody gets in the mood and shares with those around them. In that way everybody is satisfied, with some left over. Jesus is not, for them, producing food out of thin air but simply modeling helpful behavior. It's not a miracle, these people say; it's psychology.

The Miracle of the Loaves and Fishes by Tintoretto, 1581

But instead of getting stuck in those debates, let's look at the bigger picture. Is the outpouring of human compassion in sharing food with the hungry really any less wondrous than popping bread and fish out of nowhere? Don't the outpourings of gifts and kindness following a natural disaster or a horrible event like 9/11 make us feel like we've witnessed something of a miracle? Would those of us who believe Jesus is God in the flesh cancel our subscription if the story about the star of Bethlehem turned out to be a little off—or even a lot off? No Christian creed that I'm aware of has us recite, "I believe that there actually was a star/comet/insert-your-celestial-event-here that led the wise men to Jesus."

The miracle of Jesus' resurrection is a bigger deal, and we'll look at that a bit later, but for the vast majority of the miracles in both the Old and the New Testaments, we do ourselves a disservice to get caught up in trying to either prove or disprove their authenticity. For people of faith, God's ability to do things that ordinary human beings can't is usually part of the job description. But others believe differently, and we're not likely to move one another to the opposite position through rational argument. Faith and knowledge are two different spheres. Science can challenge but not disprove faith, and faith can challenge but not disprove scientific argument. If both sides exercise a little humility and respect in the debate, we can actually reap great benefits from the challenges posed by both perspectives.

MIRACLES AS SIGNS

Hands down, the most helpful contribution to the discussion of miracles in the gospels comes from the Gospel of John. John does not use the word "miracle" in his gospel. What the other writers call miracles, John calls "signs." This little shift makes all the difference in the world.

I was never bewildered by Jesus' miraculous healings, but I was puzzled and upset that Jesus seemed to pick and choose who was healed and who wasn't. And if you can walk on water, and even help your disciples do it with you, why would you ever take a boat? If you can turn water into wine, you don't ever have to worry about finding financial backing. If you can bring people back from the dead, why would you help one grieving family and not another?

What John is telling us in his gospel is that the miracles of Jesus have a purpose beyond the object of the miracle itself. They are signs of something larger. They signal to the people who witness them that this is a special person. This man may look ordinary, but he does extraordinary things.

There is no doubt that Jesus was filled with compassion when he healed people. The Bible tells us as much. He hated to see suffering, whether it was the grief of Mary and Martha at the death of Lazarus that made Jesus weep (John 11:28–36), or the misery of the blind men who called out time and time again, "Have mercy on us, Lord, Son of David!" (Matthew 20:29–34) It also seems that there were times, as in that last

Image Caption: Trafalgar Square passion play: a miracle, Jesus performs a healing miracle (scene 2 of 6)

example, that Jesus healed someone purely because he was moved by his deep compassion to do so.

However, what John shows us in using the word "signs" is that sometimes Jesus did something specifically to send a message. It might have been a message about his authority, so that people would take his teaching more seriously. Or it might have been a message about the kind of God who gave him that authority. Jesus never rains sulphur down on his enemies, for example, although I have to wonder if he thought about it sometimes.

The miracles Jesus performs often show power and authority over the elements (stilling a storm, walking on water), compassion for others (healing, feeding the hungry, providing for an embarrassed couple who ran out of wine

FOR REFLECTION

What is a miracle to you? Have you ever witnessed a miracle? Do you believe the miracle stories in the gospels? Why or why not?

at their party), or authority over the spiritual realm (casting out demons, raising the dead). The miracles signify the nature and power of the God Jesus is preaching and teaching about, while also putting people in a state of wonder in which they're willing to listen and consider seriously what he says.

Miracles may serve as signs of God-given authority, but the God Jesus speaks about doesn't seem to encourage random displays of grandeur and self-importance. We saw this in the story of Jesus' temptations in the wilderness. (Matthew 4:8–10) Jesus only calms the storm because the disciples are afraid and ask him to get up and do something about it. He walks on water to get to the disciples who are on the boat. The Gospel of Luke tells us that when Jesus appears before Herod, Herod is hoping to see some kind of miracle. Herod just wants a show and Jesus knows it. He performs no sign for Herod, even though doing so might have spared his life. (Luke 23:8–12)

It's also clear that the main purpose of Jesus' ministry was not to be a miracle worker, even when he works wonders for the welfare of others. Jesus performs many miracles in the gospel accounts, but he refrains from performing even more. Many were sick and received no healing. Many died and were not raised. Many times Jesus could have made life much easier for himself and others by changing the weather, ensuring a bumper crop, feeding the hungry, or making money appear in the pockets of the poor.

John's gospel helps us understand that the miracles of Jesus were signs, showing those around him that a loving God had come near, and to emphasize that Jesus came with God's authority. They were meant to point beyond himself to the one Jesus prayed to as "Father." They were not ends in and of themselves.

SON OF...WHO EXACTLY?

While we're on the subject of titles, it's time to look at the phrases that have provided our first three session headings, as they're all titles of a sort. At various times Jesus is referred to as the Son of Man, the Son of David, and the Son of God. We've used these titles in this course to represent Jesus as a human being, Jesus as a Jew, and Jesus as a divine figure, but let's look at what these titles would have meant to those who first used them.

SON OF MAN

The phrase "Son of Man" was around long before Jesus. In the Hebrew Bible it is used 107 times, most frequently in Ezekiel. In this phrase, the word "man" isn't the word for a male person (*ish* in Hebrew) but for human being (*adam* in Hebrew). Its use in the Old Testament seems to be simply a way of referring to a person's humanity. For example, in Ezekiel, it's God who uses the phrase to talk to Ezekiel. The New Revised Standard Version translates the phrase simply as "mortal," which sums it up. Its usage in the Old Testament seems to be a way of indicating either the limited nature of a particular human being or the race of human beings as a whole.

So the phrase "Son of Man" would have been quite familiar to at least the educated class of Jews in the first century. But in the New Testament, the phrase gets a new twist. Every single usage in the New Testament adds the definite article, so instead of just "Son of Man" it's "*the* Son of Man." It is used that way eighty-one times in the gospels and only in the sayings of Jesus. It appears only a handful of times in the rest of the New Testament (Acts, Hebrews, and Revelation), where it always refers to Jesus. The New Testament clearly wants to use the phrase in a different way. But how?

Of course nobody agrees. As early as St. Augustine in the fourth century, theologians were trying to make sense of it. Most came to believe that the phrase helped define the nature of Jesus. Remember that Christianity has taught that Jesus is both fully human and fully divine at the same time. (Don't ask me how exactly that works, I'm just reporting.) That's the doctrine, and many scholars believe that the title "the Son of Man" works together with "the Son of God" to balance out those two aspects of Jesus' nature.

Jesus is the only one who uses the phrase in the gospels. He doesn't come right out and say, "I am the Son of Man," but he seems to be referring to himself when he uses the phrase. Jesus also uses the phrase for himself in three different contexts. He uses it to talk about his basic ministry (often emphasizing its humble nature). For example, in Matthew 11:18–19, Jesus, talking about the impact of his cousin, John the Baptist, complains that there's no pleasing the current generation, saying,

> For John came neither eating nor drinking, and they say, "He has a demon"; the Son of Man came eating and drinking, and they say, "Look, a glutton and a drunkard, a friend of tax collectors and sinners!" Yet wisdom is vindicated by her deeds.

That use best fits the Old Testament understanding of the phrase. The Son of Man here is not living the ascetic lifestyle of John the Baptist, but a normal human life. Still, however, Jesus is referencing himself in a way that hadn't been done in the Old Testament texts.

A second way Jesus uses the phrase references his future (but still earthly) suffering, death, and resurrection, as seen in verses like Mark 14:21. Jesus is at the Passover meal with his disciples and has just revealed that he would be betrayed by someone seated with him. He says,

> *For the Son of Man goes as it is written of him, but woe to that one by whom the Son of Man is betrayed! It would have been better for that one not to have been born.*

As in the first instance, this passage combines an event common to human experience (a betrayal), tying it to the Old Testament usage, with a unique reference to himself.

The third way Jesus uses the phrase is to speak of his role in a final judgment, as in Mark 8:38. This also has Old Testament ties, especially to the "one like a human being" (which is "son of man" in Aramaic) in Daniel 7:13.

> *Those who are ashamed of me and of my words in this adulterous and sinful generation, of them the Son of Man will also be ashamed when he comes in the glory of his Father with the holy angels.*

That's not something we see as part of typical human life, even after death. If you imagine yourself in this role today, you usually get recommendations for therapy. But there's biblical precedent for thinking such things, even if you're not Jesus. In 1 Corinthians 6:2–3, Paul gives his congregation in Corinth a hard time about their internal conflicts and frivolous lawsuits. He then says,

> Do you not know that the saints will judge the world? And if the world is to be judged by you, are you incompetent to try trivial cases? Do you not know that we are to judge angels—to say nothing of ordinary matters?

We'll look more at Paul and his thinking in the coming sessions, but Paul holds the key to a second kind of interpretation for use of "the Son of Man" in the gospels. Paul believed Jesus is a kind of rebooting of the human race, making him a new Adam, a fresh start. He lays out his case in both Romans 5 and 1 Corinthians 15. Again, we'll look at all that when we look at Paul's teaching, but it would be another way to look at what Jesus means when he calls himself "the Son of Man" (which in Hebrew is *ben ha-adam*). "Son of Man" could easily be translated "Son of Adam."

If that interpretation is right, Jesus is not only saying that he himself has a human nature. In this model, Jesus is making a way for every human being to start over and follow his path instead of being bound to the failings of the first Adam. Jesus keeps the Old Testament meaning of the phrase that refers to all humanity, but adds himself as the originator of Humanity 2.0.

In the new model, you still live a human life and suffer a human death, but you also get the resurrection perk (denied the first Adam when he was kept away from the Tree of Life) and, if one is to believe Paul, the chance to participate in the judgment of the world. It's also worth remembering here that Luke's gospel takes pains to trace Jesus' ancestry all the way back to Adam.

Of course, some scholars argue that Jesus never said any of the verses with that phrase in them and that all the "Son of Man" references were later additions to his words. The best we can say for sure is that "Son of Man" is somehow about Jesus' life as a human being, which is why I chose it for the heading for the first session about Jesus' humanity.

SON OF DAVID

The phrase "Son of David" is much less complicated. Jesus is described this way seventeen times in the New Testament, often by those seeking healing of some kind. In Mark 10:47, the blind beggar, Bartimaeus, calls out to Jesus, "Jesus, Son of David, have mercy on me!" This kind of use is common.

Christ Giving Sight to Bartimaeus by William Blake, 1799-1800

Unlike "the Son of Man," Jesus does not refer to himself directly as "Son of David." You can argue that when he's toying with the Pharisees in Matthew 22:41–46, he's talking about himself, but only indirectly as he quotes from Psalm 110, the most frequently cited psalm in the New Testament.

Apparently enough people thought that a messiah would come from David's lineage that even a blind beggar like Bartimaeus would have heard the phrase "Son of David" used for people who seemed like good messiah candidates. Remember how Matthew begins his gospel? It's with a genealogy showing that Jesus was a descendant of David, setting up—right from the start—a messianic claim for Jesus.

So why doesn't Jesus ever make this claim himself? We can't really know for sure, but given the complex web of expectations for what any messiah would be or do—and how little most of that had to do with Jesus' actual mission and ministry—maybe he thought it better to avoid the title altogether. While those factions wanting military messiah to boot the Romans out of Israel and reestablish Jewish independence may not have been the majority, they could be quite vocal. That was not an expectation Jesus wanted to encourage. So Jesus seems to go out of his way to tone down expectations, even telling people to keep quiet about either his miracles or their belief that he's the Messiah.

If Jesus had marched around referring to himself as "Son of David," he would have been taking on a clearly political role—the heir to an earthly throne. But after his arrest, Jesus tells Pilate, "My kingdom is not from this world." (John 18:36) He had no intention of throwing more fuel on the fires of those looking for a messiah who would lead a military coup. Calling himself "Son of David" would have done exactly that. At least Matthew clearly wanted to connect Jesus to that strain of the messiah tradition, but during Jesus' lifetime it likely would have caused more problems than it would have solved.

SON OF GOD

Now it gets more complicated again. In the Bible, this title for Jesus develops right before our eyes. Think back to our discussion about the differences between the gospels. Remember that Matthew, Mark, and Luke are known as the "Synoptic" Gospels because they tell their stories in a similar way. John is very different and his use of this title for Jesus is one of those differences.

In the Synoptic Gospels, Jesus refers to God as his father and calls himself "the Son," but he doesn't call himself "Son of God." When referring to himself in the Synoptic Gospels, "Son of Man" seems to be his go-to phrase. We see Jesus shift the language very clearly in Matthew 26:63–64, which tells of Jesus' trial before the high priest.

> Then the high priest said to him, "I put you under oath before the living God, tell us if you are the Messiah, the Son of God." Jesus said to him, "You have said so. But I tell you, From now on you will see the Son of Man seated at the right hand of Power and coming on the clouds of heaven."

Those around Jesus, friend or foe, aren't afraid to make the leap to the title "Son of God." Mark, after all, begins his gospel, "The beginning of the good news of Jesus Christ, the Son of God." (Mark 1:1) The disciples, both as a group and individually, use this phrase for Jesus, and, in Matthew and Mark, so does a Roman centurion present at the crucifixion.

And it's not just mere mortals making the claim—heaven and hell weigh in on it too. In Matthew's account of Jesus' baptism (Matthew 3:17), the heavens open and a voice from heaven says, "This is my Son, the Beloved, with whom I am well pleased." And in Luke, a voice from a cloud, at the Transfiguration, proclaims, "This is my Son, my Chosen; listen to him." (Luke 9:35)

Son of God by Vicki Thomas

Even the devil gets in on the act. When he tempts Jesus in the wilderness, he begins two of his challenges with the same phrase: "If you are the Son of God…" And in the Gospel of Mark, demons call Jesus the Son of God even as he's casting them out (Mark 3:11). Jesus, for his part, doesn't refute the title, no matter who makes it. But what did it mean?

For those of us who have inherited two thousand years of teaching and tradition about what the phrase "Son of God" means, it's hard to realize that during Jesus' lifetime the phrase was more fluid. So before we see what Christians have made of it, let's look at what it might have meant back then.

For at least a thousand years, various kings and emperors around the world had claimed a special relationship to the divine. Some claimed to be gods themselves, while others claimed some kind of child-of-the-god status. The Roman emperor claimed to be *divi filius* or "son of the divine one," although there is some evidence that at least Augustus was unwilling to go the extra step of calling himself *dei filius*, or "son of god." Some later emperors took that leap with gusto.

The claim of the Roman emperor to be some kind of divine son, however, is one of the reasons that Jesus was seen as a political threat. Jesus may or may not have called himself the Son of God, but he had no qualms about calling God his father. And when you do that, and you start to gain a following in an area with a history of political revolutions and guerrilla wars, the folks in charge get nervous. Although referring to God as father wasn't part of Jewish tradition (except in the general sense that we're all God's children), Roman ears perked up when they heard it.

To Jewish ears the phrase may have meant a lot of things, just as "Son of Man" did, but it was also clear that using the title for Jesus was taking on a much more specific definition, but nobody in the Synoptic Gospels really tries to spell out what they mean when they say Jesus is the Son of God.

The Gospel of John changes all that.

While Mark begins his account simply by saying Jesus is the Son of God, John's gospel begins with a prologue that builds the foundation of what Christians believe about Jesus to this day. "Christology" is the word used for the theology about Jesus, and John begins with a Christological

> **Read John 1:1–18.**
> John's Prologue.

big bang. No angels, shepherds, and wise men here. Doing Luke one better, John goes back even before Adam and begins,

> *In the beginning was the Word, and the Word was with God, and the Word was God. He was in the beginning with God. All things came into being through him, and without him not one thing came into being. What has come into being in him was life, and the life was the light of all people. The light shines in the darkness, and the darkness did not overcome it. (John 1:1–5)*

Christ Our Light by Donald Jackson, 2002, from *The Saint John's Bible: Gospels and Acts*

In Christian teaching, this "Word" of John is none other than Jesus, in existence before the creation of the world. We know John considers the "Word" (in Greek, *logos*) to be Jesus as the prologue continues to talk about John the Baptist's predictions of Jesus and culminates in John 1:14–18:

> And the Word became flesh and lived among us, and we have seen his glory, the glory as of a father's only son, full of grace and truth…From his fullness we have all received, grace upon grace. The law indeed was given through Moses; grace and truth came through Jesus Christ. No one has ever seen God. It is God the only Son, who is close to the Father's heart, who has made him known.

Right off the bat, John claims not only that Jesus existed before creation along with God, but that Jesus actually was God. John goes on to use the title "Son of God" more than twenty times in his gospel. But to understand those references, it's important to remember the claims of this prologue.

John's gospel, of course, is the mystical and symbolic one. It's here that Jesus takes people to task for interpreting his words literally—consider Nicodemus in John 3 and the Samaritan woman at the well in John 4. John's prologue is hardly easy reading, especially for those who have just had three gospels full of "Then the disciples went…" and "Then Jesus said to them…." But in this philosophical and theological prologue, John lays out what "Son of God" means both to him and to the Christian community he represents.

Why it Matters

If you're tempted to toss theological matters like this to one side, don't. Blood has been spilled and is still being spilled today because of misunderstandings about the phrase "Son of God." The doctrine of the Trinity is rooted in the Gospel of John, and phrases later in John's gospel about Jesus as the "only begotten son" are misunderstood by legions of Christians. As a result, other faiths often get the wrong impression about what Christians believe. We need to clear that up.

> "NEVER HAS GOD BEGOTTEN A SON, NOR IS THERE ANY OTHER GOD BESIDES HIM" (Qur'an 23:91)

The Qur'an, purportedly dictated by God in the seventh century C.E. to a single scribe, the prophet Mohammad, is the primary sacred text for Muslims. A couple of years ago I decided to read the Qur'an cover to cover. Some version of the above phrase appeared time and time again as a recurring theme.

The oldest known Islamic inscription appears on the oldest Islamic building, the Dome of the Rock, which sits on the Temple Mount in Jerusalem and dates to the year 688 C.E. The inscription reads:

> *...Oh People of the Book! Don't be excessive in the name of your faith! Do not say things about God but the truth! The Messiah Jesus, son of Mary, is indeed a messenger of God: The Almighty extended a word to Mary, and a spirit too. So believe in God and all the messengers, and stop talking about a Trinity. Cease in your own best interests! Verily God is the God of unity. Lord Almighty! That God would beget a child? Either in the Heavens or on the Earth?...[1]*

---

1 Said Nuseibeh and Oleg Grabar, *The Dome of the Rock* (New York: Rizzoli International Publications, 1996).

Dome of the Rock in Jerusalem

Christians and Muslims have fought about this and their battles haven't always been limited to words. But as I read the Qur'an's repeated insistence that God did not, and in fact could not, beget a child, I found myself talking back to it and saying, "But Christians don't teach that!" Because we don't.

It is not now and has never been Christian doctrine that God physically gave birth to a child—son, daughter, none of it. As Jesus explains to the woman at the well in John 4:24, "God is spirit, and those who worship him must worship in spirit and truth." Christian faith does not teach that God is a top deity who gave birth to a second deity named Jesus or the Son or anything like it. Christians believe, just like Jews and Muslims, that there is one God. End of story.

Where it Started: Metaphors

What Christians add is not a new god, but a unique action of that one God—the action that John names in the prologue to his gospel: "And the Word became flesh and lived among us." (John 1:14) Where we start to get confused is in the next line, when John starts talking in metaphor about the glory of God. That fourteenth verse continues, "and we have seen his glory, the glory *as of a* father's only son, full of grace and truth."

John is using a metaphor, saying that the glory of God that could be seen in Jesus was the kind of thing you see when a father has one son—you're not looking at the father directly, but everything the father stands for has come to life in that man's son. We mean something similar when we say "a chip off the old block" or "the apple doesn't fall far from the tree."

John keeps the metaphor going down in verse 18, writing, "No one has ever seen God. It is God the only Son, who is close to the Father's heart, who has made him known." John then continues to use "son" language in several other places in his gospel, most famously in John 3:16. The King James Version (published in 1611) likes to use the phrase "only begotten" to translate the Greek word *monogenes* in John 3:16 and elsewhere, but that has added unnecessary problems. *Monogenes* means "unique" and has nothing to do with a person's origins.

This Son language (like the born-again language earlier in John 3) is not meant to be taken literally. It's just hard to describe what John wants to say otherwise. Think about the options. John is trying to say that God took on human form and lived a human life from birth all the way to and through death. That's quite the claim and is problematic when we try to wrap our human brains around it. We end up asking questions like, *If Jesus is God, then who is Jesus praying to? Can God die? If God is stuck inside a baby's body and mind, who's running the universe?*

Jesus had the same kinds of difficulties when he tried to describe the Kingdom of God, so he turned to metaphors as well. Over and over we hear, "The kingdom of God is like..." followed by an assortment of metaphors: A mustard seed. A treasure in a field. Leaven. A net. A field of wheat. When people of earth try to describe the things of heaven, metaphor is the best we can do. John wants to describe a heavenly mystery that would help his readers understand Christian belief about Jesus. Like Jesus before him, he reaches for a metaphor that was familiar in his age—the metaphor of a son who both is and is not his father.

It's an imperfect metaphor to be sure, but as metaphors go, it isn't bad. And, really, using metaphors for talk about God is much preferable to pretending that we can thoroughly analyze the Divine and describe God's workings like we might describe the mechanics of a toaster. That's a bit more knowledge than I believe any of us have.

Still, the devil is in the details (that's a metaphor—really, details are okay), and we human beings love our details. And so the church, beginning with the metaphor of Jesus as the Son of God, has tried to explain, right from the get-go, who, exactly, Jesus was.

Where it Led: Councils

The early church fathers gathered for a first attempt in Nicea (in modern-day Turkey) in 325 C.E. The council was called by the Roman Emperor Constantine the Great, who invited some 1,800 bishops to come together and find a consensus on several issues. At least 250 of them showed up. They took care of some business matters, like picking a consistent date to celebrate Easter, but the big theological fish they had to fry (a metaphor—they weren't frying fish) was to describe exactly how Jesus was a Son to God the Father.

This was a pressing issue because Constantine had legalized Christian worship, adopted the faith, and became the church's greatest patron. With faith and politics tied in inseparable knots, it became politically as well as religiously important to be able to know whether someone believed the "right" things or not.

Byzantine fresco of the first Council of Nicea in Church of Saint Nicholas, Demre, Turkey

Metaphors are purposely vague because they're an attempt at describing something that isn't easily described. But vague won't do if you're going to depose a prince or burn a heretic over it. Constantine couldn't rule the empire with metaphors. He had to have specifics, so he called in bishops from every part of the empire except Britain to figure out what this "only begotten Son" stuff meant.

After a full month at the council, the bishops produced what's now called the Nicene Creed, which is still recited, with some later addition, in thousands of churches every week. The part about God and Jesus reads:

> *We believe in one God,*
> *the Father, the Almighty,*
> *maker of heaven and earth,*
> *of all that is, seen and unseen.*
>
> *We believe in one Lord, Jesus Christ,*
> *the only Son of God,*
> *eternally begotten of the Father,*
> *God from God, Light from Light,*
> *true God from true God,*
> *begotten, not made,*
> *of one Being with the Father.*
> *Through him all things were made.*

For us and for our salvation
he came down from heaven:
by the power of the Holy Spirit
he became incarnate from the Virgin Mary,
and was made man.
For our sake he was crucified under Pontius Pilate;
he suffered death and was buried.
On the third day he rose again
in accordance with the Scriptures;
he ascended into heaven
and is seated at the right hand of the Father.
He will come again in glory to judge the living and the dead,
and his kingdom will have no end.

You can definitely see the influence of John's prologue in what they came up with, but if you think it's any clearer than what John wrote, you have a better mind than I. Behind the scenes they had lots of argument about the "begotten, not made" line. The point they were trying to make with that line was that Jesus wasn't part of the regular created order, the same thing John claims. But by solving that problem, they created a new one with the choice of the word "begotten."

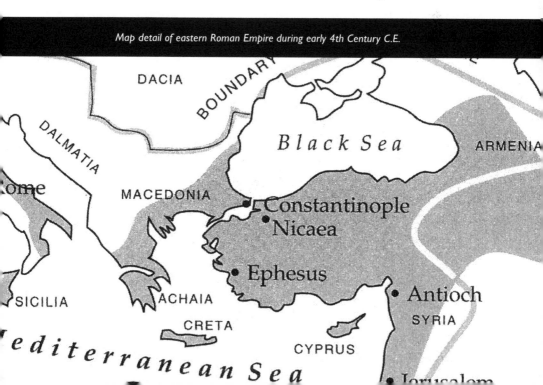

Map detail of eastern Roman Empire during early 4th Century C.E.

With the waters still muddy, the church tried to come at the issue again at Chalcedon (again in Turkey) in 451 C.E. By golly, they were going to define this thing. Here's what they came up with:

> We, then, following the holy Fathers, all with one consent, teach men to confess one and the same Son, our Lord Jesus Christ, the same perfect in Godhead and also perfect in manhood; truly God and truly man, of a reasonable [rational] soul and body; consubstantial [co-essential] with the Father according to the Godhead, and consubstantial with us according to the Manhood; in all things like unto us, without sin; begotten before all ages of the Father according to the Godhead, and in these latter days, for us and for our salvation, born of the Virgin Mary, the Mother of God, according to the Manhood; one and the same Christ, Son, Lord, only begotten, to be acknowledged in two natures, inconfusedly, unchangeably, indivisibly, inseparably; the distinction of natures being by no means taken away by the union, but rather the property of each nature being preserved, and concurring in one Person and one Subsistence, not parted or divided into two persons, but one and the same Son, and only begotten, God the Word, the Lord Jesus Christ; as the prophets from the beginning [have declared] concerning Him, and the Lord Jesus Christ Himself has taught us, and the Creed of the holy Fathers has handed down to us.

All I can say is, if you have to say that in church, God bless you.

I'm sure there are people both then and now who'd literally fight to the death to preserve the word "begotten" and the language of sonship. I actually think that language is helpful in trying to name something that is, ultimately, a mystery that Christians accept by faith.

> **FOR REFLECTION**
>
> Who is Jesus to you?

Christians just have to remember that when our faith family sits at the table with other faith families, our metaphors are not nearly so clear to them as they are to us. Others hear our language and think we worship three gods (Father, Son, and Holy Spirit) or two at the very least (God and Jesus). We don't. Just one God for us, thank you.

Christians are actually pretty much in agreement with that inscription at the Dome of the Rock that I quoted earlier. We do consider Jesus to be more than just another messenger, but we completely agree that God did not literally beget anybody. Jesus, Christians believe, is God showing up to be his own messenger. How did God manage to do that and still run the universe?

I have no clue. You'll have to ask one day when you meet. But I'm pretty sure when that day comes you won't be quizzed on Chalcedon.

DEATH AND RESURRECTION

Of course the central event of the New Testament is Jesus' own death and resurrection. We could easily do an entire course on just this event, and a large part of your third class session will focus on the resurrection story.

CHRISTIAN **SPEAK**

When studying Christian faith, you're likely to encounter some or all of the following words. They sound complicated but just represent the study of different parts of the faith.

Theology: The study of God.
Christology: The study of the nature and person of Jesus.
Soteriology: The study of salvation.
Eschatology: The study of the end times.
Ecclesiology: The study of the church.
Pneumatology: The study of the Holy Spirit.

Most of what is written in books about the resurrection of Jesus is focused on what it means. But this is not a course in theology. Our focus is biblical literacy—getting a sense of what the text says with enough background to make a confusing text a bit clearer. At this point your job is to be sure you've read what the gospels tell us about Jesus' death and resurrection (which should be covered if you've read the assignments throughout these first three chapters and have been to the class sessions), and understand the source of some Christian terms and practices.

The Passion

When the movie *The Passion of the Christ* came out in 2004, the title wasn't referring to things Jesus was passionate about or even people being passionate about Jesus. "The passion" is a specific, religious term that refers to the final events of Jesus' life from his triumphal entry into Jerusalem (celebrated in churches on Palm Sunday) through his betrayal, arrest, trial, and crucifixion. The word comes from a Greek root that means to suffer, so "the passion" as a religious term doesn't include Jesus' resurrection.

Jesus' final meal with his disciples before his arrest is known as the Last Supper and is remembered in churches on the Thursday before Easter, known as Maundy Thursday or Holy Thursday. This meal is also the root of the practice of Holy Communion. The week beginning with Palm Sunday and ending on Easter is known generally as Holy Week. The date of Easter moves and is held on the first Sunday after the full moon following the March equinox. Since the Western and Eastern churches use different calendars, Eastern rite churches often celebrate Easter on a different day than the West. Easter is preceded by a forty-day period of fasting known as Lent.

The Last Supper by Leonardo da Vinci, 1495

Crucifixion

The term "crucifixion" isn't unknown to most people. It was a very common, extremely brutal form of execution, primarily used from the sixth century B.C.E. to the fourth century C.E., when the emperor Constantine abolished it out of respect for Jesus. Unfortunately it is still used to execute people today in Burma, Iran, Saudi Arabia, and Sudan. The word "excruciating" comes from the same root, and with good reason.

The intent of a crucifixion was not just execution; it was meant also as humiliation for the condemned person and intimidation for those passing by. You were put up on a cross, often along a busy street and fairly close to the ground, and left not only to die, but to be eaten by carrion scavengers after your death. Most of those crucified received no formal burial. Crucifixion was considered too barbaric a fate for Romans, so the law forbade the crucifixion of Roman citizens.

Study for "Christ on the cross with Mourners," by Michelangelo Buonarroti, 1548

Because it was common, the vertical posts were usually already in the ground and the condemned person carried his own hundred-pound cross-beam to the particular post where he would die.

A crucified person was either tied or nailed to a cross, naked, in an agonizing and vulnerable position, and simply left in the heat to die in public. Death usually was the result of asphyxiation as the weight of the person's body collapsed the lungs. Depending on the condition of the person and the environment, there could be many other contributing factors.

Crucifixion was intentionally slow. If a crucifixion needed to conclude for religious or other reasons, soldiers would break the legs of the person being crucified, preventing people from breathing by pushing up from their feet and hastening death.

Ironically, the flogging, crown of thorns, and nails involved in Jesus' crucifixion were a sick kind of blessing, allowing him to die in several hours instead of the usual several days. Though he was offered wine mixed with myrrh, a mild analgesic, he refused it. He also received the gift of a burial in a fine tomb, donated by Joseph of Arimathea, apparently a dissenting member of the Sanhedrin, the court that put Jesus on trial.

Because Jesus is believed to have been on the cross from noon until three in the afternoon on a Friday, Christians gather the Friday before Easter (known as Good Friday) for the same three-hour period. Many churches also have a "Service of Shadows" or Tenebrae service on Good Friday evening to remember the time of mourning.

The Resurrection

Easter: the holiest of days in the Christian calendar. In many traditions there is a vigil that goes all night on Saturday and culminates in an Easter celebration at sunrise. Even churches that don't hold the vigil will generally have some form of early morning celebration in addition to later Easter services. Easter is the reason that most Christians choose to worship on a Sunday, which became known in the early church as "the Lord's Day."

The Bible tells us that early in the morning, women go to the tomb where Jesus was laid to put embalming oils on him. But when they arrive, they discover that the

> **Read the resurrection narratives in all four gospels: Matthew 28:1–20, Mark 16:1–20, Luke 24:1–53, John 20:1–31, John 21:1–24.**
> Resurrection.

large stone sealing the cave-like tomb has been moved and within the tomb they find not Jesus' body but angels telling them that Jesus has risen from the dead. John tells it a bit differently, with a longer narrative about Mary Magdalene encountering the risen Jesus and mistaking him for the gardener.

Easter in the church is not just a day—it's a season that lasts fifty days and culminates at the festival of Pentecost. We'll look at Pentecost more closely in the last session. Throughout the Easter season, the various biblical accounts of Jesus' post-resurrection appearances are usually read in churches.

The accounts themselves are pretty straightforward. No mystical metaphors here, just some amazed, scared, and baffled people. What the accounts do, however, is pose a central question of Christian faith: Did the resurrection really happen? And if it did, what does it mean? No historian or scientist can prove or disprove it; you either accept it on faith or you don't.

What is clear is that something happened to turn the disciples from a bunch of scared men, hiding from the Romans after the public execution of their leader, into an evangelistic force that literally changed the world. Christians, of course, credit an actual resurrection, complete with appearances of the resurrected Jesus as the gospels claim. Those who don't believe in an actual resurrection have to develop other ways to account for the subsequent history of Christianity.

The Atonement

This term moves us away from what technically happened and how Christians across time have interpreted the death and resurrection of Jesus. The most basic meaning in Christian faith is that the death and resurrection of Jesus was more than an earthly event, and even more than a miracle of a man coming back to life.

Christians believe that this culmination of Jesus' life and ministry had a cosmic impact that repaired the breach of relationship between God and human beings caused by sin. "Atonement" is often parsed out as at-one-ment, pointing out that the death and resurrection of Jesus brought God and people back together again, as they were meant to be at creation—before Adam and Eve decided to have a bite of fruit.

So how does that work, exactly? Well, that's where the consensus breaks down and different Christian traditions begin to talk about different "theories of atonement."

If you've ever heard the phrase "Jesus died for our sins," this represents one theory of the atonement, based in the notion of the blood sacrifice required to atone for sin laid out in the Old Testament book of Leviticus. It's the primary theory among Evangelical Christians, but not the only one out there, nor is it the oldest.

It's beyond our scope to dive into the various atonement theories. In our list of "ologies" on p. 91, it fits into the category of soteriology, the study of salvation. Suffice it to say that if you hear anything like the phrase, "Jesus saves," it represents some theory of the atonement—some way that the death and resurrection of Jesus made it possible for a perfect God and imperfect people to dwell eternally together.

So What Is the Content of this Gospel?

While the death and resurrection of Jesus are the central events of Christian faith, it's important to remember that all four gospels contain much more information about Jesus' life and teaching. Jesus himself is out preaching "the gospel" (which, remember, means "good news") and deploying his disciples to do the same well before his final trip to Jerusalem. Right at the outset of his ministry, Matthew tells us that:

> Jesus went throughout Galilee, teaching in their synagogues and proclaiming the good news of the kingdom and curing every disease and every sickness among the people. (Matthew 4:23)

The beginning of Luke 9 tells us that Jesus sends the disciples out to do the same thing, even before Peter makes his famous confession that he believes Jesus is the Messiah. It's Mark who spells out what's being proclaimed on these trips when he writes,

> Now after John was arrested, Jesus came to Galilee, proclaiming the good news of God, and saying, "The time is fulfilled, and the kingdom of God has come near; repent, and believe in the good news." (Mark 1:14–15)

The Greek word for "come near" in that verse is *eggizo*, and it means to approach, to bring near, or to join one thing to another. It's used to describe the "good news" of the kingdom of God, but it's also used in more mundane settings, to mean coming to a gate or having a person approach.

From the beginning of his ministry, Jesus announces that the kingdom of God has, in some way, arrived. Four authors depicted his life in as much detail as they could in order to get their respective audiences to believe that God's arrival was embodied in the person of Jesus who, as the Apostles' Creed claims,

> was conceived by the Holy Spirit, born of the Virgin Mary,
> suffered under Pontius Pilate,
> was crucified, died and was buried;
> he descended into hell;
> on the third day he rose again from the dead;
> he ascended into heaven,
> and is seated at the right hand of God the Father almighty;
> from there he will come to judge the living and the dead.

The ball is now in our court.

While we think on that, however, it is time to see how Jesus' disciples and those who came after him took that ball of faith and ran with it from Judea all the way to Rome and perhaps beyond. The apostles did go on foot, but even more frequently they sent their encouragement, instruction, and even chastisement in the form of a letter. Those letters came to comprise most of the rest of the New Testament, and we will turn to their authors, style, and content next.

PREPARATION FOR CHECK-IN

(Prepare for the next group session by thinking about and writing a brief response to these two questions.)

What is one thing that was new to me in this material?

What is one question that this week's topic raises for me?

HOMEWORK

(ALL STUDENTS)

☐ Read the Student Text for Session 4, including the Bible passages mentioned, and think about the reflection questions.

☐ Begin reading the book of Acts with the goal of finishing the book by the end of Session 6. Acts has twenty-eight chapters, so you'll need to read nine to ten chapters per week to get through it.

☐ Turn to the map of ancient Asia Minor on p. 100 of this book. Using the maps in your study Bible, the Internet, or other resources, label the following items on the map:

Bodies of Water	**Islands**
↳ • Adriatic Sea	✓• Crete
• Aegean Sea	⌄• Cyprus
✓• Black Sea	↳• Rhodes
✓ • Mediterranean Sea	• Samothrace

Roman Provinces *(Note that these are a Roman designation from the first century and do not reflect current geography that might have the same name.)*

• Achaia	✗ • Cappadocia	✗ • Macedonia
⤝• Asia	✗• Cilicia	• Pamphylia
• Bithynia and Pontus (shown together on the map)	✗• Galatia	⤩ • Syria
	⥾• Lycia	✗ • Thrace

You will receive the solution and develop the map further during the next group session.

EXTRA MILE

☐ Select either the city of Corinth or the city of Ephesus and research what the city of your choice was like during the first century C.E. Write a five-hundred- to seven-hundred-word description of the city in the first century, and describe the role of your chosen city in the Bible.

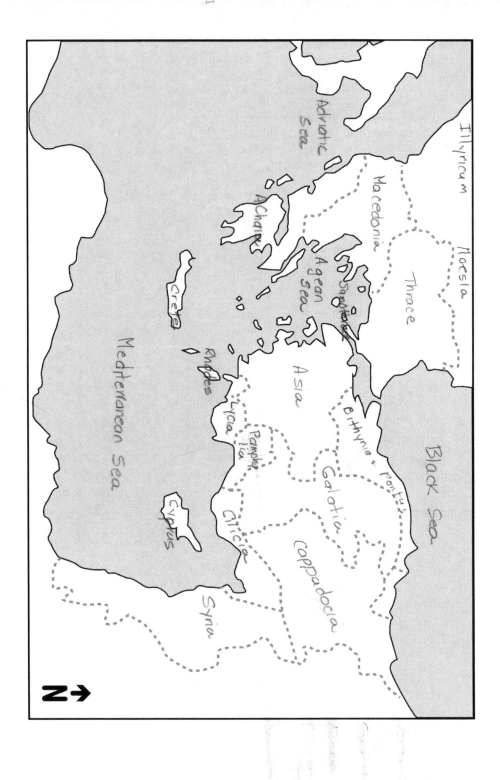

MAN OF LETTERS

Your study Bible

Responses to the check-in questions on page 131

Your filled-in map of Asia Minor from the Session 3 homework

Extra Mile homework if applicable

This Student Text

Materials for taking notes

ANCIENT WRITING

More than kisses, letters mingle souls.
—John Donne

As we shift from the Gospels to the rest of the New Testament, we pick up a type of literature that we have not encountered yet in the Bible: the letter, more formally known as the epistle. Some Bible scholars distinguish between a letter and an epistle, defining a letter being the shorter, personal correspondence and an epistle as a weightier, lengthier work sent to churches. For our purposes, though, the words are interchangeable.

There was one small letter in the section of the Old Testament that Protestants call the Apocrypha: the Letter of Jeremiah. But the New Testament takes the form to new heights, with twenty of twenty-seven books taking the form of a letter. Of the remaining seven books, four are gospels, one is history (Acts), one is a sermon (Hebrews—although some count this as a letter), and one is apocalypse (Revelation). Even the apocalypse contains seven letters to churches, as we'll see when we get there in Session 6.

As you might assume, letters are written *by* someone to someone, often with a particular purpose in mind. We'll see in the rest of the New Testament that while some letters are written to individuals (Timothy and Titus, for example), most of the longer letters are written to entire churches. We'll look at them in more depth shortly, but first let's back up and see how people wrote letters in the first century, back when fewer than 10% of people could read and write.

TO THE LETTER

Ancient letter writing was very different from modern letter writing, especially in Eastern cultures. Understanding the differences and conventions of Paul's time will help us understand some of the things he wrote a little better. To get at this, I want to literally illustrate the types of misunderstandings we have about how Paul wrote his letters.

Saint Paul Writing His Epistles by Valentin de Boulogne

This painting by Valentin de Boulogne is called *Saint Paul Writing His Epistles* and was painted in the mid-seventeenth century. There is actually a lot about this image that is historically correct, especially in the writing materials. First-century writers typically used a pen made from a reed cut into eight- to ten-inch lengths with a split cut in the end. Ten inches may seem long for a pen, but if you have to keep cutting the end to get a new sharp edge, you see the point—think of sharpening and using up a pencil.

In the image, the papers surrounding Paul are also spot-on. Up front, the item that looks like several playing cards is what a short, finished letter generally looked like. A sheet of papyrus was folded up accordion-style, then folded in half again. Because it doesn't have a string tied around and a gob of clay on the knot to seal it, we know that the letter on this desk has been opened and read. A letter from a high-ranking individual would have been sealed not by clay but wax that bore the specific mark of the sender.

So this is not only a painting of Paul *writing* a letter, this is Paul *responding* to a letter. The process is also pretty accurate. Most ancients kept notebooks so that they could jot down things they wanted to remember. Writing any letter, let alone letters the length of Paul's, took time—you wouldn't just dash one off on the road. But you might take notes while you were traveling, putting down quotes you'd heard or points you wanted to make when you had the leisure to actually write it all out. Now we often put those things in our smart phones. Back then, they used notebooks.

We know from Paul's own letters that he had notebooks, as he asked Timothy to bring them in 2 Timothy 4:13. Here he calls them "parchments," since that's what the notebooks were written on. Parchment was a much more durable material than papyrus, with the further advantage that it could be washed off and reused. It was more awkward (and expensive) for a final copy, but perfect for notes. Pieces were sewn together in a codex, which is basically a hand-written book of the style we're used to, sewn at the seams.

Paul would have kept quotations, his own rough drafts, and copies of the letters he sent off to churches in his own notebooks. That's what's on the table on the left-hand side of the drawing. In the painting Paul is referencing them as he writes.

Directly in front of him are individual sheets, another correct detail, since a draft of a letter would have been prepared on individual sheets of papyrus. Except for his letter to Philemon, Paul's epistles wouldn't have fit on a single sheet—the final copy would have taken up multiple sheets of papyrus, glued together into a vertical scroll. You can see that a scroll for the final copy is waiting on the right-hand side of the painting. Paul is working on one of the drafts.

But there are two historical problems in the representation. The most obvious faux pas is the desk. Tables certainly existed in Paul's day, but people didn't write letters at them. People wrote letters, even long ones, on their laps. Rembrandt gets that part right with this next painting, done in 1627. In that image, Paul is not just writing without a desk because he's in prison. He's writing on his lap because that's what they did, even with a perfectly good table nearby.

In Rembrandt's painting, there's a notebook and papyrus sheets on hand as Paul thoughtfully composes. But there's another historical problem in both of these paintings. Paul wouldn't have written his letters when he was all alone.

St. Paul in Prison by Rembrandt van Rijn

Teamwork

To begin with, the scene would have included a secretary. The use of secretaries in Paul's day was widespread, both for official correspondence and for private letters. Paul definitely used them—one of them is even named. Ancient secretaries had special training, which included knowing the conventions of letter writing, much as today's administrative assistants know the form of a business letter. The salutations at the beginning, the well-wishes and prayers, the greeting of individuals and groups at the end—all that followed a strict, first-century formula for letter writing.

It's unlikely that Paul included those conventions in his drafts. He'd have given the meat of the letter to the secretary (either orally or in a written draft), and the secretary would have added the standard greetings and other expected pleasantries. Then, when the letter was ready to be sent, the secretary would have brought the letter to Paul for final approval.

Co-Authors?

There were others besides the secretary hanging around. Thinking of Paul's letters as only Paul's letters is to impose a western way of thinking onto this first-century, Middle Eastern process. Eastern letter writers did not go into a back room, close the door, and write. That seems normal to us but would have baffled Paul.

Saint Paul in Prison
by Felix Emmanuel Philippoteaux,
wood engraving, 19th Century

Paul traveled with a team and wrote with a team: Timothy, Titus, Silvanus, Sosthenes, and others surrounded Paul at various times. Community is at the heart of the eastern worldview, just as individualism is at the heart of the modern West. This nineteenth-century woodcut showing Paul in conversation as he writes—even from prison—hits closer to the mark.

Paul wrote in conversation with others, who are named in the letters and who probably not only talked with Paul about what he was writing but made their own contributions to the text as well.

When a letter contains shifts in style, vocabulary, and the like, some scholars question whether Paul wrote the letter. Everybody agrees that Romans, First and Second Corinthians, Galatians, Philippians, First Thessalonians, and Philemon were actually written by Paul. There's a 50-50 split regarding Colossians and Second Thessalonians, and a majority of scholars believe that First and Second Timothy, Titus, and Ephesians were written by someone else in Paul's name.

Others, however, have suggested that we should stop talking about who "wrote" the letter and start talking about who "authorized" the letter. If we do that, a lot of things change.

Scholars like E. Randolph Richards in *Paul and First-Century Letter Writing* suggest that those people named at the beginning of a letter (rather than those who simply send greetings at the end) are colleagues of Paul who worked with him on the composition. Shifts in style or theme, Richards argues, represent an insertion by Timothy or Silvanus or Sosthenes or whoever is named at the outset as a contributor to the letter.

Although Paul's letters were frequently composed as a team effort, it was still Paul who accepted the responsibility for the contents, just as a modern CEO does when she signs a letter, even though it might have been someone else on the staff who actually composed the document. There was an ancient formula to indicate whose authority stood behind a letter—a signature of sorts—and we see it in the Bible.

Several of Paul's letters end with wording similar to the end of Colossians, "I, Paul, write this greeting with my own hand." (Colossians 4:18) He isn't referring to the whole letter but to that specific greeting—those words. That was his signature—the way a person proved to the recipient that they had read whatever the secretary or others had inserted and authorized the document. This sort of thing happens today in political ads where many people speak in the ad and then at the end you hear the politician say, "I'm so-and-so and I approve this message."

You've Got Mail

Speaking of a letter's reception, the first-century world was different on that end of the process as well. If we go back a couple hundred years before Rembrandt, we find another painting showing both the composition and the reception of letters.

This next fifteenth-century painting by Gilberti correctly shows Paul writing on his lap, and though it doesn't portray him in conversation with anyone, it puts him outdoors, where many ancients wrote their letters—after all,

St. Paul writing, and the Romans receiving, the epistle
by Petrus Gilberti, early 15th Century, located in the British Library

that was where the light was best and the smoke was least bothersome. And outside you wouldn't be alone. People would pass by, stop to chat, maybe even provide a sounding board for a particular phrase or two.

On the right-hand side of the painting, notice the other important part of the process: a human letter carrier not only brings the letter, but reads the letter to the recipients. "Reading" in the ancient world never meant a silent activity. You always read aloud, even if you were reading to yourself. Professional letter carriers were valued as much for their skills in dramatic reading as they were for their ability to get the letter to its destination.

The Romans had a postal system, but it was only for official business. Regular citizens had to either find a stranger traveling to the letter's destination or send a slave, friend, or hired hand to carry the letter there. While relying on a stranger was cheap (and surprisingly reliable), sending someone you knew had added advantages. Not only could you pick someone who could perform the reading well, one of your own people could answer questions or make clarifications on the spot.

These personal carriers sometimes had almost the entire content of the letter to convey orally, especially if the material was sensitive. The written letter might have only said, "Listen to Marcus and what he has to tell you." With that part in writing, the recipient knew that Marcus was an authorized representative of the sender, who would convey the real message more or less from memory.

I say "more or less" because sometimes the personal carriers gave out much more information than the senders intended. Barring matters of national security or other extreme circumstance, any additional verbal messages were not usually memorized verbatim. The carrier simply knew the nature of the message and delivered it in his or her own words. Recipients could ask questions about the situation and they often got more information than the sender really wanted to convey. This seems to have been the case with "Chloe's people" when they brought Paul a letter from Corinth, as we'll see shortly.

Letter writing and receiving was a big deal in the first century. There were rigid expectations and ways of going about composition and delivery that are completely foreign to the way we're used to thinking about the process

> ### FOR **REFLECTION**
>
> Does knowing about the practice of writing letters in the first century change how you think about Paul's letters? Why or why not?

today. As we look through Paul's letters and the letters of others, we should be careful not to assume that either Paul or those receiving his letters did things the way we would do them.

PAUL OF TARSUS

So what do we know about Paul himself? Between the book of Acts and Paul's own letters, we can learn a lot.

WHAT WE "KNOW"

When thinking about what we know about Paul from the Bible, most scholars believe that the letters should have more weight than Acts. Acts, many argue, was written much later than the letters, could be subject to more of the author's particular agenda, and perhaps includes legendary material. Those scholars would urge you to proceed with caution in looking to Acts for the facts about Paul's life and ministry.

Paul was born in the city of Tarsus in the Roman province of Cilicia (modern Turkey). Although born a Roman citizen, he was an observant Jew, so the New Testament refers to him both as Paul (his Roman name) and Saul (his Jewish name). Using the naming convention of the day, he would have been called Saul (or Paul) of Tarsus. There is a bit of debate about whether Paul was ever married, but his letters make it clear that, at least at the time of writing, Paul had adopted a celibate life.

What did Paul look like? Well, some people seemed to think he wrote strong letters because he didn't look like much and couldn't speak too well (2 Corinthians 10:10). For any physical description beyond that we have to look to a document written sometime before 190 C.E. that circulated widely in the early church but that never became part of the Bible: the Acts of Paul and Thecla.

Paul of Tarsus,
composite using historical sources

In this story, as Titus and Onesiphorus (who are mentioned in the Bible) were waiting for Paul to show up in Lystra, they at last see him coming and describe him as being "of a small stature with meeting eyebrows, bald [or shaved] head, bow-legged, strongly built, hollow-eyed, with a large crooked nose; he was full of grace, for sometimes he appeared as a man, sometimes he had the countenance of an angel."

In classical art Paul is usually depicted with at least some hair, but there are hints in the Bible that he may have shaved his head from time to time. On his second missionary journey, the book of Acts reports that Paul cut his hair at either the conclusion or beginning of a vow. This was most probably the Nazirite vow (not related to the town of Nazareth) described in Numbers 6:1–21.

Paul was frequently charged with either abandoning or trying to subvert Judaism. Adopting a specific Jewish discipline like the Nazirite vow could have been one way of countering that charge.

NAZIRITES

The Nazirite vow was a spiritual discipline of abstinence not unlike what many Christians observe during Lent. For a set period of time, the person refrained from all alcohol and anything related to grapes (vinegar, raisins, etc.), could not touch a dead body (even of a family member), and let his hair grow.

How long the vow lasted was up to the person, but in some cases it was adopted as a permanent way of life. This was the practice that tripped Samson up in the Old Testament when Delilah managed to cut his hair, and it's likely that John the Baptist was a life-long Nazirite as well.

The one part of Paul's physical description that we can be certain of is the "strongly built" part. If nothing else, the man had stamina. Many of his trials are recorded in the book of Acts, but he sums them up for the church in Corinth with a list that makes Chuck Norris look like a wimp:

> *Five times I have received from the Jews the forty lashes minus one. Three times I was beaten with rods. Once I received a stoning. Three times I was shipwrecked; for a night and a day I was adrift at sea; on frequent journeys, in danger from rivers, danger from bandits, danger from my own people, danger from Gentiles, danger in the city, danger in the wilderness, danger at sea, danger from false brothers and sisters; in toil and hardship, through many a sleepless night, hungry and thirsty, often without food, cold and naked. And, besides other things, I am under daily pressure because of my anxiety for all the churches. (2 Corinthians 11:24–28)*

Paul was an educated man who studied with Gamaliel, one of the most famous rabbis of the day, and emerged from his studies aligned with the Pharisees. Remember that the Pharisees were more in touch with and appreciated by the common people and that connection to regular working folk was probably enhanced by Paul's work as a tentmaker. His trade was also necessary for income. While the priests and Levites working in the Temple were taken care of through the system of tithing, rabbis and other teachers were not typically paid for their work. We see Paul trying to correct this in 1 Timothy 5:17–18. Some sort of income stream was necessary for Paul, although once he started his travels, it's likely that most of his income came as gifts.

Paul accepted gifts from churches and from friends for his work, but it appears that his income stream (or lack thereof) is a sore spot with him. He explains with an exasperated tone to the people in Corinth:

> *Did I commit a sin by humbling myself so that you might be exalted, because I proclaimed God's good news to you free of charge? I robbed other churches by accepting support from them in order to serve you. And when I was with you and was in need, I did not burden anyone, for my needs were supplied by the friends who came from Macedonia. So I refrained and will continue to refrain from burdening you in any way. (2 Corinthians 11:7–9)*

The Stoning of St. Stephen by Annibale Carracci, 1604

Defining Moments

Whether Paul was as short as the Acts of Paul and Thecla describe or not, Paul's personality was exponentially larger. Paul never just stuck a toe into a new idea. He went all-in, whatever the cause, and the book of Acts tells us that his cause took a dramatic shift in direction early in his career.

The first we hear of Paul is in Acts 7:58 where he's present at the stoning of Stephen, remembered by the church as the first Christian martyr. The account says that witnesses laid their coats at Saul's feet. It also says that he was young and that he "approved of their killing him." (Acts 8:1a) That's him in the bottom right-hand corner of the Carracci painting.

But Paul was a man of action, and tending the cloakroom at stonings was not his career goal. Stephen's stoning set off a wave of persecution against the followers of Jesus, and Paul quickly joined that effort. The next verses of Acts 8 read,

> *That day a severe persecution began against the church in Jerusalem, and all except the apostles were scattered throughout the countryside of Judea and Samaria. Devout men buried Stephen and made loud lamentation over him. But Saul was ravaging the church by entering house after house; dragging off both men and women, he committed them to prison. (Acts 8:1b–3)*

Still, however, the mission is too small. Paul is not content to just grab the offenders in Jerusalem. He wants to follow them wherever they go and drag them back to Jerusalem in chains. So he asks the high priest for permission to head north to Damascus (in modern Syria), "so that if he found any who belonged to the Way, men or women, he might bring them bound to Jerusalem." (Acts 9:2) Remember that "the Way" was the name given to the earliest Jewish followers of Jesus.

On his way to Damascus, Paul has a striking vision of Jesus that literally knocks him to the ground and leaves him blind, and his traveling

> **Read Acts 9:1–30.**
> The Conversion of Paul.

companions have to lead him by the hand to Damascus. There, God instructs a follower of Jesus named Ananias—one of the people Paul was hunting down—to find Paul and heal his blindness. I imagine the response we have in Acts 9 is a cleaned-up version of how Ananias actually responded. But he obeys, and Paul, regaining his sight, is immediately baptized.

Like a reformed smoker, Paul is now just as zealous for the Way as he had once been against it. He begins to proclaim Jesus as the Messiah in synagogues and then finally heads down to Jerusalem to meet with the rest of the disciples. Understandably wary, they're finally convinced to trust Paul by a disciple named Barnabas. Paul then starts trying to convince people in Jerusalem about Jesus to the point that threats are made on his life. Probably imagining that Paul's zeal could get them all

Conversion of Saint Paul by Caravaggio, 1600

killed, the author of Acts writes: "When the believers learned of it [the death threats], they brought him down to Caesarea and sent him off to Tarsus." (Acts 9:30)

It's about a decade from the time Paul is sent back home to Tarsus until the time he and Barnabas are singled out to spread the good news as far as they could. (Acts 13:1–3) The gospel is literally off and running.

Most of the rest of the book of Acts recounts Paul's journeys, which are typically divided into four missionary trips. Each one stretches farther west, establishing and strengthening churches along the way.

Paul always intended to visit the church that Peter established in Rome. Paul's letter to the Romans is actually Paul introducing himself and his theology to the Roman church in the hopes that they will accept him and that their community will serve as home base for Paul's hoped-for mission to Spain.

Paul does get to Rome, but not in the way he'd planned. Captured by the authorities in Jerusalem and put on trial, he spends two years in prison in Caesarea, appealing his case all the way to Rome. Paul arrives in the capital as a prisoner and continues writing letters during his confinement, though at first he was given a fair amount of freedom, and may even have been released for a few years. Tradition records that Paul was either arrested again or at least more severely limited, then finally beheaded by Nero about 67 C.E. Being a Roman citizen earned him a more merciful execution than many others experienced.

DEAR CHURCH

As we've seen, most of the "books" of the New Testament are actually letters. Let's look at the letters attributed to Paul that were sent to churches. In the next session we'll look at letters attributed to Paul that were sent to individuals, as well as those attributed to other writers. We'll examine the letters to churches in the order in which they appear in the Bible, which happens to be the order from longest to shortest.

Paul references several letters that are unknown to us. First Corinthians 5:9 refers to an earlier letter sent to that church. Second Corinthians 2:4 and 2 Corinthians 7:8–9 refer to a "severe" letter to Corinth that we don't appear to have either. Ephesians 3:3–4 references an earlier letter to that congregation and Colossians 4:16 mentions a letter to the church at Laodicea that is unknown to us. If you should run across them, I hear desert caves make for great long-term storage options.

Romans

Although this is the first of Paul's letters to appear in the Bible, it was written relatively late in Paul's career—probably between 54 and 58 C.E. It's the longest of Paul's letters and has historically had the most influence. Romans is the only book that actually names the secretary Paul used (Tertius), and the only book in which Timothy is present but not listed at the beginning as a co-author.

Paul appears to be writing this letter from Corinth, right before he returns to Jerusalem with the special offering he's been collecting from the churches in Asia Minor for the poor in Jerusalem. When Paul takes the money back to Jerusalem, he'll be arrested and eventually taken to Rome, so this is his last pre-arrest letter.

Romans is different than Paul's letters to other churches. As we'll see, most of Paul's letters are written specifically to deal with some issue, often in reply to a letter that church has sent him. With the exception of Colossae, all of Paul's other letters are to churches that he himself founded. Although local leadership took charge of those congregations, Paul felt personally responsible for what was happening there in a way that a modern bishop might be concerned for what is happening in the various churches of a diocese.

But Rome was different. Paul didn't found the church in Rome, had never been there, hadn't received correspondence from them, and, apart from Priscilla and Aquila, didn't seem to know anybody there. And yet, chapter 16 has the longest list of greetings of any of Paul's letters. What's going on? Why is Paul writing his longest letter to the Romans?

The Colosseum, Rome

The first thing to remember is that Paul's composition in Romans really ends with his "Amen" at the end of chapter 15. All of chapter 16 is the sort of material that a secretary like Tertius would have added on Paul's behalf. Paul was not familiar with the church at Rome, but it's clear that Tertius was, perhaps being a member of that church himself. But it's extremely unusual for a secretary to insert his own greeting into a letter as Tertius does in Romans 16:22. One explanation for it here is that, unlike Paul, Tertius is the one who knew these people and added greetings to all those whose inclusion would have been beneficial to Paul.

Some have even suggested that it was the presence of Tertius in Corinth that prompted Paul to write the letter in the first place. Paul badly wanted to go to Rome. He had covered Asia Minor and was ready to take the gospel further west, at least to Spain and possibly further. To travel west of Rome, however, a home base in Antioch or even in Corinth wasn't practical. Rome had a large enough Christian community to provide financial sponsorship for his travels and was a much easier travel hub for locations in Europe and even northern Africa.

If it is true that Peter was the one who founded the church in Rome as tradition claims, put yourself in Paul's shoes. Imagine that you want to establish base camp in Rome. There's a strong church there, but you didn't found it. Plus, you've had some conflict with the person (Peter) who did. Paul and Peter were both very strong personalities, and Galatians 2:11–14 tells us about Paul getting right in Peter's face and accusing him of hypocrisy. Now Paul wants favors from the church that looked to Peter rather than himself for guidance. Awkward.

Now imagine that while you're trying to figure out how to make nice with the church in Rome, you come across one of their members, traveling abroad—a member who also has the skills to write letters and who may even be willing to carry the letter back home with him. A good reference, a good scribe, and a perfect letter carrier, all in the same person and right there in Corinth. Opportunity knocked.

Of course it may not have happened exactly that way, but Paul's purpose in writing to Rome seems to be to show that he believes the same things that Christians there do in the hopes that they'll be willing to support his planned mission west. He describes much of this purpose in the fifteenth chapter. That's why most of Romans reads more like a theological treatise than a letter.

Romans isn't a quick note that Paul penned overnight—it's crafted and structured more carefully than any of the other letters. Probably it took months of notes and working with Tertius on drafts to put together something that Paul could be comfortable sending to Rome as the summary of his core beliefs. Any person preparing to write a grant proposal knows you don't do it with haste—at least not if you want to succeed.

Since Paul was taken to Rome as a prisoner, we'll never know if his letter persuaded the church to support a further mission or not. But we do know that it has persuaded a whole lot of people ever since, both to adopt Christian faith and to use Paul's strength of conviction to work toward reform.

It was Romans 3, after all, that lit a fire under Martin Luther and kicked off the Protestant Reformation in the sixteenth century. It was listening to someone read Luther's commentary on the book of Romans that "strangely warmed" the heart of John Wesley (the founder of Methodism and the root of the Pentecostal movement) two centuries later, giving him the strength to challenge the Church of England and institute social reforms from the prison overhauls to women's work cooperatives.

It's impossible to imagine any evangelistic movement or reform movement in the history of the church that hasn't been deeply rooted in Paul's Letter to the Romans. On the flip side, there are also many internal and external church conflicts that also trace their origins to Romans.

> **Read the following chapters of Romans: 2, 3, 7, 8, 11, 12, 14.**

To all of it, I think there is one basic response, which comes, of course, from the book of Romans:

> *Rejoice in hope, be patient in suffering, persevere in prayer. Contribute to the needs of the saints; extend hospitality to strangers. Bless those who persecute you; bless and do not curse them. Rejoice with those who rejoice, weep with those who weep. Live in harmony with one another; do not be haughty, but associate with the lowly; do not claim to be wiser than you are. Do not repay anyone evil for evil, but take thought for what is noble in the sight of all. If it is possible, so far as it depends on you, live peaceably with all. (Romans 12:12–18)*

Corinth

The New Testament contains two letters from Paul to the church at Corinth, aptly named First and Second Corinthians. Sitting on a tiny bit of land only four miles wide that connected the northern and southern parts of Greece, Corinth was founded about 6500 B.C.E. The first triremes, Greek battleships, were built there. By the classical age the city rivaled both Athens and Thebes in wealth and in architecture—the city is known for developing the Corinthian order, the most elaborate of the Greek architectural styles.

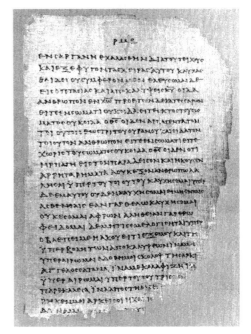

Papyrus 46

Corinth was also known for the more than one thousand temple prostitutes, especially a woman named Lais, who was so famous that medieval painters portrayed her and today she has her own Wikipedia entry. In keeping with that part of its reputation, Corinth added a new word to the Greek language. *Korinthiazesthai* (to live like a Corinthian) meant to live a life of wealthy, drunken debauchery.

The poet Horace (65–8 B.C.E.) wrote, "Not everyone is able to go to Corinth," referring to the cost of living. In the Roman period it was a bustling center of trade, with large populations of Romans, Greeks, and Jews and smaller populations of almost everyone else. It isn't surprising that the church Paul established there had some troubles.

Both First and Second Corinthians were written before the letter to the Romans. We know that because both mention the ongoing collection Paul was taking for the poor in Jerusalem, which was complete at the time Romans was written. Most scholars date First Corinthians around 53–54 C.E. and Second Corinthians a year or two later.

Remember that there are two letters to Corinth that Paul mentions that we don't appear to have. One apparently came before what we call First

Corinthians; the other Paul describes as a "severe letter." Some claim that we do indeed have this severe letter and that it's included as chapters 10–13 of Second Corinthians. That section is harsher than the rest of the letter, and everybody seems to agree that it doesn't flow easily from chapters 1–9 and was probably written at a different time.

Some scholars believe that 2 Corinthians 10–13 is the severe letter. Some just believe it's a third letter, but not the severe one that Paul mentions. Still others believe it was tacked on as a postscript because new information came to Paul's attention before he had the chance to send the first nine chapters. After all, you couldn't just drop a letter in a postbox any old time. You had to wait for a carrier, and those carriers could experience long delays. All three theories are possible and no one option substantially affects our understanding the letter.

Paul tells us that he's writing First Corinthians in Ephesus (16:8), just across the Aegean Sea from Corinth. His co-writer is Sosthenes, believed by most to be the synagogue leader in Corinth named in Acts 18. Remember that it was expected that letter carriers who knew the sender would bring additional information and be able to interpret the meaning and intent of the letter for the recipients. In verse 11 of chapter 1, we learn that "Chloe's people" (most likely Chloe's slaves who served as carriers for the letter from Corinth to Paul) have spilled more information than perhaps the church wanted conveyed.

Paul responds to the letter from Corinth and to the questions the church meant to ask him—but he doesn't even get started until chapter 7. The first six chapters all address the church in-fighting and other issues that Paul learned about from "Chloe's people." After reading those chapters, I shudder to think what the "severe letter" was like!

Not surprisingly, the church in Corinth had issues with sexual immorality and prostitution, but there was also bickering about which apostles were more important and a bit of "my baptism is better than your baptism" arguing, based on who performed the rite. As some of the dissension in the church escalated, church members were taking each other to court, which really upsets Paul. In 1 Corinthians 6:7–8, he writes: *"In fact, to have lawsuits at all with one another is already a defeat for you. Why not rather be wronged? Why not rather be defrauded? But you yourselves wrong and defraud—and believers at that."*

Starting in chapter 7, we see that the church has asked some specific questions of Paul, from sexual and marital ethics to a host of other concerns. One that may puzzle modern readers is the lengthy section about animals sacrificed to idols and its suitability for Christian meals.

The Jewish sacrificial system and the pagan system had one thing in common: only a small portion of the animal was given away. Most of it went back to the donor, who used the meat for as long as it lasted. Meat from a sacrifice might even end up in the marketplace. If you had a dinner invitation, it would be difficult to—even if you were the host serving the food—know if the food you were eating had been offered up to Jupiter that morning.

Ancient Corinth, Fountain of Peirene

Further, even if you did realize that the food had come from a pagan sacrifice, you could easily end up causing a major offense by refusing a meal. These were not the days when you could list your dietary preferences on your RSVP. Hospitality was (and still is) an extremely important virtue in eastern cultures, and much of society's functioning depended on it.

Neither Jewish nor Gentile Christians wanted to be seen as supporting idolatry, but neither did they want to be inhospitable, either by refusing or by serving food that had been sacrificed to idols. But, they wondered, maybe it didn't matter? If those pagan gods were really just lumps of wood or stone, what's the harm? They asked Paul, who responds in chapters 8–10. He sums up the issue this way:

> Eat what is sold in the meat market without raising any question on the ground of conscience, for "the earth and its fullness are the Lord's." If an unbeliever invites you to a meal and you are disposed to go, eat whatever is set before you without raising any question on the ground of conscience. But if someone says to you, "This has been offered in sacrifice," then do not eat it, out of consideration for the one who

informed you, and for the sake of conscience—I mean the other's conscience, not your own. For why should my liberty be subject to the judgment of someone else's conscience? If I partake with thankfulness, why should I be denounced because of that for which I give thanks? So, whether you eat or drink, or whatever you do, do everything for the glory of God. (1 Corinthians 10:25–31)

Paul revisits this warning not to become a stumbling block to the faith of others in Romans 14, an indicator that he sees this concept as having a wide application in the Christian community and not just local importance to the situation in Corinth.

But while they're on the subject of food, Paul comes down hard on the Corinthians for the way they celebrate the Lord's Supper (Holy Communion), another bit of info probably provided by Chloe's helpful letter carriers.

While the practice of churches today is to give everyone a small wafer or bit of bread and wine or juice, this wasn't always so. Originally it was a full meal, just as it had been when Jesus ate with his disciples. The custom only changed to be the small token of a meal we have now when the churches were being persecuted and had to meet secretly. A full meal would be too obvious and participants might be caught.

But when Paul is writing to Corinth, the church gathered in homes and had dinner. Everyone brought something to share. Whether you call it potluck or covered dish, anyone who's part of a church community in the West today knows the drill—and knows that this is often where our deepest fellowship takes place.

The problem in Corinth was that the wealthy, who didn't need to work, came early—and started eating early. They also brought the larger (and better) amounts of food. By the time the poorer members of the community got to the house with their meager portions, the bulk of the food was gone. Paul even reports that by the time the poor got there, the richer members were not only stuffed, but drunk. Paul lets them have it:

What! Do you not have homes to eat and drink in? Or do you show contempt for the church of God and humiliate those who have nothing? What should I say to you? Should I commend you? In this matter I do not commend you!

For I received from the Lord what I also handed on to you, that the Lord Jesus on the night when he was betrayed took a loaf of bread, and when he had given thanks, he broke it and said, "This is my body that is for you. Do this in remembrance of me." In the same way he took the cup also, after supper, saying, "This cup is the new covenant in my blood. Do this, as often as you drink it, in remembrance of me." For as often as you eat this bread and drink the cup, you proclaim the Lord's death until he comes.

Whoever, therefore, eats the bread or drinks the cup of the Lord in an unworthy manner will be answerable for the body and blood of the Lord. (1 Corinthians 11:22–27)

Many Christians today worry about taking Communion because they fear they are somehow "unworthy" and that in this passage Paul is warning them to stay away. But that's not his message. Unless you come in drunk and pick the pockets of those who have gone up ahead of you, this passage isn't talking about you. Paul is talking about very specific, and very obnoxious behavior.

In the remaining chapters of First Corinthians, Paul covers spiritual gifts, the metaphor of the church as the Body of Christ, the nature of love, the structure of a worship service, and the meaning of Jesus' resurrection for all Christians. He concludes with instruction about the offering he's collecting, his itinerary, and the usual greetings and benedictions.

> **Read I Corinthians 12–14.**

In Second Corinthians, which Paul writes with Timothy, we see that Paul's planned visit discussed at the end of First Corinthians has gone awry and the relationship between Paul and Corinth has taken a hit. Though he does seem to have managed a visit, he describes it in 2:1 as "painful" and decides that maybe he should just write a letter instead of coming back in person.

The latter chapters of Second Corinthians are believed to be either another letter copied in or a postscript added by Paul after the first nine chapters were ready to send.

Paul's letters to the church in Corinth give us a wonderful picture of both the challenges and blessings of the early Christian movement. They show us that struggles with sexuality, leadership, and worship in the church are not at all new. While Paul's specific solutions may be questioned in a modern setting, there's a reason that we still hear 1 Corinthians 13 read at weddings and 1 Corinthians 15 read at funerals. And Paul's language in 1 Corinthians 11 gives the church its Communion liturgy even today. Romans may forge the soul, but it's the letters to Corinth that forge the church.

Tel at the site of ancient Lystra, located in modern-day Turkey

Galatians

While some of Paul's letters to churches probably circulated from one city to another, with Galatians, we're sure that's the case. Galatia wasn't a city; it was a Roman province. Lystra, Derbe, Iconium, and Pisidian Antioch all are located in the southern part of this region, and this letter would have been brought to all of them. Paul visited Galatia on his first missionary journey and frequently returned there, as it wasn't far from his home city of Tarsus.

The date and place of writing depends on an interpretation of a trip to Jerusalem that Paul mentions in Galatians 2:1–10. Depending on what events he is referencing, Galatians could be the very first of Paul's letters, written in the late 40s C.E. or it could be closer to the time of the writing of Romans in the mid to late 50s.

There's one central question that makes up the focus of the six chapters of this letter. Remember that Jesus and all the first Christians were Jews, and "the Way," as the earliest Christian movement was called, was one of many first-century Jewish sects. As Paul—and to some extent Peter—took the message about Jesus out into Gentile territory, the question arose about whether someone wanting to convert to the Way had to strictly follow Jewish law. In other words, did you have to first become a Jew in order to be a Christian?

This question was so divisive that a council was convened in Jerusalem to deal with it, and we'll look at that in depth in the last session. In fact, whether Galatians 2 is referencing that Jerusalem council (discussed in Acts 15) is part of the issue in determining when this letter was written. The question of that council is the central question of this letter.

It's easy for us today to misunderstand the question. We often want to see the question as either/or—either Christians were supposed to be Jewish or they were not. When both Paul and the Jerusalem council determine that one can be a Christian without adhering to the entire Law of Moses, we tend to think that all Jewish Christians changed their practice. Not so.

The result of the Gentile challenge was that Christians could include both Jews and Gentiles. Jewish Christians like Paul continued their Jewish practices. They continued to circumcise their children, to keep the food and purity laws, to honor the Sabbath, and so on.

It seems from the letter that Paul had first established an understanding in Galatia that Gentiles could become Christians without having to become Jews. However, once Paul moved on to other regions, other voices rose up to challenge that assumption and the churches in the region were both confused and in conflict about it. Paul spends a fair amount of Galatians defending his authority as an apostle, so it may be that some of those other voices carried authority in the Jerusalem church, and Peter and Barnabas both apparently had been swayed to this other opinion, at least for a time (Galatians 2:11–14).

Galatians can be difficult for a modern reader to follow. Paul uses arguments from Jewish history and practice both to convince the Jews he is still Jewish and to convince the Gentiles that Jesus' mission is to unify all people. He complains that Christians miss the entire point of unity in Christ if they circumcise themselves to try to conform to only one way of being a Christian. In Christ, Paul believes, it is not either/or but both/and. As he says in Galatians 3:28–29,

> There is no longer Jew or Greek, there is no longer slave or free, there is no longer male and female; for all of you are one in Christ Jesus. And if you belong to Christ, then you are Abraham's offspring, heirs according to the promise.

The takeaway: In Christ a person becomes free. If you freely submit to the Law of Moses, well and good. But if you join with the Body of Christ as a Gentile, that is also well and good. Law and freedom, Jew and Gentile; Paul walks the fine line between opposing concepts in the book of Galatians.

Read Galatians 4–5.

Ephesians and Colossians

We're going a bit out of order here, since the letter to the Philippians comes in between these two, but there are reasons to look at these letters together.

Ephesians and Colossians—cities some 100 miles apart in the Roman province of Asia—have a lot of overlapping material, with over fifty-five verses that are exactly the same. They had the same letter carrier (Tychicus) and both were written during the early 60s, while Paul was in prison in Rome. Paul founded the church in Ephesus, but never even visited the Colossian church.

Roman Amphitheatre at Ephesus

Scholars have questioned whether Paul is the author of these letters. Some evidence that guides their queries: The earliest Greek manuscripts of Ephesians actually don't mention Ephesus in verse 1 at all, raising some questions about the audience originally intended. Ephesians is also quite impersonal, implying that the author doesn't even know the congregation. But Paul actually spent years in Ephesus. Could Ephesians be a draft that would be personalized later? Puzzling! The Colossian letter, on the other hand, is much more personal and names Timothy up front as a co-author. For this reason, more scholars accept Paul as the author of Colossians than they do Ephesians.

If those kinds of questions interest you, there are plenty of places where you can dig in and do research. The explanation I find most compelling is that we have evidence of some kind of circular letter. The church in Laodicea was also nearby, and I bet if we ever find a copy of that letter it will have the same core fifty-five verses. With those verses as a base, other specifics could be added to fit a particular city—and Tychicus could have been dispatched to deliver all three. At the end of Colossians, Paul directly tells the people to swap letters with the Laodicean church—that's

> **Read Ephesians 4–5 and Colossians 2–3.**

how we know one is missing. Or maybe there is no missing letter and on some copies of Ephesians, the first verse said Laodicea instead of Ephesus. Only Tychicus knows for sure, and he's not talking.

If you read the chapters suggested here, you'll hear themes repeated in other letters: law and freedom, the Body of Christ, love as a guiding principle, unity in the church, and so on. Whether Paul actually composed either Ephesians or Colossians is, at least to me, a secondary concern, especially given the group-think of first-century letter writing. Paul's themes are here in these letters, and the church has turned to them time and time again for inspiration, instruction, and a reminder to:

Lead a life worthy of the calling to which you have been called, with all humility and gentleness, with patience, bearing with one another in love, making every effort to maintain the unity of the Spirit in the bond of peace. (Ephesians 4:1–3)

Saint Lydia of Thyatira

Philippians

Philippians was also written while Paul was in prison—probably in Rome, but possibly in Caesarea. Paul is writing in response to a gift that was sent to him from the church in Philippi, carried to him by Epaphroditus.

Actually, Epaphroditus was part of the gift. The church was sending him to be a servant of Paul (clearly we have to adjust our view of "prison" during this time—it was more of a house-arrest at first). Epaphroditus became quite ill, however, so Paul sent him back with enough commendation to be sure he was received well on his return.

With a carrier available and a thank-you required, every bit of first-century etiquette demanded that Epaphroditus get a letter from Paul to take back with him. As we see from the opening verse (and letter writing conventions), Paul and Timothy write this together and Paul's authorship is not disputed.

The city of Philippi is in Macedonia and here was the first church Paul established on European soil. The story of Paul's stay there is in Acts 16. It is in Philippi that Paul meets Lydia, the

> **Read Philippians I and 2.**

businesswoman from Thyatira who dealt in purple cloth and who became an important patron of Paul.

Unlike Paul's relation with the church in Corinth farther south, Paul and the folks in Philippi were tight. Paul seeks to strengthen them in the face of persecution, and clearly loves them. The most famous section of Philippians is at the beginning of chapter 2 and talks about the "mind of Christ." Most scholars believe that in verses 6–11 of chapter 2, Paul is quoting a very early hymn of the church.

Thessalonians

Thessalonica is south of Philippi but north of Corinth in the province of Macedonia. It is a coastal city, known for hot springs and a famous port, with a population of as many as two hundred thousand. Situated on what was known as the Via Egnatia, or Egnatian Road, a critical trade route connecting Rome to Byzantium (now Constantinople) and the east, it was a center of trade by both sea and land.

Paul established a church in Thessalonica on his second missionary journey and if you go with a later date for the book of Galatians, First Thessalonians

Ancient vs. Modern Thessalonika

is the first letter of Paul's that we have. The first letter was probably written in the early 50s and the second letter shortly thereafter to clear up some questions in the first. Paul was probably writing from Corinth, or maybe Athens, but he was close enough that his carrier wouldn't have needed much time to run letters back and forth. Both letters are the joint work of Paul, Silvanus, and Timothy and were probably written within weeks of each other.

Paul writes to strengthen the church, since Acts tells us that Paul had to leave Thessalonica abruptly. The letters show his anxiety—was he there long enough, he wonders, for his teaching to really stick? These letters are unique in their discussion of the Second Coming of Jesus. We'll look at the concept in depth when we consider the book of Revelation, but Paul addresses it in both his first and second letters to the Thessalonians. In fact, it's rather ironic. Paul begins the last chapter of First Thessalonians by saying,

> Now concerning the times and the seasons, brothers and sisters, you do not need to have anything written to you. For you yourselves know very well that the day of the Lord will come like a thief in the night. (1 Thessalonians 5:1–2)

Well, apparently they did need to have something written to them about it and must have made that clear in their return letter to Paul. Most of Second Thessalonians deals with exactly that, although it should be noted that many scholars think Paul was not involved in the writing of 2 Thessalonians.

Read 2 Thessalonians 2.

Those are Paul's letters to churches, but Paul didn't limit his encouragement and teaching to groups. He also wrote to his co-workers in the mission field, and it's to those people and letters, as well as the letters attributed to other writers, that we turn in the next chapter.

PREPARATION FOR CHECK-IN

(Prepare for the next group session by thinking about and writing a brief response to these two questions.)

What is one thing that was new to me in this material?

What is one question that this week's topic raises for me?

HOMEWORK

(ALL STUDENTS)

☐ Read the Student Text for Session 5, including the recommended Bible passages, and think about the reflection questions.

☐ Continue reading in the book of Acts, with the goal of finishing the book by the end of the course. To avoid last-minute overload you should be around chapter 20 by the time you show up to the Session 5 class.

EXTRA MILE

(CEU AND CERTIFICATE STUDENTS)

☐ Several books of the New Testament are attributed to John: the Gospel of John, the three letters of John, and the book of Revelation. Some believe these are all the same John and some believe they are different people. Research this question and in five hundred to seven hundred words summarize the arguments for both positions.

LEADERSHIP

Your study Bible

Responses to the check-in questions on page 166

Extra Mile homework if applicable

This Student Text

Materials for taking notes

The remaining letters of Paul are all addressed to individuals: Timothy, Titus, and Philemon, although the salutation in Philemon does include other family members as well as the church that meets in their house. We will look at the first two together and then examine Philemon on its own.

THE PASTORALS

Unlike a priest who intercedes with God on behalf of the people, the role of a pastor is more that of a spiritual director and guide, taking its imagery from the shepherd guiding sheep to good pasture and keeping wolves and thieves at bay. Paul served as pastor for the churches he founded and then found others like Timothy and Titus to take on that role in certain places. Paul then became the pastor to the pastors and wrote them with instruction for leading their respective flocks.

"Saints Paul and Timothy" from the *Bible Historiale,* 14th Century, located in the Abbaye de Saint-Omer, France

The letters to Timothy and Titus are known generally as the "pastoral epistles," because Paul writes to them with guidance in leading the churches in Ephesus and Crete, where they had pastoral authority. (Sometimes Philemon is grouped in with them, just so there's not a stray letter of Paul left hanging without a category—but Paul writes to Philemon for other reasons.)

Remember that most scholars doubt that Paul was responsible for writing these letters, at least in the form we currently have them. Those doubts go way back to the early centuries of the church. There are several reasons that Paul's authorship is questioned.

First, the letters talk about an elaborate church structure and hierarchy—too elaborate, many feel, to have developed during Paul's lifetime. Others point to the fact that the letters seem to warn Timothy and Titus against Gnosticism, a system of belief that developed later. Scholars of the Greek language also notice that the style and word usage in the pastoral letters are very different than Paul's other letters.

Plus, none of the pastoral letters bears the "signature" present in other pieces of Paul's writing—there's no "I Paul am writing this with my own hand" or similar statement. So scholars are skeptical. And yet, there's a warmth and personal connection in the letters, especially to Timothy, that wouldn't have made sense coming from someone else. It's a puzzle.

The true solution to that puzzle will probably never be known, but we may be misled if we think of the question in either/or terms. We tend to want to take sides and say that either Paul wrote it all or that Paul didn't write any of it. But we've already seen in the letters to the churches (and ancient letter writing in general) that the notion of "authorship" was communal, not individual.

Nobody back then would have cried "Forgery!" if a disciple wrote in the master's name. It was common to do so. People just assumed that the content added by a disciple reflected the beliefs and teaching of the master. It would also have been common for Paul to have been the person who attached his name to lend his approval and authority to someone else's message. I think in these letters—and maybe in all of the letters—we have a combination of Paul's own words and the words of others.

For our purposes, it's enough to know that there are questions about who composed these letters—and a variety of ways to answer those questions. Whether Paul wrote all, part, or none of them doesn't change the fact that they ended up in the Bible and have been used for millennia to teach and encourage the church. So let's move on.

Who were these men and why did Paul write to them? That's what we'll look at next.

TIMOTHY

By all accounts there was no human being emotionally closer to Paul than Timothy. Timothy was from Lystra in the province of Galatia, so Paul probably met him on his first missionary journey with Barnabas, although we don't know for sure. Because Paul talks about Timothy's mother and

Saint Timothy window by Edward Burne-Jones, located at Christ Church Cathedral and College, Oxford, UK

grandmother, many have assumed that Paul stayed in Timothy's home at some point. Maybe that's how they met. They formally became a team during Paul's second journey, when he again visited Lystra:

> Paul went on also to Derbe and to Lystra, where there was a disciple named Timothy, the son of a Jewish woman who was a believer; but his father was a Greek. He was well spoken of by the believers in Lystra and Iconium. Paul wanted Timothy to accompany him; and he took him and had him circumcised because of the Jews who were in those places, for they all knew that his father was a Greek. (Acts 16:1–3)

There was a significant age difference between Paul and Timothy and it seems that Paul became a father figure to the young disciple. In his letter to the Philippians, Paul writes, "But Timothy's worth you know, how like a son with a father he has served with me in the work of the gospel." (Philippians 2:22) That is just one of many times that Paul uses close father–son language to describe his relationship with Timothy. We don't know the age difference exactly, but Timothy was young enough that Paul felt some might question his authority. Paul writes, after all, in 1 Timothy 4:12, "Let no one despise your youth."

Timothy becomes not just a loving son to Paul, but a responsible delegate whom Paul could send to deliver his letters and help deal with issues and controversies arising in the various churches. Paul sent Timothy to try to straighten out the mess in Corinth and to check on progress in Thessalonica. When Paul is in prison, Timothy comes to his side.

Timothy is named as a co-author in six of Paul's letters, showing the degree of trust Paul had in him not just as a person but also as a teacher and evangelist of the faith.

TIMOTHY **TRADITION**

A book outside of the Bible, the Acts of Timothy, claims that Timothy was stoned to death at the age of eighty by a mob when he tried to prevent a pagan procession in Ephesus in 97 C.E.

Remembering the angry mob shouting "Great is Artemis of the Ephesians!" when Paul threatened the idol-making livelihood of a silversmith there (Acts 19:23–41), the stoning of Timothy for such reasons sounds plausible.

The Temple of Artemis in Ephesus was one of the Seven Wonders of the Ancient World and a huge number of people came to Ephesus to visit it. Paganism in Ephesus wasn't just religion; it was big business. The temple was the city's pride and the chief source of income for thousands of residents.

Paul and Timothy both had the courage to take it on and both were met by fierce mobs. Paul escaped. Timothy did not.

Right at the outset of First Timothy, Paul tells Timothy to stay in Ephesus and tradition names him as the first bishop of that city. Because Paul tells his friend in 1 Timothy 5:23, "No longer drink only water, but take a little wine for the sake of your stomach and your frequent ailments," Timothy is considered the patron saint of stomach problems.

The Letters

We have two letters to Timothy in the Bible. The purpose of the first letter seems to have been to sort out some problems in church administration and to address a false teaching—most scholars assume this teaching was some form of Gnosticism—being confronted.

The second letter is the most personal of all the Pastoral Letters and implies that Timothy has oversight of several congregations. Remembering that the churches at Colossae and Laodicea are close to Ephesus, it's possible that Timothy had some degree of oversight of these congregations as well. Paul encourages Timothy to stay strong in the face of opposition, and urges him to visit—and to bring supplies—before winter.

Scholars think both letters were written during Paul's imprisonment in Rome, and it's clear from Second Timothy that Paul knows his time is drawing short.

> As for me, I am already being poured out as a libation, and the time of my departure has come. I have fought the good fight, I have finished the race, I have kept the faith. From now on there is reserved for me the crown of righteousness, which the Lord, the righteous judge, will give me on that day, and not only to me but also to all who have longed for his appearing. (2 Timothy 4:6–8)

We'll look at some of the specific instructions for running a household (a common theme in a number of the letters) in the next chapter.

TITUS

We know much less about Titus than we do about Timothy. Titus isn't mentioned at all in Acts, but is named as a companion and helper of Paul in the letter to the Galatians and in Second Corinthians. We know from Galatians 2 that he was a Greek and was not circumcised. Titus seems to have played a large role in actually collecting the offering for the poor in Jerusalem that Paul organized across the churches of Asia Minor.

Church of Saint Titus, Crete

From the letter that bears his name, we know that at some point Paul was in Crete with Titus and left him there to put the believers of Crete in order. The short letter to Titus sounds similar to First Timothy in that regard. Titus became the bishop of Gortyn in Crete and died there about 107 C.E. at the ripe old age of ninety-five. That would make him about five years older than Timothy.

Although we know little of him, Titus must have been a strong personality because the people of ancient Crete had a reputation:

> It was one of them, their very own prophet, who said, "Cretans are always liars, vicious brutes, lazy gluttons." That testimony is true. For this reason rebuke them sharply, so that they may become sound in the faith. (Titus 1:12–13)

It wasn't just Paul who had issues with the people of ancient Crete. Paul is quoting a Greek poet named Epimenides who lived about 600 B.C.E. Their lack of character was so legendary that it made its way into the Greek language with the word *kretizein*, which meant to lie and to cheat.

Perhaps that is why almost the entire letter to Titus is a reminder about the nature of Christian character. Titus had his work cut out for him, which may be the reason that Titus is the patron saint of the US Army Chaplain Corps. He was both faithful and tough.

Philemon is unlike any of Paul's other known letters. Philemon didn't travel with Paul and, although a church apparently met in his home (which was probably in Colossae), the letter isn't about church leadership or ministry. This is a private letter about a private matter—or at least as private as anything got in that day and age. We see from the outset that Paul, writing again from prison, composed the letter with Timothy, whose church in Ephesus is close to Colossae.

"Saint Philemon welcoming Saint Onesime,"
Bible Historiale, Guiard de Moulins, 14th Century

Paul's letter to Philemon, the only personal letter that everyone agrees Paul wrote, is his shortest, with only one issue to be addressed. It centers on a man named Onesimus, who somehow stumbled on Paul in his travels, and became both beloved and useful to Paul. Many believe Onesimus was a household slave of Philemon, while other scholars believe Philemon and Onesimus are brothers. But don't get too hung up on Paul "using" Onesimus. It's a pun. The name Onesimus means "useful."

There's undoubtedly an interesting backstory to this letter, but we don't know it. Many assume Onesimus is a runaway, but the text doesn't say that. We have only pieces of the one side of a conversation we get to hear: Paul's letter to Onesimus' master, Philemon.

While we might have wished for Paul to use this occasion to speak against slavery and remind Philemon that in Christ "there is no slave or free," he doesn't do that, except for a vague reference in verse 16. Paul does, however, artfully box Philemon into a corner where it would be very difficult for him to either punish Onesimus, if indeed he was a runaway, or even to continue to keep him as a slave. Remember that Onesimus is carrying the letter back to his master.

I am appealing to you for my child, Onesimus, whose father I have become during my imprisonment. Formerly he was useless to you, but now he is indeed useful both to you and to me. I am sending him, that is, my own heart, back to you. I wanted to keep him with me, so that he might be of service to me in your place during my imprisonment for the gospel; but I preferred to do nothing without your consent, in order that your good deed might be voluntary and not something forced. (Philemon 1:10–14)

Here's what Paul is saying: Onesimus has become dear to me and I want to keep him here. But he's your slave, so that would be stealing if I didn't have your consent. Protocol dictates that I have to send him back to you. I have done what is necessary, now *you* do what is befitting of a Christian leader and send him back to me.

Paul goes on to write:

So if you consider me your partner, welcome him as you would welcome me. If he has wronged you in any way, or owes you anything, charge that to my account. I, Paul, am writing this with my own hand: I will repay it. I say nothing about your owing me even your own self. (Philemon 1:17–19)

Masterful! Paul has just implied that Philemon himself really should be Paul's slave, and he throws in more obedience language in verse 21: "Confident of your obedience, I am writing to you, knowing that you will do even more than I say." No parent ever laid a better guilt trip on a person than Paul has put on Philemon if he doesn't both welcome Onesimus graciously and then turn around and send him back to Paul. And in case Philemon thought of wavering, Paul adds:

One thing more—prepare a guest room for me, for I am hoping through your prayers to be restored to you. (Philemon 1:22)

Slam dunk. Remember that letters were read aloud to the recipients, and the recipients in this case included a woman named Apphia, who, tradition says, was Philemon's wife; Archippus, whom Paul describes as a "fellow soldier" and who may have been Philemon's son; and the whole church that met in their house. For Philemon to do anything but take the high road here would have made him look like a cad who was thumbing his nose at Paul, just when Paul was in his time of greatest need.

We don't know the end of the story. Tradition says that all of them— Philemon, Apphia, Archippus, and Onesimus—were martyred in Colossae during Nero's reign. Some make the case that Philemon was from Laodicea rather than Colossae, that this is the lost letter to Laodicea, and that

Onesimus was sent back to Paul and eventually became the same Onesimus who was bishop of Ephesus after Timothy!

Whatever the truth may be, this letter shows that Paul's epistles, even the short, personal ones, were artfully crafted to achieve his ends. From puns on a person's name to the skillful presentation of a request that made it impossible to refuse, Paul was a master letter-writer. And it was with letters that Paul encouraged, chastened, and built the church—both then and now.

THE GENERAL EPISTLES

Paul gets two categories of letters all to himself (epistles to the churches and the pastorals), but he wasn't the only person with a pen and a supply of papyrus. Apart from the book of Revelation, which we'll look at in the final chapter, the rest of the New Testament books—Hebrews, James, First and Second Peter, First, Second, and Third John, and Jude—are known as the General Epistles. They are also known as the Catholic Epistles (the word catholic here means "universal"), since most seem to be addressed to a general population of Christians rather than to a specific church or person.

This isn't completely true, however. Most had a specific audience in mind, even if we can't directly identify it. Some scholars have suggested that they're known as the General or Catholic Epistles not because they had a universal intended audience, but because they gained universal acceptance in the church. You see the complexities of biblical scholarship when we can't even agree on why a group of letters has the name that it does. Whatever the reason for the category title, we'll look at these letters now in their biblical order.

HEBREWS

Some of the early church fathers tried to attribute the book of Hebrews to Paul, but no scholar on any side of the aisle today believes that to be the case. The book itself names no author, and the conditions in the church that are addressed by the book happen after Paul's time. Some claimed that Paul wrote an original in Hebrew and Luke translated it into

> **Read Hebrews 11–13.**

Greek, but that seems like a stretch to help get this book that the early church loved into the accepted canon of Scripture.

It's easy for the modern reader to forget that the books of the Bible didn't drop from the sky in one bound volume. (We covered all that in the first course *What Is the Bible?*, if you want to know more.) For our purposes here, just remember that it took centuries for the books of the Bible as we know them to be accepted as a set. Even as late as the sixteenth century, people like Martin Luther were lobbying to toss out certain books (Luther was not a fan of Hebrews, James, Jude, or Revelation) and it was later than that when Protestants decided to stop printing the Apocrypha in the Bibles they were using.

But back to Hebrews. This letter was circulated and loved in the early church, but with no author's name attached and no real way to link it to Paul, its credibility was often questioned by those seeking to establish an authoritative canon for the church. It wasn't until the fourth century that the book settled in to stay. Later scholarship hasn't cleared up any of its mysteries; today we still know next to nothing about the author or the circumstances of its writing.

The closing mentions that Timothy has been "set free." Neither Acts nor Paul mention any imprisonment for Timothy, so we can assume that the letter was written after Paul's lifetime, but obviously within Timothy's. But that mention would preclude Timothy as an author. Some of the early church fathers thought Barnabas wrote it; others held out for Apollos. The German scholar von Harnack put forward that Priscilla and Aquila wrote it together (the work uses the word "we" a lot) and that it has no author's name or initial greetings because associating it with a woman would have blunted its impact.

Orthodox Icon of Saint Priscilla

The long and short of it is that we don't know and, short of finding an ancient copy with that information added, we likely never will. What we can say is that the Greek is flawless, and the author was obviously very familiar with Jewish faith and practice.

You'll notice I've called it a book rather than a letter. It's called the letter to the Hebrews (the earliest title was just "To the Hebrews"), and it has some short greetings at the end, but apart from that it reads like a sermon rather than a letter. What we do know is that the intended audience has been through a time of persecution for their faith. There are indicators that some are buckling under the pressure, and the author seeks to encourage and strengthen them against outside forces.

Hebrews describes Jesus' role as that of a high priest—even as it seeks to make Jesus more accessible to the average person than any high priest ever was. A beautiful example of that is at the end of chapter 2:

> Since, therefore, the children share flesh and blood, he himself [Jesus] likewise shared the same things, so that through death he might destroy the one who has the power of death, that is, the devil, and free those who all their lives were held in slavery by the fear of death. For it is clear that he did not come to help angels, but the descendants of Abraham. Therefore he had to become like his brothers and sisters in every respect, so that he might be a merciful and faithful high priest in the service of God, to make a sacrifice of atonement for the sins of the people. Because he himself was tested by what he suffered, he is able to help those who are being tested. (Hebrews 2:14–18)

After those words of encouragement and support, however, the author hits pretty hard. Given all that Jesus has done for them, those listening had better get their act together:

> About this we have much to say that is hard to explain, since you have become dull in understanding. For though by this time you ought to be teachers, you need someone to teach you again the basic elements of the oracles of God. You need milk, not solid food; for everyone who lives on milk, being still an infant, is unskilled in the word of righteousness. But solid food is for the mature, for those whose faculties have been trained by practice to distinguish good from evil. (Hebrews 5:11–14)

Ouch. This tone continues, ending with a metaphor about the ground in 6:8 with "But if it produces thorns and thistles, it is worthless and on the verge of being cursed; its end is to be burned over." Now that the people are hiding under their pews, the sermon backs up and says, in 6:9, "Even though we speak in this way, beloved, we are confident of better things in your case, things that belong to salvation."

And so it proceeds. There's further discussion of Jesus as a high priest, a lengthy examination of Psalm 110, more exhortation, a dollop of encouragement, and then at last it concludes with a benediction that I have heard used as a benediction in more churches than I can count:

> *Now may the God of peace, who brought back from the dead our Lord Jesus, the great shepherd of the sheep, by the blood of the eternal covenant, make you complete in everything good so that you may do his will, working among us that which is pleasing in his sight, through Jesus Christ, to whom be the glory forever and ever. Amen. (Hebrews 13:20–21)*

JAMES

While people were debating whether Hebrews belonged in the canon of Scripture, the book of James was in the same boat. Like Hebrews, it was finally accepted during the fourth century, and, like Hebrews, that acceptance didn't keep Luther from calling it a "straw epistle," and grouping it with "secondary" works at the end of his German Bible along with Hebrews, Jude, and Revelation. Luther was never shy about saying what he thought, and his reasons are clear in his preface to the book of James:

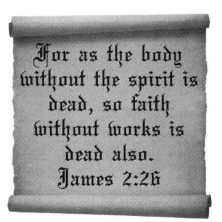

For as the body without the spirit is dead, so faith without works is dead also.
James 2:26

> *In sum: he [James] wishes to guard against those who depended on faith without going on to works, but he had neither the spirit, nor the thought, nor the eloquence equal to the task. He does violence to Scripture, and so contradicts Paul and all Scripture. He tries to accomplish by emphasizing law what the apostles bring about by attracting man to love. I therefore refuse him a place among the writers of the true canon of my Bible; but I would not prevent anyone else placing him or raising him where he likes, for the epistle contains many excellent passages. One man does not count for every man even in the eyes of the world; how then shall this single and isolated writer count against Paul and all the rest of the Bible? (Martin Luther, Preface to the book of James)*

Tell us what you *really* think, Dr. Luther.

Also like Hebrews, James doesn't bear much resemblance to a letter. Hebrews has a concluding greeting but no opening and James is the opposite, with an opening greeting "to the twelve tribes in the Dispersion," but no closing. Unlike Hebrews, however, the style and tone is more like Wisdom literature than sermon. You can pull out single statements in James in the way you would a proverb. In Hebrews, you need to look at multiple paragraphs together (if not larger chunks) to understand the point being made.

We're a bit closer to identifying the author of James, since the book begins "James, a servant of God and of the Lord Jesus Christ," but we still don't know *which* James—after all, it was a common name. Like Mary and (as we'll see shortly) John, there are lots of people named James in the New Testament— five, all told. Two were numbered among Jesus' twelve disciples. Two of the five have various traditions lobbying for authorship of this book.

The first possibility is James, son of Zebedee and brother of John. These two brothers, along with Peter, comprised the inner circle of Jesus' disciples. Whenever Jesus is with just a select few, it is these three. Many of the verses in James sound like things Jesus would say, especially regarding the disparities between rich and poor. The writing in James also strongly echoes the ethic of most parables that faith is about what you do instead of about what you think. "Faith" in James is an action verb, and "Faith without works is dead," probably the book's most famous line, lays that out plainly.

Head of St. James the Less by Leonardo da Vinci

If you listened to Jesus teach day in and day out, that might be reflected in your thought and your writing. But the difficulty with making the author James the son of Zebedee is that he was martyred about 44 C.E. Of course he still could have written the letter (which would make it the earliest book of the New Testament) or his thoughts could have been collected and circulated by someone else later.

An early composition could account for the disconnect between this book and the writings of Paul, whose first missionary journey began after this James the son of Zebedee was martyred. This letter is addressed to "the twelve tribes in the Dispersion," which meant any Jews living outside of Palestine. Paul certainly made those rounds on his trips through Asia Minor, and it seems odd not even to mention Paul in a letter so widely circulated in areas that he traveled. Unless, of course, the letter was very early and few had even heard the name Paul of Tarsus.

The other main contender for authorship is Jesus' brother James, also known as James the Just. Some believe this James to be the other James among the twelve, the one described in the gospels as being the son of Alphaeus. That would involve some complex family dynamics, but families were complicated back then just as they are now, so anything is possible. The gospels tell us next to nothing about James the son of Alphaeus (commonly referred to in the listings of disciples as James the Less), so this possibility would fill out his story a bit.

In any case, James the Just emerges in the book of Acts as not just a supporter and believer, but the leader of the church in Jerusalem. He, too, is martyred, but about twenty years later than James the son of Zebedee, giving more time for Christian communities and their leaders to become established and occasions for writing letters to arise. Certainly the leader of the Jerusalem church had things to say and would have had an audience for anything he wrote. It would also make sense that the leader of the church in Jerusalem would be writing to Jews in the Diaspora, as the greeting describes—sort of a letter from home.

There's a bit of a literary connection to this James in the greeting. While Paul typically has a religious greeting—"Grace and peace to you" or something like that—this letter has a secular greeting that says just "Greetings." We know that James the Just sent one other letter to be read far and wide—the letter drafted by the Council of Jerusalem in Acts 15, a council over which James presided. That letter began with exactly the same greeting as the book of James (Acts 15:23).

Of course there are scholars who think the author was neither James but instead the letter was penned later by a lesser-known person who attached a respected name to the work. This could have been because the person was a disciple of one James or the other, or someone who had access to some of

James' thoughts and writings and polished it up for distribution later. These scholars argue that either James the son of Zebedee or James the Just would have identified themselves more clearly at the outset of the letter to bolster its authority.

Whoever wrote it, I think James had trouble getting in (and staying in) the Bible because it tells us things we don't generally like to hear. James doesn't allow us to wander off in intellectual debates, condemn heretics of days gone by, or sit comfortably on our own righteousness. Instead, James warns us to be "quick to listen, slow to speak, slow to anger, for your anger does not produce God's righteousness." (James 1:19–20) More than half of what we hear on the airwaves today wouldn't pass that test.

Good with anger management? How about James 2:1–4, 9–10? Have you visited this church?

> *My brothers and sisters, do you with your acts of favoritism really believe in our glorious Lord Jesus Christ? For if a person with gold rings and in fine clothes comes into your assembly, and if a poor person in dirty clothes also comes in, and if you take notice of the one wearing the fine clothes and say, "Have a seat here, please," while to the one who is poor you say, "Stand there," or, "Sit at my feet," have you not made distinctions among yourselves, and become judges with evil thoughts?...But if you show partiality, you commit sin and are convicted by the law as transgressors. For whoever keeps the whole law but fails in one point has become accountable for all of it.*

James isn't done. Especially in this land of "free speech," we don't like to have restraints put on our tongues. But most of chapter 3 deals with the troubles our tongues get us into.

How great a forest is set ablaze by a small fire! And the tongue is a fire. The tongue is placed among our members as a world of iniquity; it stains the whole body, sets on fire the cycle of nature, and is itself set on fire by hell. For every species of beast and bird, of reptile and sea creature, can be tamed and has been tamed by the human species, but no one can tame the tongue—a restless evil, full of deadly poison. With it we bless the Lord and Father, and with it we curse those who are made in the likeness of God. From the same mouth come blessing and cursing. My brothers and sisters, this ought not to be so. Does a spring pour forth from the same opening both fresh and brackish water? Can a fig tree, my brothers and sisters, yield olives, or a grapevine figs? No more can salt water yield fresh. (James 3:5b–12)

Let's turn to the courtroom, shall we? James 4:1–3:

Those conflicts and disputes among you, where do they come from? Do they not come from your cravings that are at war within you? You want something and do not have it; so you commit murder. And you covet something and cannot obtain it; so you engage in disputes and conflicts. You do not have, because you do not ask. You ask and do not receive, because you ask wrongly, in order to spend what you get on your pleasures.

By this point we'd be quite pleased to have a discussion about food sacrificed to idols or something—anything—that doesn't have quite as much practical application to our daily lives. But we get no such reprieve. James 4:13–17:

Come now, you who say, "Today or tomorrow we will go to such and such a town and spend a year there, doing business and making money." Yet you do not even know what tomorrow will bring. What is your life? For you are a mist that appears for a little while and then vanishes. Instead you ought to say, "If the Lord wishes, we will live and do this or that." As it is, you boast in your arrogance; all such boasting is evil. Anyone, then, who knows the right thing to do and fails to do it, commits sin.

I don't know about you, but that last line in verse 17 leaves me gasping for air. And the beginning of chapter 5 sounds like it's straight out of the Old Testament prophets.

Come now, you rich people, weep and wail for the miseries that are coming to you. Your riches have rotted, and your clothes are moth-eaten. Your gold and silver have rusted, and their rust will be evidence against you, and it will eat your flesh like fire. You have laid up treasure for the last days. Listen! The wages of the laborers who mowed your fields, which you kept back by fraud, cry out, and the cries of the harvesters have reached the ears of the Lord of hosts. You have lived on the earth in luxury and in pleasure; you have fattened your hearts in a day of slaughter. You have condemned and murdered the righteous one, who does not resist you. (James 5:1–6)

I think it is this strong, prophetic voice, which slices and dices our way of life today just as it has in every age, that made people set the book of James to one side. Whether it came from James the son of Zebedee, James the Just, or some guy named Ralph doesn't really matter. James calls out the hypocrisy of the believer and warns us that if our words and actions don't match up, our faith is only so much hot air. When a pastor preaches from James, the sermon rarely makes the greatest hits album. As they say in the South, "Now you've gone to meddlin'!"

PETER

By now you should be able to write the first paragraph of this section yourself. Who wrote First and Second Peter? You know the answer. Some scholars stick with the attribution in the two letters and believe that they were written by Simon Peter, the disciple of Jesus who founded the church in Rome. Other scholars say that's impossible and that someone decades later wrote the letters in Peter's name. Still others split the difference and say that Peter wrote the first one and someone else wrote the second.

It does bear repeating that people writing in somebody else's name wasn't as scandalous back then as it is to us. Our first response is "plagiarism!" but writing in the name of a respected ancient scholar or leader was a common and accepted practice in ancient times. If a student were heavily influenced by the thought and instruction of a teacher and the student wrote something representing the teacher's thinking, it would have been more arrogant and scandalous for the student to attach his own name to the document. Leaving your own name off and putting the name of the original thinker on your work was considered a way of showing respect. It was the ancient way of doing footnotes, a way of saying, "Don't give *me* credit for this. I could never have come up with this on my own. So-and-so taught me this."

That's not to say that Peter *didn't* write these letters. Maybe he did. But we shouldn't dismiss the other possibilities as heretical thoughts dreamed up by liberal scholars who don't believe the Bible. As we've seen time and time again in the courses of Exploring the Bible, these writings are both old and foreign to Western readers. If any one of us were sent back in a time machine to first-century Palestine, we'd be completely lost and probably dead within a week for our lack of understanding of even basic life skills of the time. When it comes to reading the Bible, almost all our automatic assumptions are at least partially wrong.

The First Letter

In First Peter we see right off that we're looking at a conventional letter. The traditional elements we first saw in Paul's letters are back—the naming of the sender, the greeting, the thanksgiving, the closing. In the closing element, Peter says the letter is written "through Silvanus," which could mean Silvanus was the secretary, the letter carrier, or both. Since the Greek here is much more polished than you'd expect from a Jewish fisherman, the letter may have been written by a different author or Silvanus may have played a more substantial secretarial role in its composition.

SILVANUS

So who was Silvanus? If you've been reading the book of Acts, you've encountered him already under the other form of his name: Silas. A Roman citizen, Silas/Silvanus is first mentioned in Acts 15:22, when the elders in Jerusalem pick him to go with Paul and Barnabas to deliver the letter about their decision regarding the Gentiles. (More about that in the final session.) Later, when Barnabas splits from Paul over a dispute about John Mark's

Midnight Song, bronze sculpture by Tom White, Tom White Studios, Inc. (tomwhitestudio.com)

involvement, Paul takes Silas along instead on his second missionary journey.

It's Silas who is imprisoned with Paul in Philippi. Acts 16:25ff tells us that a miraculous earthquake freed them—that's why you sometimes see images of Silas holding broken chains. Joined by Timothy, Paul and Silas travel from Philippi to Thessalonica, where Paul has to make a hasty exit without either of his companions. They join up with Paul again in Corinth, where the three of them probably sat down together to compose the letters to the Thessalonian church. Remember, after all, that both Timothy and Silas/Silvanus are listed with Paul as co-authors of both Thessalonian letters. Paul's second letter to the Corinthians mentions Silas preaching in Corinth (2 Corinthians 1:19), and tradition says he was the first bishop there.

This matters to First Peter for two reasons. First, it shows Paul's confidence in Silas. He doesn't just send greetings from Silas; he lets him preach in the churches he founded and seeks his help drafting important letters. Clearly Silas was literate, eloquent, and a respected leader in the early church, making him a natural co-author of First Peter.

Second, the Thessalonian letters, especially Second Thessalonians, are the epistles of Paul's that most dwell on the question of Jesus' return or Second Coming (known more technically as the Parousia). That emphasis is the motivating factor behind both of Peter's letters as well. We know this was important in the theology of the early church and Silas apparently didn't let any letters he had a hand in go out without a discussion of it. Silas is recognized as a saint in the church; his feast day is July 13.

The audience for First Peter is basically the same as for James—those in the Diaspora—but in First Peter the recipients are more clearly defined: "To the exiles of the Disperion in Pontus, Galatia, Cappadocia, Asia, and Bithynia." (1 Peter 1:1) If you still have your maps from Session 4, you'll remember that these are the names of Roman provinces, not cities or continents.

The closing greeting in First Peter also mentions a sister church in Babylon—but not the historical place known as Babylon, which sits in modern Iraq. Among Christians of the time, Babylon was a derogatory nickname for Rome. We'll see it used extensively in this way in the book of Revelation.

The first letter of Peter makes plain that the recipients are in some kind of distress. They're being persecuted in some way, although there's debate about whether that persecution is physical or verbal. Clearly, though, Peter is preparing them to face persecution in all its forms, urging them to continue a holy life in the face of harshness as a witness to the way Christ suffered yet remained pure.

In chapter 4:12–19 we see Peter's approach to these challenges:

> Beloved, do not be surprised at the fiery ordeal that is taking place among you to test you, as though something strange were happening to you. But rejoice insofar as you are sharing Christ's sufferings, so that you may also be glad and shout for joy when his glory is revealed. If you are reviled for the name of Christ, you are blessed, because the spirit of glory, which is the Spirit of God, is resting on you. But let none of you suffer as a murderer, a thief, a criminal, or even as a mischief maker. Yet if any of you suffers as a Christian, do not consider it a disgrace, but glorify God because you bear this name. For the time has come for judgment to begin with the household of God; if it begins with us, what will be the end for those who do not obey the gospel of God? And "If it is hard for the righteous to be saved, what will become of the ungodly and the sinners?" Therefore, let those suffering in accordance with God's will entrust themselves to a faithful Creator, while continuing to do good.

We'll save the discussion of the end times for our final session, where we'll also look at the category of "household rules" that we see in a number of these letters, including First Peter. In the meantime, there's one other part of this letter that we should notice here.

DESCENDED INTO HELL

The Apostles' Creed is a very early creed of the church. It came before the Nicene Creed and the debates about the nature of Jesus that we talked about in Session 3, and probably existed in a number of variant forms before it became the creed spoken in many churches today.

I mention it in connection with First Peter because it's in this book that we find the biblical support for a line of the creed that confuses many people. A number of Protestant churches actually leave it out in their versions of the creed. The line? "He descended into hell."

As the creed relates the experiences of Jesus, it proclaims that Jesus was not idle in between the time of his death on Friday and his resurrection early on Sunday. Where was he? In hell, preaching to all those who had died before him, giving them a chance at the salvation that all who came later would enjoy. While "hell" is the English word used, the place meant in the creed is not the fiery punishing place of the damned. It is, rather, the Old Testament concept of Sheol—that gray, nondescript place that's neither heaven nor hell.

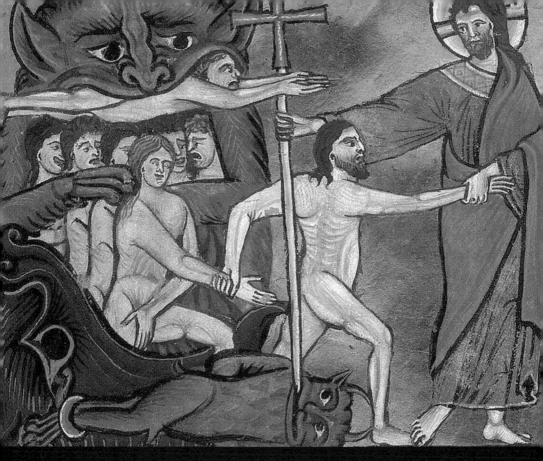

The Harrowing of Hell, ca. 1240, British Museum

Some versions of the creed say, "He descended to the dead" instead of "He descended into hell" to make that more plain.

This bit of Jesus' itinerary is news to most people, though the line appears in the most frequently recited creed of the church, The only real biblical support for the concept comes from 1 Peter 3:18–20:

> For Christ also suffered for sins once for all, the righteous for the unrighteous, in order to bring you to God. He was put to death in the flesh, but made alive in the spirit, in which also he went and made a proclamation to the spirits in prison, who in former times did not obey, when God waited patiently in the days of Noah, during the building of the ark, in which a few, that is, eight persons, were saved through water.

It's that "proclamation to the spirits in prison" part that provides the support, especially with the connection way back to Noah. Those people lived a long time back then, but two thousand years would be a stretch even for them. So the assumption was that Jesus, in the ultimate act of fairness, gave the opportunity for salvation to all human beings who came before.

While the passage in Peter is the only biblical support for the idea, there were additional writings that spelled out the events more plainly, most notably in a section of the apocryphal book titled the *Gospel of Nicodemus*. From those sources and the brief mention in First Peter, the tradition took off, and by medieval times references to Jesus' descent to the netherworld could be found in poems, plays, art, and music.

Known to scholars from the early church onward as the "harrowing of hell," it's described in the Catechism of the Roman Catholic Church,

> By the expression "He descended into Hell," the Apostles' Creed confesses that Jesus did really die and through his death for us conquered death and the devil 'who has the power of death.' In his human soul united to his divine person, the dead Christ went down to the realm of the dead. He opened Heaven's gates for the just who had gone before him.

The event is also a prominent part of Orthodox tradition, with a specific remembrance of it at services on Holy Saturday, when the priest scatters laurel leaves around the sanctuary, symbolizing the broken gates of hell.

A number of Protestants embraced the idea as well. Martin Luther said, "We believe simply that the entire person, God and human being, descended to Hell after his burial, conquered the devil, destroyed the power of Hell, and took from the devil all his power." (Solid Declaration, Art. IX)

Geneva reformer John Calvin also took up the cause with a slightly different twist: "Christ's descent into Hell was necessary for Christians' atonement, because Christ did in fact endure the penalty for the sins of the redeemed." (Book II, chapter xvi, 8–12 of the *Institutes of the Christian Religion*)

Back in Session 4 we mentioned that there were a number of different theories of atonement—the way Christians view what it means to be "saved" by the work of Jesus. Here we see two of them. The Catholic and Lutheran position is often called Christus Victor, that is, Jesus descends into hell, destroys hell, death, and the devil, assuring victory over those things for all of us. Almost every Easter hymn I'm aware of has this victory theme in its lyrics.

Jesus and Satan arm wrestling, artist unknown

The Calvinist position, reflected in much of Paul's writing, is called "substitutionary atonement." In that view, Jesus descends to hell not as the last part of a victory lap but as a condemned sinner himself—taking the sins of humanity on himself, and dying, condemned, in our place. This is the atonement theory of most Good Friday hymns.

Enter the Mormons, who basically go with the Christus Victor approach, but with a difference. For them, Jesus not only preached to the dead himself, but he organized the righteous among them to keep right on preaching, since Jesus himself had a resurrection and ascension to attend. In Mormon theology a crew of righteous spirits are still preaching to the dead at this very moment.

St. Augustine certainly had his theories of the atonement, but for him the whole harrowing of hell thing was allegory, not history, and a number of other traditions have followed that line of thought.

FACING THE END

Whatever Peter actually meant by his comments about those "spirits in prison," he is writing here to those still in living bodies who are trying to find a faithful way during a difficult time. The theme of the letter is nicely summed up in chapter 4, verses 7–11, right before the "fiery ordeal" passage quoted earlier:

The end of all things is near; therefore be serious and discipline yourselves for the sake of your prayers. Above all, maintain constant love for one another, for love covers a multitude of sins. Be hospitable to one another without complaining. Like good stewards of the manifold grace of God, serve one another with whatever gift each of you has received. Whoever speaks must do so as one speaking the very words of God; whoever serves must do so with the strength that God supplies, so that God may be glorified in all things through Jesus Christ. To him belong the glory and the power forever and ever. Amen.

Second Peter

The second letter bearing Peter's name gets very little attention. With it we're back to a letter that has an opening greeting, but no closing, and the opening is very general and perfunctory. It does reference the existence of an earlier letter in 3:1, but its style, tone, and content don't look anything like the letter we have as First Peter.

Like Hebrews and James, 2 Peter was late to the party. We have no reference to it before the year 200 and the early church fathers were quite skeptical of it. It wasn't until about the year 400 that it settled into its place as official Scripture, the very last to get in before the door closed.

While scholars debate whether Peter actually wrote First Peter, no scholar believes that Peter actually wrote Second Peter. Nobody. Not conservative, not liberal, not Orthodox, not Catholic, not Protestant. Everybody agrees that it was written very late—probably the latest of all the New Testament books, and decades after Peter's lifetime. They also agree that 2 Peter has copied and revised sections of Jude, which is why they think 2 Peter was written so late. Such scholarly agreement across theological lines might indeed mean that the end is near!

The content of the letter deals with an issue of heresy. The problematic teaching isn't identified directly, but the entire letter is an attempt to get the recipients back on board with orthodox belief. Also of interest is a remark about Paul. Not far from the end of the letter we read,

So also our beloved brother Paul wrote to you according to the wisdom given him, speaking of this as he does in all his letters. There are some things in them hard to understand, which the ignorant and unstable twist to their own destruction, as they do the other scriptures. (2 Peter 3:15–16)

Many today would agree with that. It just wasn't really Peter who said it.

If you said to someone, "Hey, I went to school with John!" the first response you'd get would be "John who?" There are lots of people named John around, so your listener would naturally want more details. Even if you said, "You know, the famous John," the matter still wouldn't be settled. John Lennon? John Kennedy? John Wayne? John Grisham? The list goes on and on.

The Bible, too, is full of people named John. It's also full of famous people named John. We have John the Baptist, John the son of Zebedee (one of Jesus' twelve disciples), and John Mark as characters within the Bible, and we have five books of the New Testament which various traditions credit to someone named John: the Gospel of John, the book of Revelation, and the three letters we will look at here called…wait for it…First, Second, and Third John. Are they all the same person? All different? A combination? It depends who you ask.

Apart from their book titles, First, Second, and Third John don't actually have John's name within them. Nobody is listed as the author of First John, and the other two (much shorter) letters claim to be from the "Elder." That elder is not named. Even so, the three are enough alike that just about everybody accepts that they were all written by the same person.

Did that person also write the Gospel of John? There is no consensus. There are enough similarities in images and themes to make that plausible and some would say the differences can mostly be accounted for by assigning different times to the writing. But if you start asking, "Which came first? The gospel or the letters?" even those agreements go out the window. Remember that the Bible is not put together chronologically. Just because the letters come later in the Bible doesn't mean they were written later. They were just grouped with all the other letters, and the people who put the New Testament books together thought the gospels should come first.

In the end, it doesn't really matter. The letters are easily understood when intertwined with John's gospel, and it's the content, not the date of composition, that is sacred. First John was known, accepted, and associated with the Apostle John very early, despite the absence of his name in the book. Second and Third John took a bit longer to become generally accepted but basically rode the coattails of First John into the canon.

St. John the Evangelist at Patmos by Alonzo Cano, ca. 1645

First John

Both Second and Third John are short letters that would have occupied just a single sheet of papyrus. First John isn't huge, especially by Paul's standards, but it is meaty and deep and is home to the verse that anchors all of my own theology: "Beloved, let us love one another, because love is from God; everyone who loves is born of God and knows God. Whoever does not love does not know God, for God is love." (1 John 4:7–8)

One of the reasons we don't have an author named in First John is that this book has even less resemblance to an actual letter than Hebrews does. While there are passages that say things like, "Beloved, I am writing to you…" there are none of the conventions of letter writing that we've come to recognize. No "From" or "To," no greetings, no thanksgivings, no signatures, no nothing. The last verse is not a lovely benediction, but just a one-off verse that says, "Little children, keep yourselves from idols."

Like Hebrews, First John sounds more like a sermon than a letter, and my guess is that it was probably both. There's no reason that a powerful message from a revered leader in the church wouldn't be written out and circulated around, even if it were not originally conceived as a letter.

First John contains a lot of the images and themes that we see in the Gospel of John: dark and light, sight and blindness, truth and falsehood, water and blood, all woven together with strands of love. With his deft use of imagery, a touch of mysticism, and its loving tone, John manages to say a lot of things that we heard in James—without having people hate him for it. Consider this paragraph from 1 John 2:3–6:

> Now by this we may be sure that we know him, if we obey his commandments. Whoever says, "I have come to know him," but does not obey his commandments, is a liar, and in such a person the truth does not exist; but whoever obeys his word, truly in this person the love of God has reached perfection. By this we may be sure that we are in him: whoever says, "I abide in him," ought to walk just as he walked.

James just takes one line to say all that, "Faith without works is dead" (James 2:26), and Luther wanted to boot him from the Bible for it. John has the exact same message, but it sails on through with no poison pen letters in response.

First John, like Thessalonians and First Peter, makes quite a few references to the imminent end of the world, embellishing that scene with the first mentions of the character known as the antichrist. That's one theme that would tie the author of First John to the book of Revelation, but we'll look at those issues more closely in the next session. Just note here that John supports the belief of the earliest Christians that Jesus would return within their lifetimes, putting an end to an evil age and ushering in the reign of God.

First John is about living purely, resisting false teaching, and abiding in God. In it we find a robust role for the Spirit, a call to perfection, a strong condemnation of Christian hypocrisy, and the sure conviction that the love of God conquers all.

Second John

John's second letter is a whopping thirteen verses long and, unlike First John, this one is truly a letter. Almost half of those thirteen verses are devoted to letter conventions.

The message is the same as First John: Abide in Christ, love one another, and resist false teaching. The antichrist gets a mention even in this tiny space. But the thing scholars want to talk about in Second John is not the content of the letter but the recipient.

Verses 1–3 read:

> The elder to the elect lady and her children, whom I love in the truth, and not only I but also all who know the truth, because of the truth that abides in us and will be with us forever: Grace, mercy, and peace will be with us from God the Father and from Jesus Christ, the Father's Son, in truth and love.

After reading First John, it is easy to recognize that the reference to "children" means those in the faith community of the recipient, not the person's literal offspring. The basic assumption is that the "elect lady" at the beginning and the "elect sister" referenced at the end are churches and the "children" are the members of those church communities.

Maybe. But there's also a line in verse 5 that begins, "But now, dear lady…," and it sounds equally plausible that the letter might have had a particular individual in mind. But who? There are three women named in the Bible who have churches in their homes: Phoebe, Priscilla, and Lydia. Priscilla was part of a team with her husband, Aquila, so the absence of a joint greeting makes it seem less likely that she was the "elect lady" of Second John.

Phoebe was from Cenchrea (just south of Corinth) and Lydia was further north in Philippi. Writing to either of them would have required a trip across the Aegean Sea from John's likely location in Ephesus. Of the two, I would favor Lydia, because Lydia's hometown of Thyatira is relatively close to Ephesus. A more local community that knew Lydia and her family could explain the reference to the "elect sister" who was sending greetings at the end.

Of course church tradition tells us that John was not wanting for the company of elect women closer to home. As he was dying on the cross, Jesus put his mother under John's care (John 19:26–27), and the church has always held that both the Virgin Mary and Mary Magdalene lived out their lives with John in Ephesus. Was one of them the "elect sister" sending greetings? We'll never know.

Third John

Third John is fifteen verses long and begins, "The elder to the beloved Gaius, whom I love in truth." Isn't it nice when people name the recipients of their letters? Still, Gaius was a common name and, again, we have three of them mentioned in the Bible—one in Ephesus, one in Derbe, and one in Corinth. It could be any of them or another Gaius entirely.

The opening and closing sections are like Second John, only instead of "children," the talk is of "friends." It seems that Gaius was a church member rather than a church leader, but he's getting a letter because he's a personal friend of John's. The letter's purpose is to encourage Gaius to welcome and support some traveling missionaries coming his way.

Apparently there was another letter about the issue (which we don't have) written to the church where Gaius was a member. Someone named Diotrephes, "who likes to put himself first," and who didn't acknowledge John's authority, was spreading false rumors. This Diotrephes was not only refusing to welcome the missionaries, but was kicking others who wanted to welcome them out of the church. So John is going around official channels by enlisting the help of Gaius. As we saw in Corinth, church conflict is not a new thing.

The closing section of the letter says, "I have much to write to you, but I would rather not write with pen and ink; instead I hope to see you soon, and we will talk together face to face" (v. 13). That is almost identical to the closing of Second John, making it seem all the more likely that both were written by the same person to specific individuals within a church community.

Now to him who is able to keep you from falling, and to make you stand without blemish in the presence of his glory with rejoicing, to the only God our Savior, through Jesus Christ our Lord, be glory, majesty, power and authority, before all time and now and forever. Amen. (Jude, verses 24–25)

Those verses, so often recited as a benediction at Christian services, are the only thing most people would recognize about this one-chapter letter. Those are the final verses, so again we have a case where the conventions of a letter aren't all present.

There is a greeting at the beginning which, though it specifically names the sender, is vague about the recipients:

Jude, a servant of Jesus Christ and brother of James, to those who are called, who are beloved in God the Father and kept safe for Jesus Christ: May mercy, peace, and love be yours in abundance. (Jude, verses 1–2)

The two most common assumptions about the authorship of this book are either that Jude (which is short for Judas) is another of Jesus' brothers (mentioned in Matthew 13:55 and Mark 6:3) or that the letter was composed by an anonymous writer putting the name of Jude on the document. There are all kinds of other options, since there are other people named Jude in the Bible (including some of the twelve disciples) and, as we've seen, other people named James. But most scholars fall into one of the first two camps.

If you read this little book, you'll notice the tone is similar to other General Epistles. Jude warns his listeners about false teachings and unrighteous living and talks a bit about the end of all things. The message is akin to Second Peter on many levels. But in Jude, you'll also see a couple of verses that will probably make you scratch your head:

But when the archangel Michael contended with the devil and disputed about the body of Moses, he did not dare to bring a condemnation of slander against him, but said, "The Lord rebuke you!" (v. 9)

It was also about these that Enoch, in the seventh generation from Adam, prophesied, saying, "See, the Lord is coming with ten thousands of his holy ones, to execute judgment on all, and to convict everyone of all the deeds of ungodliness that they have committed in such an ungodly way, and of all the harsh things that ungodly sinners have spoken against him. (v. 14–15)

The Burial of Moses by William Blake, 1805

If those events seem like news to you, you're not alone. They are not found within the Bible as we know it. Instead, Jude is quoting from two apocryphal books: the Assumption of Moses (v. 9) and the Book of Enoch (v. 14–15). Because of his use of these books and the question of authorship, Jude is another book that was very late securing a place in the canon.

IN FORMATION

What we see across all these letters is a picture of the fits and starts of an emerging religion. Begun as a movement within Judaism, this new belief system required the earliest Christians to struggle to define what they did and didn't believe, what voices they could or couldn't trust, what behaviors were and weren't acceptable, and what documents would be authoritative for their common life and practice.

Clearly there were books not in our current Bibles that some turned to for inspiration—even some of the Bible writers themselves relied on those sources as we see in Jude and elsewhere. What was "true" belief and what was heresy was still very much in flux in these early years, and it took several centuries of debate, questions, and councils before the Bible we have today and orthodox belief took a firm shape. Even then there were respected church leaders and reformers who continued to question the authority of some texts across the next thousand years and more.

> ### FOR REFLECTION
>
> You have now read all or parts of many letters.
>
> Do you have a favorite?
>
> Are there any you would like to toss out, as Luther did?
>
> Did anything surprise you?
>
> Who do you think wrote these letters?

In the letters, we've been looking at church beliefs and struggles on a very local and personal level. In the final session we'll back up to get a broader overview of the Christian movement and that bewildering vision of the end of all things known as Revelation.

PREPARATION FOR CHECK-IN

(Prepare for the next group session by thinking about and writing a brief response to these two questions.)

What is one thing that was new to me in this material?

```
[                                                              ]
```

What is one question that this week's topic raises for me?

```
[                                                              ]
```

HOMEWORK

(ALL STUDENTS)

- ☐ Read the Student Text for Session 6, including the Bible references mentioned.
- ☐ Think about the questions for reflection.
- ☐ Do a bit of online research and find one person (there are many) born after 1900 who has been called the Antichrist.
- ☐ Finish reading the book of Acts.

EXTRA MILE

(CEU AND CERTIFICATE STUDENTS)

- ☐ Do some research and find as many people as possible (of any era) who have been called the Antichrist.
- ☐ Reflect on the letters to the seven churches in Revelation 2–3. Considering the strengths and weaknesses of your own faith community or other group, write the letter you think God might send to your assembly.

EXPERIENCING
CHURCH

THE BIG PICTURE

For the past two sessions we've been using a magnifying glass to examine the letters of Paul and of others. We've seen their lives; we've heard about the conflicts in Corinth, the reputation of Crete, and the details of a runaway slave named Onesimus. But for this last chapter, it's time to pull back to the big picture.

Across these last three sessions, your homework has included reading the entire book of Acts. The stories and travels related there give us the basis for interpreting much of what we read in the letters and for helping to place the letters in time, space, and context. When we pull back from those details, we see that Acts, and even many of the letters themselves, are also pieces of a larger puzzle. They show us the conception, birth, and early formation of the Christian church.

As we've mentioned before, there is no book of the Bible that shows us with certainty that Christianity is completely separated from its Jewish roots. But we can see how those who became disciples of Jesus began to organize, practice, and describe their religious experiences in ways that set them apart from more traditional Jewish faith and practice.

While a history of the church is beyond the scope of this series, we've structured the courses with the assumption that part of basic biblical literacy is connecting the dots from the Bible to the religion that holds it sacred. Your biblical education is incomplete at best if you can't walk across the Bible bridge to better understand the religion of over two billion people worldwide, whether you profess that religion or not. I'll grant you that understanding the Bible may make the actions of some of those two billion people even more mystifying—and I'll guess that a good number of those two billion people have never read the collection of texts they claim informs their faith. All of those are reasons the *Exploring the Bible: The Dickinson Series* was created.

In any case, we turn now to what the Bible tells us about the earliest Christians and the emerging church that would bear their name. You can decide for yourself whether that early church bears any resemblance to what you see in Christianity today.

Tongues of Fire, Christ Church Amsterdam

HAPPY BIRTHDAY, CHURCH

While the church celebrates the birthday of Jesus on December 25, there is another day that is considered to be the birthday of the church: Pentecost. Pentecost is the Greek name for the Jewish festival of Shavu'ot or the Festival of Weeks. The Greek name *pentekoste* means fiftieth, and reflects that it is celebrated seven weeks (roughly fifty days) after Passover. Pentecost is the Jewish festival that celebrates the giving of the Torah to Moses on Mt. Sinai. To understand how this particular festival became the birthday of the church, we have to look to the second chapter of the book of Acts.

Remember that Acts is written by Luke and is generally seen as the second volume of his gospel. The first verse of Acts lays that out plainly: "In the first book, Theophilus, I wrote about all that Jesus did and taught from the beginning." Acts is the sequel. The first chapter of Acts wraps up the earthly life of Jesus by describing his ascension into heaven and the selection of a disciple to replace the betrayer Judas (who had committed suicide) in the band of twelve. Remember from the Old Testament course that twelve is a symbolic number, so the apostles can't just leave it at eleven. They cast lots—similar to drawing straws, only trusting that God is guiding the selection—and pick a man named Matthias.

"Jesus' followers continued to meet and chose Matthias to replace Judas Iscariot," from *Bible Stories for Children*

The selection of Matthias seems to have had little impact, and I'm probably not the only one who'd argue that God's choice to fill the slot would've been Paul. But there are two other things mentioned in Acts 1 that are important for what follows. One is a prediction of Jesus before he ascends and the other is a prediction of the angels who show up once Jesus disappears.

Luke tells us in Acts 1:4–5 that after Jesus had been with them forty days after his resurrection, he told them the following:

> While staying with them, he [Jesus] ordered them not to leave Jerusalem, but to wait there for the promise of the Father. "This," he said, "is what you have heard from me; for John baptized with water, but you will be baptized with the Holy Spirit not many days from now."

Remembering all the various strains of expectations for a messiah that we talked about in the chapters about Jesus, it's not surprising that the disciples have some idea about what this might look like. They ask in verse 6: "Lord, is this the time when you will restore the kingdom to Israel?" But Jesus responds instead with the last thing his closest disciples ever hear him say,

> "It is not for you to know the times or periods that the Father has set by his own authority. But you will receive power when the Holy Spirit has come upon you; and you will be my witnesses in Jerusalem, in all Judea and Samaria, and to the ends of the earth." When he had said this, as they were watching he was lifted up, and a cloud took him out of their sight. While he was going and they were gazing up toward heaven, suddenly two men in white robes stood by them. They said, "Men of Galilee, why do you stand looking up toward heaven? This Jesus, who has been taken up from you into heaven, will come in the same way as you saw him go into heaven." (Acts 1:7–11)

Ascension of Christ by Benvenuto Tisi da Garofalo, ca. 1510-1520

While we might have wished for the guys in the robes to stick around and give a few more details, apparently they don't. But it's impossible to overestimate the power of this account for the formation of the expectations of the early church. While Jesus talked some about the end of days and those sorts of expectations during his ministry, the disciples at that point were still trying to figure out who this guy Jesus was. But here, there are no more doubting Thomases.

These are the guys who saw Jesus arrested and crucified and ran away, afraid for their own lives. These are the ones who last encountered a couple of folks in white robes at an empty tomb, angels who asked them, then as now, why they were gawking when Jesus had risen and gone ahead of them to Galilee. That turned out to be pretty good information, and now they were back.

Jesus had already disappeared and reappeared to them relatively quickly. Now Jesus is making them a mysterious promise about a huge power coming for them, shortly, that will take them to the ends of the earth with their witness. And angels are again predicting that they haven't seen the last of Jesus. No questions this time around. Verse 12 has the disciples obediently returning to Jerusalem to an upstairs room where they were staying.

The Pentecost by unknown French goldsmith, 1150-1160

All the remaining eleven disciples were staying in that upper room, where, according to verse 14, they "were constantly devoting themselves to prayer, together with certain women, including Mary the mother of Jesus, as well as his brothers." Verse 15 tells us that the "believers" at this stage numbered about 120 people.

Acts 2 begins on the day of Pentecost, with the whole crew gathered together in one place. The account goes on,

> *And suddenly from heaven there came a sound like the rush of a violent wind, and it filled the entire house where they were sitting. Divided tongues, as of fire, appeared among them, and a tongue rested on each of them. All of them were*

filled with the Holy Spirit and began to speak in other languages, as the Spirit gave them ability.

Now there were devout Jews from every nation under heaven living in Jerusalem. And at this sound the crowd gathered and was bewildered, because each one heard them speaking in the native language of each. Amazed and astonished, they asked, "Are not all these who are speaking Galileans? And how is it that we hear, each of us, in our own native language? Parthians, Medes, Elamites, and residents of Mesopotamia, Judea and Cappadocia, Pontus and Asia, Phrygia and Pamphylia, Egypt and the parts of Libya belonging to Cyrene, and visitors from Rome, both Jews and proselytes, Cretans and Arabs—in our own languages we hear them speaking about God's deeds of power." All were amazed and perplexed, saying to one another, "What does this mean?" But others sneered and said, "They are filled with new wine." (Acts 2:5–13)

Peter gets up to answer those questions and preaches a sermon that goes on for almost the rest of the chapter. In wind and flame, the church is born.

IT'S ABOUT THE EXPERIENCE

The key to understanding Christianity is the recognition that, for all its (appropriate) attention to the Bible, Christian faith is first and foremost about the religious *experience* of the believer. Of course people of all faiths have religious experiences, and this is not to say that Christian experience is better or worse than the others. Christian experience, however, is distinct from the others in that it is formed, verified, and transmitted through bodily, relational, outward experience.

The Hebrew Scriptures are full of such religious experiences, and an intersection for Jews and Christians is the common belief that God is willing to enter into relationship with at least some human beings, and work in and through human history. For both Jews and Christians, God is personal and interacts with human beings in tangible, physical ways.

Christians take this relational God a step further. It's not just the Word, but rather the Word made *flesh* that forms the Christian worldview. And it's not just the Word made flesh in Jesus, but the belief that what happens to the believers in Acts 2—receiving the power of God's Spirit—is a universal opportunity. That universal opportunity generates the universal mandate—to go into all the world, to witness to that opportunity "in Jerusalem, in all Judea and Samaria, and to the ends of the earth." As Paul begins to articulate in his letters, Christians believe that they become the "body of Christ," and through the guidance of the Holy Spirit, continue to be the hands and feet of Jesus in the world.

Christian faith began in the experience of Pentecost by those who had first-hand experience of Jesus and believed

TIMELINE FOR **PAUL'S MINISTRY**

Christ has no body but yours,
No hands, no feet on earth but yours,
Yours are the eyes with which he looks
Compassion on this world,
Yours are the feet with which he walks to do good,
Yours are the hands, with which he blesses all the world.
Yours are the hands, yours are the feet,
Yours are the eyes, you are his body.
Christ has no body now but yours,
No hands, no feet on earth but yours,
Yours are the eyes with which he looks
compassion on this world.
Christ has no body now on earth but yours.

(St. Teresa of Avila, 1525–1582)

that, because of that encounter, they'd been given first-hand experience with God. When Paul and the other apostles spread the gospel message, it was a message that experiencing God directly was possible ("the Kingdom of God has come near"). And when people wondered what the nature of this God was like, experiencing the love and care of the Christian was supposed to provide the answer.

That experiential core has never changed. Whether Christians do this well or poorly is of course debatable, but the point remains. Christianity holds that the believer is, in a mystical way, the continuing incarnation of Christ in the world. The old identity is washed away in the waters of baptism and thereafter the Christian is reminded of his or her new identity in the ritual of Holy Communion, ingesting the body and blood of Christ (or its symbols, depending on your theology). That makes Christ's body, literally, a part of the believer.

Which is not to say that all Christians express this belief the same way. In some Christian traditions the experience of faith is highly ritualized, emphasizing the awe and mystery of standing in the presence of God. Typically in these settings the experience of faith touches all the senses: the visual beauty of art and architecture, the soaring spirit of music, the scent of incense that literally becomes the air participants breathe.

In some traditions the experience of God evokes a strong sense of humility and almost stunned silence. These believers turn their reflection inward and their sanctuaries are often without ornament and sometimes, as in the case of the Quakers, mostly without sound. There are those who take the specific experience of speaking in other languages in Acts 2 to be their primary expression; when someone from one of the quieter traditions enters these sanctuaries, they have a similar reaction to the observers in Acts 2. It seems like mayhem, and they wonder what the people have been smoking. The Old Testament called such expressions of God's spirit a "prophetic frenzy."

Whether it's through praise bands or classical choirs, learned sermons or lay testimony, stained glass or plank walls, shouting, silence, or responsive prayers, all Christian traditions proclaim that you enter Christian faith through the portal of experience.

For some, that experience is dramatic, like Paul getting knocked off his horse on the road to Damascus. For others, it's a long process of thought and questioning, like Thomas asking to see and touch Jesus' wounds. For still others, it's the experience of warmth and community in a family, a person, or a church community. Christians can (and do) sometimes argue about what constitutes a "valid" Christian experience, but it's all rooted in experience nonetheless.

I think this is why Christians are also more susceptible to stepping out of the portal of Christian faith in the wake of difficult or negative experiences. The experience of feeling excluded from a church community, the tragic death of a loved one, becoming the victim of senseless violence, being betrayed and harmed by a Christian leader—all those things and more have resulted in some abandoning Christian faith altogether. Those who adhere to traditions not as strongly rooted in religious experience often have difficulty understanding this.

> **FOR REFLECTION**
>
> What experiences, religious or otherwise, have shaped your life and belief about the world?
>
> Do you share your experiences with others? Why or why not?

This is also why many atheists feel like they're banging their heads against a wall when talking to Christians. Atheists pride themselves in looking to facts and rational argument to determine what they believe to be "true." But when they interact with Christians, they're talking to people who find their "truth" through their own experiences and the experiences of their faith community and tradition. Both are valid kinds of truth, but it's apples and oranges. Ideally, each has something to offer to the other, but often interactions just end up with the atheist claiming the Christian has no brain and the Christian claiming the atheist has no soul.

GENTILES AND THE COUNCIL OF JERUSALEM

The importance of experience is clear in Acts 10–15. The sequence begins with an experience of Peter, who has a vision of a sheet being lowered from heaven, full of all the foods that the laws in the Torah called "unclean." The vision is accompanied by a voice telling Peter to eat the unclean foods. Peter does what any good Jew would do when offered a plate of bacon. He says, "By no means, Lord; for I have never eaten anything that is profane or unclean." The voice responds, "What God has made clean, you must not call profane." (10:14–15) This whole scene replays itself three times—like *Groundhog Day*—and then stops.

While Peter tries to figure out the meaning of his vision, a real-life event happens outside his gate. During Peter's vision, God sends word to a very pious but very Gentile Roman centurion named Cornelius, telling him to send somebody to Joppa to find a person named "Simon, who is called Peter," who's staying with Simon the tanner in a house on the coast. In response, Cornelius sends out two slaves and a devout soldier to complete the task.

So while Peter is contemplating pork and shellfish, those messengers from Cornelius arrive, asking Peter to return with them to visit Cornelius. Peter obliges, saying nothing further about the vision until he arrives at the home of Cornelius. There, he begins to speak to the crowd Cornelius has gathered, saying,

> You yourselves know that it is unlawful for a Jew to associate with or to visit a Gentile; but God has shown me that I should not call anyone profane or unclean. So when I was sent for, I came without objection. (Acts 10:28–29)

JEWS AND **GENTILES**

While it is clear in this passage that Peter believes his Jewish faith prohibits him from visiting a Gentile, it is clear in other passages of Scripture that such prohibitions were not generally known or practiced.

continued on page 178

The Vision of St. Peter by Tintoretto, ca. 1556

In Luke 7:1-10, Jesus is headed to the home of a Roman centurion and we learn that the centurion actually built the local synagogue. Nothing is said to indicate that either thing was out of the ordinary except the centurion's generosity.

The Temple included a special place, the Court of the Gentiles, where Gentiles were encouraged to enter and pray, and a number of Old Testament passages (like Zecharaiah 8:23) talk of Jews and Gentiles going together into God's presence.

One glance across the Christian landscape shows that the doctrines, creeds, and laws associated with Christian practice vary widely, even regarding something as basic as Christian baptism. We've already seen that there was, likewise, a wide array of Jewish belief and practice in the first century.

To assume that Peter's statement represents all of Judaism, even all of Judaism back in the first century, would be to misread the text. There may have been particular circles in Peter's time that forbid Jews to associate with Gentiles—the first century was a long, long time ago and there is much we don't know. But it is clear that it was not the norm.

Peter goes on to preach to the crowd, beginning with his newfound understanding:

> I truly understand that God shows no partiality, but in every nation anyone who fears him and does what is right is acceptable to him. (Acts 10:34–35)

What is notable for our discussion about experience is what happens at the end of his message:

> While Peter was still speaking, the Holy Spirit fell upon all who heard the word. The circumcised believers who had come with Peter were astounded that the gift of the Holy Spirit had been poured out even on the Gentiles, for they heard them speaking in tongues and extolling God. Then Peter said, "Can anyone withhold the water for baptizing these people who have received the Holy Spirit just as we have?" So he ordered them to be baptized in the name of Jesus Christ. Then they invited him to stay for several days. (Acts 10:44–48)

When Peter goes back to Jerusalem, his critics demand, "Why did you go to uncircumcised men and eat with them?" (Acts 11:3). Peter tells them the whole story, ending with "If then God gave them the same gift that he gave us when we believed in the Lord Jesus Christ, who was I that I could hinder God?" (Acts 11:17) That satisfies the critics: "When they heard this, they were silenced. And they praised God, saying, 'Then God has given even to the Gentiles the repentance that leads to life.'" (Acts 11:18)

St. Peter and Cornelius the Centurion by Bernardo Cavallino, 1640s

The next few chapters of Acts move on to describe mounting persecution, and the narrative moves away from Peter and on to Paul and his first missionary journey. It's not until Paul and Barnabas return from this trip that the issue of Gentile believers flares up again.

> Then certain individuals came down from Judea and were teaching the brothers, "Unless you are circumcised according to the custom of Moses, you cannot be saved." And after Paul and Barnabas had no small dissension and debate with them, Paul and Barnabas and some of the others were appointed to go up to Jerusalem to discuss this question with the apostles and the elders. (Acts 15:1–2)

The resulting council in Jerusalem has an uncanny resemblance to current debates between Christians. On the one side are those who say, "The Bible says…" and on the other are those who point out that their experience points to a different conclusion. The "Bible says" folks in Jerusalem were the Pharisees, who quoted the Law of Moses that demanded circumcision of any who wanted to be considered the people of God.

Those Pharisees were absolutely right. There's nothing quite so clear in the Old Testament, from the call of Abraham to the day of that Jerusalem council, as the fact that circumcision was the sign of the covenant. Read Genesis 17 if you doubt me. And it doesn't say this is something subject to change down the road. It's an "everlasting covenant" to be kept "throughout your generations."

Remember, this is a Jewish council with the Jewish leaders of a new Jewish sect. Those who followed "the Way," as it was first called, became known as "Christians" in Acts 11:26. But they're still not a separate religion. If they were, the Pharisees wouldn't have cared what they did. But these folks are Jews, so the Pharisees take their argument back to the source—to the Torah and God's everlasting sign of the covenant established with Abraham. Scripture is clear, end of argument.

Except that it isn't. After they debate for a while, Peter gets up and tells about his experiences with Gentiles saying, "And God, who knows the human heart, testified to them by giving them the Holy Spirit, just as he did to us; and in cleansing their hearts by faith he has made no distinction between them and us." (Acts 15:8–9) Then Paul and Barnabas get up and tell about their experiences of God blessing and accepting Gentiles.

Then James, who's leading the council, makes a brilliant move. Staying within Scripture, he moves the discussion from the law to the prophets and re-shapes a quote from Amos 9:11–12, which opens the door, "so that all other peoples may seek the Lord." After tying the experiences of Peter and Paul to God's intention expressed through the prophets, James makes the following decision:

> *Therefore I have reached the decision that we should not trouble those Gentiles who are turning to God, but we should write to them to abstain only from things polluted by idols and from fornication and from whatever has been strangled and from blood. (Acts 15:19–20)*

We've already seen how Paul pushes the limits of even these commands, in his discussions of food sacrificed to idols, and in the discussion in Romans 14 about being a stumbling block. Note that *porneia*, the Greek word translated as "fornication" here, is a general term for illicit sexual activity, and also used in the Bible in the symbolic sense to represent idolatry. The admonition to

Taking the Council's decision to the churches from The Brick Testament.

abstain from "whatever has been strangled and from blood" is a reference to the laws of meat preparation that demand that blood be drained from an animal at the time of slaughter and cooked out of the meat. The rest of the council agrees with James and a letter is prepared and sent out as official instruction to all the churches.

For these early Christians, experience doesn't trump Scripture. But the experience of God's spirit was powerful enough to make devout Jews, even a former Pharisee like Paul, question an interpretation of Scripture that had been in place for over two millennia. James anchors his decision in a different part of Scripture—one that acknowledges that God has bigger plans for the future—and thereby validates both those who looked to the Scriptures and those who had new experiences of God's current work.

Christianity that's merely *practiced* is not Christianity. From the commands of Jesus onward, Christianity has been a faith that is *lived*. Remember that James said, "Faith without works is dead." He wasn't entering into the faith-or-works debate of the Protestant Reformation. He wasn't even contradicting Paul's claim that people are saved by faith. He was saying that faith for the Christian isn't an intellectual proposition, an assent to a set of doctrines, or a simple adherence to rules.

For the Christian, faith *is* works—an on-going experience of God's spirit that changes the way the believer lives in the world. It alters relationships, social class distinctions, business practices, and every other life experience up to and including the experience of death. And, sometimes, it alters which verses in the Bible guide our common life together.

HOUSEHOLD RULES

With talk of Christianity altering relationships and class distinctions, let's go back and look at a section of a number of the New Testament letters that we glossed over in the last couple of chapters.

In five of the New Testament letters— Ephesians, Colossians, First Timothy, Titus, and First Peter—there's a series of instructions about how Christians should behave in various relationships. These instructions are called "household rules" because they mostly deal with relationships within a household. But they're also grouped together because "household rules" or "household codes" represent a form of instruction common in the Greco-

Roman world, not just within the pages of the Bible.

When we have a literary genre in the Bible that's also found in non-biblical cultures, we can find meaning most easily by looking at the places where the biblical accounts are *different* from those other sources. It can also be helpful to look at the specific context in which these works of literature were written—both the context of letters written to specific people for specific reasons, and the context of the ancient world itself.

HOUSEHOLD CODES

Read the following passages containing household codes:

Ephesians 5:21–6:9
Colossians 3:18–4:1
I Timothy 2:1–6:2
Titus 2:1–10
I Peter 2:13–21, 3:1–7

So, for a moment, put your assumptions about and experiences with these texts aside. Cast off any righteous indignation that sees these passages as legitimizing slavery and subjugating women. Yes, they have been horribly used for those ends. Worse, they still are used in that way in many quarters. In my time as a mediator for the Atlanta courts, I watched ordained ministers instruct women in their churches to remain with husbands who beat them because 1 Peter 3:1–2 says if you stick it out you'll change him. I have seen it and heard it, and I've had these verses used against me in my own ministry.

Even worse, these portions of Scripture are too frequently used hypocritically. People have frequently based their opposition to my ordination and ministry by quoting 1 Timothy 2:11–12, which says Paul did not permit a woman to teach or have authority over a man. (Note: The words for man and woman in this passage are sometimes translated as husband and wife in other parts of the Bible. This could be about marital relations, not about church leadership.)

FOR **REFLECTION**

What are the "household codes" generally accepted in your culture? How about in your religion? Are the codes for your culture in conflict with those for your religion?

If you got to set up household codes for everyone to live by, what would they be? Why?

There's evidence that Paul *did allow* women like Phoebe, Priscilla, and Lydia to run churches. Yet many of those quoting First Timothy at me have been women. But not a single one of those women who sought to apply 1 Timothy 2:11–12 to me applied 1 Timothy 2:8–9 to themselves. Those passages tell women they shouldn't braid their hair or wear gold, pearls, or expensive clothes. The same adornment rules are in 1 Peter 3:3—again, right after the verses that some like to throw around to force women to stay with abusive men. Though the verses are right next to each other, in the same paragraph, some people seem to think that the clothing and adornment rules only applied in ancient times, while the prohibition against women's authority applies in all times and places. Uh…no.

I understand those of you who are no fan of these passages. But rather than cast them aside, let's see if there's something in the first-century context that can help us understand them in a different light.

Household codes were common in the Greco-Roman world, and while the New Testament codes are similar in many ways, they have some striking differences. The first difference: the audience. Roman codes were addressed to the head of the household only—that is, to the man. All others—wives, slaves, children—were mentioned in the third person. In the Bible, though, wives, children, and slaves are directly addressed in the second person, as you. It may seem like a small thing, but this subtle shift grants personhood to those seen in the surrounding culture as only property.

Have you ever been in a hospital or nursing home where everyone around talks *about* the patient and not to the patient? It's dehumanizing. Roman codes were like that for everyone except the man who headed the household. Christian codes, on the other hand, begin by recognizing that, whatever the secular law might say, members of the household are people, not property.

Consider the way Greco-Roman and Christian household codes treat the question of slavery. While Aristotle specifically said that "a slave is a living possession" (*Politics* 1.4), there is no evidence in the New Testament rules of that concept. Instead, slaves are addressed directly and told to obey their masters. That sounds abhorrent to modern ears, but it implies that slaves are people who can and *should* make their own, independent decisions and moral judgments—a concession that Aristotle and the like would never have made.

Relief sculpture of ancient Roman family

There is also a balance in the New Testament codes that was not present in their ancient counterparts. For example, every place that tells a woman to submit to her husband also tells the husband to love and care for his wife. Ephesians states this about as strongly as anywhere:

> Husbands, love your wives, just as Christ loved the church and gave himself up for her, in order to make her holy by cleansing her with the washing of water by the word, so as to present the church to himself in splendor, without a spot or wrinkle or anything of the kind—yes, so that she may be holy and without blemish. In the same way, husbands should love their wives as they do their own bodies. He who loves his wife loves himself. For no one ever hates his own body, but he nourishes and tenderly cares for it, just as Christ does for the church, because we are members of his body. For this reason a man will leave his father and mother and be joined to his wife, and the two will become one flesh. This is a great mystery, and I am applying it to Christ and the church. Each of you, however, should love his wife as himself, and a wife should respect her husband. (Ephesians 5:25–33)

In a culture where a wife was considered property, this is radically progressive teaching. And there is similar balance in every category. Children are told to obey their parents, but then fathers are told not to provoke their children to anger. Slaves are told to obey their masters, but masters are told to treat their slaves well. Why? Again Ephesians explains in a word to slave masters, "Stop threatening them, for you know that both of you have the same Master in heaven, and with him there is no partiality." (Ephesians 6:9)

That's a stunning message. It not only limits the actions of the master, it asserts that in the eyes of God, there is no difference between the master and the slave. That's what Paul said in Galatians 3:28: "There is no longer Jew or Greek, there is no longer slave or free, there is no longer male and female; for all of you are one in Christ Jesus." Wife and husband are one body; slave and master have one Master who sees them both the same. And we've already seen how the "no longer Jew or Greek" line played out in the Council of Jerusalem and the ministry to the Gentiles.

These codes appear in Paul's letters for several reasons. First is Paul's desire to show that in the life of the Christian, relationships are transformed. While the outer structure of the household may still be bound by the customs of the age and culture, the way that structure is experienced in Christian households is dramatically different, because the claim that all Christians are one body in Christ is a dramatically different worldview.

Second, Paul is also dealing with some practical issues. Especially in the churches outside Judea, congregations were a melting pot of Roman, Greek, and Jewish cultures. They were also a melting pot of various classes of society. Though we may talk about the Greco-Roman world as one distinct culture, it was actually composed of an amalgam of cultures with many different household customs and different expectations about both gender roles and slavery. Then throw in Jewish customs that were different than those of both the Greeks and the Romans. And remember that even within one of those cultures, different classes had different expectations and—often—different laws.

For now, however, it's important just to recognize that when all those different expectations came together in a single church, there were bound to be at least questions if not outright conflicts about how to run a household and what to teach the children. The household codes in the New Testament letters provide an answer to the specific problem of clashing cultures.

Some letters also seek to address problems that exist in one particular place, but that may not exist elsewhere. First Timothy is a case in point. Timothy's church (assumed to be in Ephesus) has issues with false teaching, gossips, busybodies, and immorality in leadership. Because we don't understand exactly what was going on, the directions given in First Timothy to counter those problems can baffle us.

We can assume that some of the issues were with widows, since a huge chunk of chapter 5 is devoted to an odd discussion that begins, "Honor widows who are really widows." (1 Timothy 5:3) This letter also sets out firm behavioral standards for church leaders. While it's fair to assume that the overall attitudes expressed about proper behavior would be standard, there may well be specific injunctions intended only for a particular time and place, due to the problems that exist there but perhaps not elsewhere.

In general, these household codes work within the cultural norms while simultaneously undermining the assumptions on which those cultural norms are based. Paul and the other New Testament writers were not political activists trying to get into the Roman senate to change the laws. They were pastors and church leaders trying to help struggling churches find a moral compass in the midst of colliding cultures and religions.

Moreover, they were doing so in a world where the refusal to worship the emperor could—and often did—get you killed. If Christians completely subverted the social structures of the empire, things would get even worse. So they picked their battles and, in my opinion, used these codes to strike just the right balance between keeping the outward structure and changing the inward heart for the age in which they were written.

CHURCH COMMUNITY AND LEADERSHIP

The way early churches were structured evolved over time. This should go without saying—it's the same in any organization, sacred or secular. But with today's massive church hierarchies and the overall age of the institution of the church, it's easy to forget that the first time people gathered to share their experiences of Jesus, they didn't call a pastor, draft a creed, or open to page 86 of the hymnal.

This is in part true because the earliest Christians never intended to form a new religion. They were Jews, and Judaism was already well established in its form, leadership, and law. They were, at the outset, Jews who had a set of experiences with Jesus of Nazareth and who came to believe certain things about him as a result of those experiences. Of course they wanted to share those things with each other, but Jesus had also mandated that they share their experiences with the world.

And so we mostly stop hearing about "disciples," which means those who learn from a master, because with Jesus' ascension and the day of Pentecost, school is officially over. Now the language shifts to "apostles," which means those who are sent out. Those who were once disciples are deployed as apostles to share the gospel as they've known and experienced it. But if you read Acts carefully, the apostles almost always begin their sharing in synagogues, and their first outreach is close to home.

The account of the day of Pentecost, with its wind, fire, and tongues, wasn't just notable for those miraculous signs. It was also notable because, despite the presence of the most significant figures from the gospel narratives, the power of the Holy Spirit singled out no one. It didn't even distinguish Jesus' original disciples from other believers. It fell on the whole lot of them at once and without distinction.

That equality in the eyes of God is reflected in the very earliest Christian community, described in Acts 2:44–47:

> *All who believed were together and had all things in common; they would sell their possessions and goods and distribute the proceeds to all, as any had need. Day by day, as they spent much time together in the temple, they broke bread at home and ate their food with glad and generous hearts, praising God and having the goodwill of all the people. And day by day the Lord added to their number those who were being saved.*

The early Christian community is described again in Acts 4:32–35, although in this passage we see that the apostles had primary responsibility for administration:

> Now the whole group of those who believed were of one heart and soul, and no one claimed private ownership of any possessions, but everything they owned was held in common. With great power the apostles gave their testimony to the resurrection of the Lord Jesus, and great grace was upon them all. There was not a needy person among them, for as many as owned lands or houses sold them and brought the proceeds of what was sold. They laid it at the apostles' feet, and it was distributed to each as any had need.

This communal living and sharing was the norm at the outset, but it wasn't required. We know this because of the rather chilling story of Ananias and Sapphira told in Acts 5. This couple, like others, sold their property and brought proceeds to the apostles. Unlike the others, however, they didn't give it all, they brought only part of the proceeds to donate.

Many a church today would beg for that level of generosity in its members, but apparently Ananias and Sapphira were trying to make the apostles believe that they were giving all the proceeds when, in fact, it was only part. Peter responds to Ananias,

The Death of Ananias by Raphael, 1515-1516

"Why has Satan filled your heart to lie to the Holy Spirit and to keep back part of the proceeds of the land? While it remained unsold, did it not remain your own? And after it was sold, were not the proceeds at your disposal? How is it that you have contrived this deed in your heart? You did not lie to us but to God!" Now when Ananias heard these words, he fell down and died. (Acts 5:3–5)

Three hours later, Sapphira comes in and Peter asks her to come clean. When she doesn't, she drops dead, too. But Peter's words show that Ananias and Sapphira weren't forced to sell their property and give it to the community. They could have kept it, or they could have sold it and given part. But they claimed to be giving it all, and that was the issue. As they say, "It's not the crime; it's the cover-up."

We don't know if those who kept all or part of their property got fewer community benefits or how the system worked, but in terms of the structure of the first community of believers we see that there was an option (but not a mandate) to live in radical community, without private property, and with those who had more taking care of those who had less. Most believers, it seems, took this option.

The letters show us that, although this form of community didn't extend out to the new churches formed across Asia Minor, the practice of taking care of any believer in need became a hallmark of early Christianity. Paul organizes a huge offering across all the churches in Asia Minor to send back to the poor in Jerusalem. Later, the church in Rome is reported to have given regular support to 1,500 distressed persons in 250 C.E. alone.

And it wasn't just Rome. In his book *The Early Christians In Their Own Words*, Eberhard Arnold writes:

> *Even in the smallest church community, the overseer had to be a friend of the poor, and there was at least one widow responsible to see to it, day and night, that no sick or needy person was neglected. The deacon was responsible to find and help the poor and to impress on the rich the need to do their utmost. Deacons also served at table. There was no excuse for anyone because he had not learned or was unable to do this service. Everybody was expected to go, street by street, looking for the poorest dwellings. As a result, Christians spent more money in the streets than the followers of other religions spent in their temples.[2]*

---

2 *(Farmington, PA: Plough Publishing, 1997), 15.*

We'll look at the role of deacons and other leaders in a moment, but first one more quote from Eberhard that might help us understand how far most modern Christian practice is from its earliest roots:

> *The rank afforded by property and profession was recognized to be incompatible with such fellowship and simplicity, and repugnant to it. For that reason alone, the early Christians had an aversion to any high judicial position and commissions in the army. They found it impossible to take responsibility for any penalty or imprisonment, any disfranchisement, any judgment over life or death, or the execution of any death sentence pronounced by martial or criminal courts. Other trades and professions were out of the question because they were connected with idolatry or immorality. Christians therefore had to be prepared to give up their occupations. The resulting threat of hunger was no less frightening than violent death by martyrdom.[3]*

Advocating this lifestyle would empty most of America's pews. But the numbers in the early church grew. And as they grew, Peter and the other apostles began to have issues. Conflicts began to arise and charges of unfair distribution were raised so that even the staff of the twelve apostles was strained. Here is the beginning of Acts 6, where we see the very first division of labor in the church—apostles and deacons.

FOR REFLECTION

What do you think of these descriptions of the early church? Are they viable today? Why or why not?

Which parts of the early church lifestyle would you find fulfilling? Which would you find difficult?

> *Now during those days, when the disciples were increasing in number, the Hellenists complained against the Hebrews because their widows were being neglected in the daily distribution of food. And the twelve called together the whole community of the disciples and said, "It is not right that we should neglect the word of God in order to wait on tables. Therefore, friends, select from among yourselves seven men of good standing, full of the Spirit and of wisdom, whom we may appoint to this task, while we, for our part, will devote ourselves to prayer and to serving the word." What they said pleased the whole community, and they chose Stephen, a man full of faith and the Holy Spirit, together with Philip, Prochorus, Nicanor, Timon, Parmenas, and Nicolaus, a proselyte of Antioch. They had these men stand before the apostles, who prayed and laid their hands on them. (Acts 6:1–6)*

---

3 Ibid., 15–16.

So the first division of labor in church leadership was recognizing that preaching is a full-time job, and it takes others to carry out the visitation and other charitable works of service in the community. These people who administered the charity of the church—the ones who found out who needed what, found the resources to meet those needs, and oversaw their distribution—were called deacons. To this day there is an international program to train Christian caregivers called Stephen Ministry, named after this first deacon, who also became the first Christian martyr. First Timothy 3:8–13 describes the importance of having temperate, faithful deacons, and it seems clear from the appearance of verse 11 in the middle of this description that women also served in this role.

"I can't stand to listen to anyone else preach.
You reckon that means the Lord is calling
me to the ministry?"

First Timothy also talks about bishops, but if you think of a modern bishop when you read this, you'll be far from the mark. The word in Greek is *episkopos*, which simply means overseer. This term could obviously take many forms and, unlike the work of a deacon, the Bible doesn't spell out a job description. We simply know that bishops existed, and it would be surprising if they had not. In any organization, after all, someone has to keep the ball rolling.

Other words are also used to describe church leaders. The most common is "elder," but we also find "shepherd" and "steward." While it's possible that these all had distinct roles and duties, it's more likely that they were just different words used for very similar forms of oversight of a Christian community. We have a similar situation today where someone who leads a Christian congregation might be called a priest, minister, pastor, elder, bishop, apostle, and more, depending on the particular community. In some Christian traditions, there are distinctions between those terms and in other places there are not.

Apart from deacons, we simply can't say for certain what the various terms for church leaders meant in New Testament times. What we can say is that the church had both local and regional leaders, that their character and integrity were important for their selection (or were supposed to be), and that they had greater responsibility for church governance, but not greater value in the eyes of God.

HOW LONG, O LORD, HOW LONG?

Jews and Christians share a history of persecution. We have persecuted each other, sadly, but we have also each been targeted by empires—even otherwise tolerant empires—for giving our allegiance to God above any emperor or king.

Damnatio ad bestias. 3rd-Century C.E. mosaic in the Museum of El Djem (Tunisia)

For Rome, which generally had a live-and-let-live policy when it came to religion, the new Christians were an even greater threat than the other branches of Judaism, because the Christians were actively trying to spread their religion. Traditional Judaism has always welcomed converts, though they didn't usually solicit them actively. But, spurred by the final words of Jesus and the account of the angels at Jesus' ascension, the Christians took evangelism to new heights. For Christians, spreading the gospel was a divine mandate, the last word and command given by Jesus. And that often got them into trouble.

Acts 19 describes the riots in the streets of Ephesus as Christians, urging people to turn away from local deities, threatened the pagan tourist trade surrounding the goddess Artemis. But Christian zeal didn't just cause conflicts with pagans. There were about thirteen synagogues in Rome when the Christians came with their message. Their first stop: the synagogues, where they shared the gospel. Some of the synagogues embraced the message; others rejected it.

Tensions began to rise between those synagogues who accepted the message about Jesus and those who did not, and it began to get ugly. We know from the Roman historian Suetonius and others that about 49 C.E. the conflict was affecting the city to such a degree that the emperor Claudius expelled all the Jews in Rome, some forty to fifty thousand people, "because they were constantly rioting at the instigation of Chrestus," a reference to Christ. But for Claudius this was not a matter of religion, it was simply a matter of keeping the peace in the city. Suetonius explains that it was, at its root, an immigration problem, with the blame placed not just on religion but on foreigners.

This expulsion affected all Jews—traditional Jews who wanted nothing to do with Jesus as well as Jewish Christians—although it's not clear how strictly this expulsion was enforced. But many, many Jews left, and this is how Priscilla and Aquila, who were part of the Roman church, ended up in Corinth, where they met Paul. The expulsion lasted five years. At the beginning of Nero's reign, in 54 C.E., Jews were allowed to return to Rome. And then the killing started.

REVELATION

You may have noticed that there's one book of the Bible we haven't talked about yet—that wild and wooly vision called Revelation. I've placed it here because part of understanding what on earth (or in heaven, as the case may be) is going on in Revelation is understanding the context in which it was written.

Popular culture has portrayed this book in terms of horror and terror. The Greek word for Revelation is *apocalypsis*, and when someone outside of church talks about an apocalypse, they are usually talking about a summer blockbuster where the world comes to a dramatic end. That's how we've come to use the word, in no small part because of the dramatic disasters visited on the world in this final book of the Bible.

"My wife just left me, I lost my job, I need surgery, and my spirits have hit bottom? Pastor, you've gotta help me. What's the difference between pre-, post-, and amillennialism?"

"Irony of Doctrinal Divisions" by Doug Hall, 1986

APOCALYPSE IS A THING

But the Greek word *apocalypsis* actually means "to uncover" or "to disclose knowledge," thus the usual name of the book—Revelation. We spent quite a bit of time with this book in the first course of this series, *What Is the Bible?*, and I have reproduced that chapter here in Appendix 1 on p. 205.

There we learned that apocalypse is actually a type of literature that emerged about 250 B.C.E. and continued into Jesus' time and beyond. You know you're reading an apocalypse because of the highly symbolic language, a focus on upheaval or destruction of the world, and the fact that the community to whom the work is addressed is undergoing persecution or some other extreme difficulty.

We saw in the Old Testament course that there were some examples of apocalyptic literature in parts of Isaiah, Daniel, and Zechariah. There were more full-blown apocalyptic works in both Old and New Testament times that didn't make it into the Bible. The New Testament ones are described in Appendix 3 on p. 239.

What I'm getting at is that an apocalypse was a thing—a genre, to be precise. Revelation happens to be the only fully formed apocalypse that made it into the Bible, but there were others like it that were known to early Christians, including writings attributed to both Peter and Paul. If you read mystery novels or fantasy novels or romance or sci-fi, you see that each genre of literature has certain things you can count on.

In a good whodunit, you won't learn who the killer is and how the crime was committed until the end. If you're reading horror, the murder might be the first thing you read. If you read fantasy, you know that some kind of hero will go on some kind of quest, and so on. Apocalypse was a type (genre) of literature that had the certain set of conventions we mentioned before.

For the past two sessions we've seen the kind of conventions that were common to another genre of literature—the letter. Revelation has its own set of conventions, but we don't have much in our Bibles to compare it to.

What we have in Revelation is the apocalypse of John. The text tells us that John, who isn't identified in the text beyond that first name, has been persecuted for his faith and exiled to the island of Patmos. Is this the same John who wrote the gospel and the three letters? Some say yes, some say no.

What we know is that this apocalypse takes a step out of the general apocalyptic form by including letters to seven churches in and around the area where tradition places the Apostle John after Jesus' death: Ephesus, Smyrna, Pergamum, Thyatira, Sardis, Philadelphia, and Laodicea. Some of these locations are already on your maps from Session 4; others are not.

> **EXERCISE**
>
> *Read Revelation 1–3.*
>
> Using the maps in your study Bible and/or the Internet or other atlas, find the general locations of Smyrna, Pergamum, Sardis, Philadelphia, and Laodicea and put them on your Session 4 map. Also locate the island of Patmos.

But the list does offer an expanded sense of where actual churches were formed in the Roman province of Asia.

We also know that the book relies heavily on the Old Testament. Of the 404 verses in the book of Revelation, 275 include one or more allusions to the Old Testament. If you are one of the people who see the Old Testament as being irrelevant to Christian faith, you're at risk for a gross misunderstanding of the New Testament writings and message. Too many Christians read the Old Testament (if they read it at all) through the lens of the New, when really it should be the other way 'round.

Apocalypses were written in times of persecution and difficulty, which is one of the chief reasons they're so confusing. As we saw with letters, this wasn't an age where you could shoot someone an e-mail or put up an anonymous blog post. Whether you were sending a letter or trying to circulate a different kind of message to a community, you had to write it down (or have someone write it for you), send it with a human courier, and have it read aloud at its destination.

I think this is why New Testament letters from both Paul and Peter take pains to say that the recipients should obey the governing authorities. Since both of them ended up in prison and executed by the Roman government, it's clear that neither of them saw that obedience as absolute. But if you're sending a message in the first century, it is public by default. No need to ruffle official feathers as the messages were read aloud. Life was hard enough.

But what do you do when you're going through persecution? How can a religious leader, himself in exile away from his community, strengthen his flock? If he writes that God has given him a vision of Roman condemnation and destruction and calls the emperor the ultimate evil, his exile will turn to execution—both his and his recipients'. So you do what every nation does in wartime to protect messages from enemy interception. You put your messages in code.

Cryptography of Géza Gardonyi (1863-1922), Hungarian writer

An apocalypse is an elaborate code. The trouble is, we don't have the key for many of the symbols. We know that for the early church the code name for Rome was Babylon. Through Old Testament references and other writings we can pick up a few other tidbits. A horn symbolized a king, for example, and adultery and prostitution were general symbols for idolatry. So the "great whore of Babylon" in Revelation 17 is not some woman running a brothel in ancient Iraq. It's a reference to—and a condemnation of—the pagan religion of the Roman Empire, especially the notion that Caesar was a god. The refusal of Jews, including Christian Jews, to make an offering to Caesar as a god was what got them in trouble in the first place. And as you got truly nasty Caesars in power—like Nero and Domitian—that refusal could cost you your life.

The book of Revelation is a coded message to early Christians enduring persecution. Bad persecution. Nero, for example, was known to cover Christians in tar, stick them on posts in his garden, and set them on fire for a little evening ambiance. We're not talking about minor inconveniences here. Part of the debate about Revelation is whether it was written during the persecutions of Nero, Domitian (a couple decades later), or someone else.

But no matter when it was written, the intent was the same. The overall message is that God sees and hears what is going on and the persecutors will ultimately get what's coming to them. Revelation is meant to answer the question posed by the martyrs that John sees in his vision in Revelation 6:9–10:

When he opened the fifth seal, I saw under the altar the souls of those who had been slaughtered for the word of God and for the testimony they had given; they cried out with a loud voice, "Sovereign Lord, holy and true, how long will it be before you judge and avenge our blood on the inhabitants of the earth?"

The answer is that those who committed such horrors will receive justice equal to their atrocities and those who have been faithful will see a day when the true and merciful God, not the fake and cruel Caesar-god, rules the kingdom. Revelation is meant as a message of hope. When contemporary film,

The Fitfth Seal, The Douce Apocalypse, Bodleian Library (Oxford, Great Britain), Ms. Douce 180, p. 17.

literature, or groups use Revelation to instill fear of being "left behind" and being subject to the horrors described, they are misusing the book. Revelation is not a message of warning to the persecutors to scare them into righteous living. If it were, the code language wouldn't have been needed. It's a message of hope to those enduring great suffering for their faith—a message that God has not abandoned them and that they will, one day, see justice and peace.

For all its incomprehensible symbols and language, the book of Revelation is woven into the fabric of Western civilization. On the darker side is the *Left Behind* series of books and films (which are *fiction*, by the way) and the common usage of words like "apocalypse," "Armageddon," and "the Four Horsemen." On the beautiful side is Handel's Messiah and symbols like the tree of life. And of course every joke that has St. Peter stationed at the "pearly gates" is referencing Revelation 21:21 as it describes the New Jerusalem:

> And the twelve gates are twelve pearls, each of the gates is a single pearl, and the street of the city is pure gold, transparent as glass.

BEASTS AND ANTICHRISTS

The king of the symbols in the book of Revelation is the terrible and mystifying beast of Revelation 13. Revelation 13:18 taunts us when it says that anyone who's wise will be able to figure out the identity of this beast, who goes against everything Christ ever taught, by recognizing him in the number 666. People both love and hate this number. They love to decipher a secret code in the name of their enemies, making the letters in the name add up to the cryptic number 666—and then proclaiming that person to be the Antichrist. That game isn't new. Someone has done it for every bad person (or every person someone thinks is bad) from Nero to now, and for every US president from Ronald Reagan to Barack Obama.

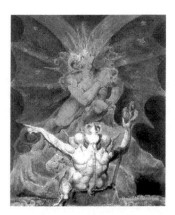

The Number of the Beast is 666
by William Blake

But 666 is also a number people run from. For forty years, 666 was the local telephone exchange for a small town of about 450 homes in Louisiana. In 2007 the little village of Reeves was finally successful in their petition to have that number changed and it hasn't ever been reassigned. Wherever the number appears, someone gets nervous. On the flip side, Satanists and those seeking to instill fear embrace the number and use it for precisely those ends.

So what are we to think? Well, as far as the number 666 goes, a quick Internet search will show you that there's no shortage of theories, but apart from a general understanding of biblical numerology, the code for this number is lost to us. For the general concept of antichrist, though, we do have some biblical references. I've mentioned them briefly as we passed them, but let's go back and pull them all together to find a better definition.

Newsflash: The word "antichrist" (*antichristos* in Greek) appears five times across four verses of the Bible. None of those times is in the book of Revelation. None, as in zero. While the beasts of Revelation 13 are clearly not Christ-like figures, nowhere in the book are they identified as the Antichrist. Their actions of brutal control, economic coercion, and forced worship, though, easily describe the Caesar du jour.

All the biblical appearances of the word *antichristos* are in John's letters. (Find them in 1 John 2:18, 1 John 2:22, 1 John 4:3, and 2 John 1:7.) It's clear from those verses that there's no single Antichrist with a capital A. John talks about it in 1 John 4:3 as a "spirit of the antichrist, of which you have heard that it is coming; and now it is already in the world." Antichrist in the Bible is not a single person who comes and deceives nations at the end of the world. Antichrist in the Bible is the spirit of any and all persons who stand in opposition to Jesus.

This entire discussion still creates difficulties for interfaith relations. John, in his letters, gives readers a litmus test for divine favor—those who are for Christ are in and those who are anti-Christ (that is those who don't profess faith in Jesus) are out. But given that John also says, "Everyone who loves is born of God and knows God," (1 John 4:7) I think that our interpretations of what "faith in Jesus" means for John can be a lot more inclusive. That debate, though, is beyond our scope here. My point: The use of the word "antichrist" in the Bible doesn't support the contemporary trend of trying to delegitimize a world leader by declaring him to be evil incarnate and the agent of the world's end.

The symbolism of the Beast in Revelation 13 does point to the ruler of a nation. But there is no indication that it refers to a leader far in the future. Remember, after all: Any number of Roman emperors fit the bill. Clearly there are parts of John's vision that envision a future age—belief in a future glorious time of the reign of God had, for many years, been part of Jewish belief, stronger in some branches of Judaism than others. But that doesn't mean that every part of Revelation belongs to that future age.

We've already seen that the eventual glorious reign of God was a particular focus of the Essenes, the monastic Jewish sect whose members lived in the desert. And both Paul and Jesus predict that such a time is coming soon, although Jesus points out that no one but God the Father knows when that time will be. Spurred on by reports of the words of the angels at Jesus' ascension, though, the early church would have probably denied across the board that Jesus' return would be delayed more than 2,000 years.

Paul was so convinced that the final age would come quickly that he even advised people against getting married. No time to worry about marriage and families—just get your spiritual house in order and prepare for the coming of the Lord. The ending sections of Revelation represent that common belief, adding a more specifically Christian spin to the events. But many if not most scholars put the trials and tribulations of the central chapters of Revelation squarely on the Roman Empire of the first and perhaps second centuries. The readers in the churches of Asia Minor would have understood the code and recognized the players as living among them.

Remember the context—always remember the context. Christians are being persecuted. Tortured. Killed. Driven into poverty. Think of the message of Revelation as similar to that of a parent who holds a child close after witnessing some horror of war. "Shhhhhh… it will be okay. Everything's going to be all right. They'll catch those bad guys so they can't hurt us anymore. We'll move to a place where clean water flows like a river and nobody needs money to get food. Everybody will help one another there, and the bad people won't be allowed in. We're going to move there—yes, baby, we are. Just you wait and see."

Mother's Goodnight Kiss
by Mary Cassatt, 1888

The truth is, nobody knows that it will be okay. The parent may in fact know the opposite to be true. Both parent and child might be blown to little bits in the next minutes or hours. The bad guys might literally get away with murder. But we comfort one another in terrible times with words that have deeper and sometimes different meanings than the plain facts before us. We know somehow that if we are to survive, hope will be the attitude that gets us through. There are times when even false hope is preferable to despair. And, after all, who can say that we're wrong in that hope? Who can say that hope for a future of peace, mercy, and justice for all is false?

FAITH, HOPE, AND LOVE ABIDE

And so we come to the end of our overview of the New Testament. We've read and learned a lot, but still have barely scratched the surface. It's easy to look at individual passages and books and get caught up in the questions, controversies, and theologies that spring from their pages. There are literally thousands of books—probably tens of thousands of books—devoted to studying those individual parts. Many of those books contradict each other, sometimes with respectful disagreement, other times with rancor.

Reading the New Testament today, we have to come to grips with the fact that there are some questions that we simply cannot answer with certainty. It may be called the "New" Testament, but it is still ancient. Some answers are lost in the sands of Judea and Asia Minor. We also have to recognize that sometimes we look to the Bible for answers to questions that never would have occurred to the original writers or listeners to ask—let alone answer.

The answers we seek sometimes aren't there, or are confusing because we don't understand ancient culture and/or Eastern ways of thinking. Sometimes we stumble because we want answers to questions that don't have answers— never did and never will. For instance, we want to know the exact nature of God, as if God were something that could be placed under a microscope and dissected, categorized, and predicted.

In my book (both literally and figuratively), the most eloquent summation of the gospel message of the New Testament comes in Paul's first letter to the Corinthians—although, as someone who embraced Judaism to his death, Paul wouldn't have made any distinction between this message and the message of the Hebrew Scriptures.

> *If I speak in the tongues of mortals and of angels, but do not have love, I am a noisy gong or a clanging cymbal. And if I have prophetic powers and understand all mysteries and all knowledge, and if I have all faith, so as to remove mountains, but do not have love, I am nothing. If I give away all my possessions, and if I hand over my body so that I may boast, but do not have love, I gain nothing.*
>
> *Love is patient; love is kind; love is not envious or boastful or arrogant or rude. It does not insist on its own way; it is not irritable or resentful; it does not rejoice in wrongdoing, but rejoices in the truth. It bears all things, believes all things, hopes all things, endures all things.*
>
> *Love never ends. But as for prophecies, they will come to an end; as for tongues, they will cease; as for knowledge, it will come to an end. For we know only in part, and we prophesy only in part; but when the complete comes, the partial will come to an end. When I was a child, I spoke like a child, I thought like a child, I reasoned like a child; when I became an adult, I put an end to childish ways. For now we see in a mirror, dimly, but then we will see face to face. Now I know only in part; then I will know fully, even as I have been fully known. And now faith, hope, and love abide, these three; and the greatest of these is love. (1 Corinthians 13:1–13)*

PREPARATION FOR CHECK-IN

(Prepare for the next group session by thinking about and writing a brief response to these two questions.)

What is one thing that was new to me in this material?

What is one question that this week's topic raises for me?

EXTRA MILE WRAP-UP
(CEU AND CERTIFICATE STUDENTS)

☐ In an essay of five hundred to seven hundred words, describe your experience of the New Testament in this course. What was new to you? What was familiar? Did you find your beliefs challenged? Supported? If you could take one lesson from this course back to your own faith community, what would it be? If you are not part of a faith community, would you recommend that others read the New Testament? Why or why not?

APPENDIX I

This is the chapter introducing the New Testament in the first course of *Exploring the Bible: The Dickinson Series, What Is the Bible?* If you have not taken that course, you should read this chapter before beginning this course.

AND NOW FOR SOMETHING COMPLETELY DIFFERENT

The divisions of the New Testament are not quite as standardized as those of the Old Testament, but the differences don't really cause issues. There are the four Gospels, which tell of the life of Jesus, one book of history (Acts of the Apostles), a pile of letters, and then the final Apocalypse (Revelation).

Some divisions put the Gospels with Acts and call it all history, and most groupings separate the various letters, but not all in the same way. The most common way to divide the letters is to separate out the letters of Paul and the letters of everybody else. There are a number of scholars who question whether some of the letters attributed to Paul are really his, so the list of books under a category called Paul's Letters can be different depending on where you look.

The letters that everyone agrees are *not* written by Paul are Hebrews; James; 1 and 2 Peter; 1, 2, and 3 John; and Jude. They are usually called "general letters."

Unlike the Old Testament, which very literally spans millennia, the New Testament covers a period of only fifty to sixty years. The decisions about which books would be included and which would not were made centuries after the events described rather than millennia afterward, as was the case with the Hebrew Bible. In the formation of the New Testament, there wasn't time for long-term historical reflection on the events described, so you don't have the kinds of sweeping historical books that you do in the Hebrew Bible. The New Testament is more immediate, encompassing the writings about the life of Jesus, the very earliest accounts of the Christian movement (begun as a Jewish sect called the Way), letters to both churches and individuals, and a pretty wild prophetic vision at the end. Let's look at each of the groups of books that comprise the New Testament.

GOSPELS AND THE ACTS OF THE APOSTLES

The word "gospel" comes from the Old English *god-spell* (thus the Broadway musical about Jesus by that name) and means "good news." The Greek word is *evangelion* and it occurs seventy-six times in the New Testament. In literary terms, the word Gospel refers to writing about the life and teaching of Jesus. There were many, many gospels written but only four made it into the official compilation

SYNOPTIC **GOSPELS**

Matthew, Mark, and Luke.

The word "synoptic" means to see things in a similar way. The first three Gospels are very similar in content and style. Since the Gospel of John is so different, the first three are often grouped together under this heading.

> **Read the parable of the Prodigal Son in Luke 15:11–32.**

we call the New Testament: Matthew, Mark, Luke, and John. It is generally assumed that the Gospel of Mark is the earliest of the four and that the other three writers had access to it when they wrote their accounts.

Matthew, Mark, and Luke each address their gospels to different constituencies, and they choose to include different stories or to emphasize different ideas or events. But they read in a similar way and the timeline of

Jesus' life is roughly the same. For that reason, those three gospels are called the "Synoptic Gospels"—from *syn* (same) *optic* (see).

The Gospel of John is a whole different kettle of fish. John is the last of the gospels to have been written, probably by a good many years. It is likely that John had not only Mark to look at but Matthew and Luke as well. It has often

> **Read John 1:1–18.** This is all you get of Christmas in John.

been suggested that John is more like a commentary on the other gospels— that while the first three gospels tell us what Jesus did and what he said, John tells us what it all means. John is deeper and more philosophical than the other gospels. The ordering of events is different and there is layer upon layer of meaning.

Luke also deserves special mention because of its relation to the book of Acts. Most scholars agree that Luke (possibly a Greek physician who traveled with Paul) wrote both Luke and Acts. In fact, you'll sometimes see reference to just one book called Luke-Acts. In antiquity you could fit thirty sheets of papyrus into a single scroll. Luke fills thirty sheets, the assumption being that the only reason we have two books (Luke and Acts) instead of one is because Luke ran out of scroll.

In fact, the beginning of Acts is a continuation of the life of Jesus recorded in Luke, and it is addressed to the same person (Theophilus) and mentions the author's "first" book. Acts begins with the ascension of the resurrected Jesus into heaven before it moves on to tell of the lives of the disciples after Jesus was gone.

> **Read Acts 9:1–19.** The story of Saint Paul's conversion.

A "disciple" is one who learns from a master. An "apostle" is one who is sent out on a mission. In the book of Acts, we see the disciples from the gospels come to the end of their training with Jesus. Then the narrative turns to show how

THE **FOUR EVANGELISTS**

The early church held the four Gospel writers in high regard and believed them to have a special place in heaven.

Because of texts in Ezekiel and Revelation that described four heavenly beings in the presence of God, Matthew, Mark, Luke, and John became equated with those symbolic figures. Christian art is full of the representation of Matthew as a human or cherub, Mark as a lion, Luke as an ox, and John as an eagle as you can see in the four corners of the illustration on the following page.

Christ enthroned amongst the Four Evangelists, from the Codex Bruschal, ca. 1220

they are transformed into apostles and sent out to spread that gospel—the good news that they learned from him. Acts shows us how the early church was begun, how those who were not Jews got into the act, and how a Pharisee named Saul (whose name is later changed to Paul), who actively persecuted the first Christians, became one of Christianity's most ardent defenders.

The four Gospels in our New Testament were the second set of writings (after the letters of Paul) to be collected together and deemed authoritative. It wasn't an easy process. An early Christian writer and theologian from Assyria named Tatian didn't like the thought of having several "different" gospels put out there, so in 170 C.E. he tried putting Matthew, Mark, and Luke together in one cohesive narrative with some other bits of oral tradition thrown in. It didn't gain any traction, and by the end of the second century, it was accepted that we had a "four-fold gospel," composed of four books. Each piece of the single "four-fold gospel" tells the narrative of Jesus' life according to the perspective of a given writer. So today you see the Gospel "according to Matthew" or the Gospel "according to Mark," and so on.

LETTERS

Paul was a Pharisee—someone who was trained in and who interpreted Jewish law. He was an educated man and considered himself a Jew, even after he became a follower of Jesus. Paul was literate, learned, and zealous. Probably he was difficult to live with, but his fierce determination to tell the world about Jesus and his resurrection from the dead lit a fire under all of Asia

> **Read I Corinthians 13:1–13.**
> The nature of love.

Minor—modern-day Turkey—as well as parts of Greece and even Rome as he traveled and founded churches in place after place.

The Acts of the Apostles is largely devoted to his story, and much of the rest of the New Testament is composed of the letters he wrote to both the churches he founded and the pastors he sent to care for them as he moved from one community to another. Paul is a love-him-or-hate-him kind of guy, but there is no denying his prominence, both in the New Testament and in the founding of the early church.

Paul's letters were the first writings of the New Testament to be gathered together in a collection and were most probably the first books of the

New Testament written in their completed form. At the beginning of the second century C.E., ten of Paul's letters were grouped together as a set of authoritative writing: Romans, 1 and 2 Corinthians, Galatians, Ephesians, Philippians, Colossians, 1 and 2 Thessalonians, and Philemon. The earliest of Paul's letters were written about 50 C.E., with many claiming the first was Galatians and others claiming it was 1 Thessalonians. Both were written close to that time.

The letter to Titus and the two letters to Timothy are often dubbed the "Pastoral Epistles," and weren't as readily accepted. By the end of the second century, however, they were recognized as authoritative for the

> **Read I Timothy 4:1-16.**
> Words to encourage a young pastor.

church, although the question over whether Paul actually wrote them is still a matter of debate among scholars. Likewise the letter to the Hebrews, whose author is unknown, gained its acceptance in that same late-second-century time frame.

Paul was the most prolific letter writer of the New Testament, but he was not the only one. The letters of Peter, John, James, Jude, and whoever wrote Hebrews fill out the picture with a variety of perspectives. Most of these "general letters" (sometimes called

> **Read James 2:14-26.**
> Faith and works.

the "catholic epistles" because they were written to all churches rather than a particular congregation) weren't readily included in the New Testament.

It wasn't universal, but most Christian communities accepted 1 Peter and 1 John during the second and third centuries. However, James, 2 Peter, 2 and 3 John, and Jude were way down on the list and parts of the church were still rejecting them as late as the sixth century. Even as late as the sixteenth century C.E., Martin Luther had to be arm-twisted to include James in his German translation of the Bible.

REVELATION

Another book that Martin Luther (and those earlier Christians who didn't like many of the general letters) would sooner have left out of the Bible is Revelation. Many Christians today would like to remove it as well. This book of the Bible is responsible for some of the most beautiful things in American culture, yet some would say it is also responsible for some of the oddest.

Revelation represents a genre of literature that we saw a bit of in the Old Testament. It is called apocalyptic. The Greek word *apocalypse* means "revelation," thus the book's title. It represents a prophetic vision of a time to come that relies heavily on symbolic language.

The Old Testament contains quasi-apocalyptic literature in portions of Isaiah, Jeremiah, Joel, and Zechariah, plus a full-blown apocalypse in the book of Daniel.

In American culture, the book of Revelation shows up in two primary ways. One is in the "Hallelujah Chorus" of Handel's *Messiah*, which is from Revelation 11:15; 19:6; and 19:16. The "Worthy Is the Lamb" chorus in the *Messiah* can also be found there, in Revelation 5:12–13.

In the twentieth century, however, more people became familiar with Revelation as a horrifying picture of the end times: the Four Horsemen of the Apocalypse (shown on the following page), the Mark of the Beast, 666, people being "left behind" in the rapture (even though the passages that comprise the basis for the rapture are not in the book of Revelation), and a multi-million-dollar business in scaring people into thinking we are living in the end times.

Radio broadcaster Harold Camping made over $70 million by claiming that he had cracked the code of Revelation and knew the end of the world would be May 21, 2011. Even though he had already unsuccessfully predicted such an end on May 21, 1988, and on September 7, 1994, people believed him and sent him money to promote his message. He was not the first such opportunist and he will not be the last.

The book of Revelation begins innocently enough, with seven letters from God to seven churches in seven locations around Asia Minor. They reference sects and heresies that we can only speculate about today but otherwise are pretty straightforward and are helpful reminders of the priority God should have in the lives of the faithful.

Next come several chapters of praise as the vision shifts to a scene in heaven of God surrounded by all sorts of creatures engaged in worship and Jesus in

Four Horsemen of the Apocalypse, ca. 1497-98, Albrecht Dürer

a prominent place. A lot of this section is poetry and some of it can be found in hymns as well as classical music.

The Antichrist and Conspiracy Theories

Then it gets strange. The vision shifts to angels who pour out bowls of disasters on the earth, and earthly events are described in terms of multi-horned beasts, whores, and some kind of evil mark you must have to buy or sell anything. A friend who worked in a Christian bookstore in Georgia reported that a customer returned a whole pile of books she had bought the day before. The reason for the return? She was aghast to find that books she had bought—from a Christian bookstore, mind you—bore the mark of the beast. The mark? The UPC barcode.

I don't doubt that the woman was sincere in her faith, but she had been duped into looking for signs of the end at every turn. I feel for her. I was swept up in that kind of thinking in my earlier years and became so caught up in looking for the end times that I was very little good in the present.

And then there's 666—the number of the beast. Revelation 13:18 practically begs for people to run wild with this. The verse reads, "This calls for wisdom: let anyone with understanding calculate the number of the beast, for it is the number of a person. Its number is six hundred sixty-six." Never mind that some ancient manuscripts have 616; the 666 is what has stuck. And who doesn't want to be considered wise? Everyone wants to be the person who figures it out.

> **HEXAKOSIOIHEXEKONTAHEXAPHOBIACS:**
>
> The term for people with a debilitating fear of the number 666.

Every time things get bad, people begin to wonder if this is it. Paul thought the end times were so close to his day that he advised people not even to get married. (1 Corinthians 7:8) And it has been that way ever since. When someone rises to prominence, those who hate him figure out a way to work the numbers so that his name equals 666. It's been going on for centuries.

Nero has been identified as the Antichrist, as have any number of popes and even the papal office itself. Of course it was done for Hitler, Mao Zedong, Stalin, and even for tyrants in general. As US politics became more partisan, Ronald Reagan got the treatment (full name: Ronald Wilson Reagan; each of his three names has six letters) as well as every subsequent US president. Henry Kissinger, various General Secretaries of the United Nations, and Bill Gates can be made to fit the number. Someone even did it for Barney the Dinosaur. Take "Cute Purple Dinosaur," take out all the letters that are not Roman numerals (converting the u's to v's), convert those to Arabic values and then add them up. That's right. 666.

It's Supposed To Be Hopeful

There are a number of scholars who believe the predictions of the time of tribulation in Revelation were predictions of the fall of Rome—and that event is over and done with. Of course many see it as a time yet to come. What gets lost in all of that is that the message of Revelation is meant to be one of hope. The book ends

> **Read Revelation 21:1–6.**
> The New Jerusalem.

with a new heaven and a new earth, lit by the glory of God. It was written to a people undergoing fierce and terrible persecution, who needed to know that God heard their cries and that there would be justice for those who were cruelly murdering them and their families solely because they would not bow to the Roman emperor as god.

What comfortable twenty-first-century Americans see as a time of terror and a chance for conspiracy theories, the original, persecuted recipients cheered as a promise of justice, just as there was literally dancing in the streets of the United States when Osama bin Laden was killed. Other parts of the Bible warn us against rejoicing in the destruction of our enemies, and Revelation does not encourage that. But it's understandable that those who were dipped in tar and set aflame to light Emperor Nero's garden might appreciate a God who was fighting mad about it.

FORMING THE CANON: BIBLE BY COMMITTEE

After a few centuries had passed since the life of Jesus, later generations of Christians had to finally decide which writings would be considered official and included in their sacred Scriptures—and which would not. It was a complicated process. Those writings that were seen as representing those who had direct knowledge of the events or had been with Jesus either directly or indirectly tended to carry more weight, as did writings addressed to the entire church. Over time, these came to be valued above the others. Of course it was only a matter of time before someone asked, "Are you *sure* John (or whoever) wrote this?" and then the debate about the official canon (from a Greek word meaning "measure" or "rule") was off and running. What books would comprise the canon, or rule, for Christian faith?

We've seen that over the first few centuries C.E., at least basic agreement began to coalesce around certain collections of writings. As we also have seen, however, there was disagreement among various Christian communities about which writings should be accepted as authoritative. There were many, many other writings out there and you can find them in a variety of collections today. Plus, there were church leaders like Marcion taking the matter into their own hands and expunging references to the Hebrew Scriptures from New Testament writings.

Not to be outdone, in 367 C.E., the bishop of Alexandria, Athanasius, sent out an Easter letter in which he named the twenty-seven books we have today as the "canon" of the New Testament. His listing enjoyed a much better reception than that of Marcion, but it still did not settle the matter in all sectors and a number of councils were held in ensuing centuries to try to keep the debate down to a dull roar.

By the fifth century, acceptance of those twenty-seven books listed by Athanasius was pretty much universal, but it wasn't firmly settled until the Council of Trent (1546) for Roman Catholics, the Thirty-Nine Articles (1563) for the Church of England, the Westminster Confession of Faith (1647) for Calvinism, and the Synod of Jerusalem (1672) for the Eastern Orthodox Church.

FOR **REFLECTION**
Does knowing how the Bible was put together make you think about it differently? In what way?
Does this issue raise any questions for you?
Does it settle any questions for you?
What do you suppose it was like sitting in on a council that was deciding on the canon of Scripture?

It's important to remember that when you encounter a reference to "Scripture" in the New Testament (as in 2 Timothy 3:14–17), the writer is referring to the Hebrew Bible. There was no "New Testament" at that point. What you had were prominent figures in the early church recording events or sending letters to fledgling Christian communities for a variety of purposes.

APPENDIX 2

WHO DAT? BIOGRAPHIES OF JESUS' BEST-KNOWN DISCIPLES

ANDREW

Unlike his brother, Simon Peter, Andrew has only his Greek name, which means manly or brave. Like his brother, Andrew was a fisherman. Matthew, Mark, and Luke have Andrew and Peter called to discipleship together. John, however, tells us that Andrew was first a disciple of John the Baptist, and that it was Andrew who brought Peter to Jesus (John 1:35–42). Whether Andrew was the very first or simply among the first disciples called, the Orthodox tradition names St. Andrew *protokletos*, or first-called.

Tradition and the early church fathers describe Andrew as preaching in Scythia, all around the Black Sea and along the Dnieper River all the way to Kiev and Novgorod. He is also recorded as being in Byzantium and Thrace. All that travel got him named as the patron saint of Ukraine, Romania, Russia, and the Patriarchate of Constantinople.

Andrew was martyred by crucifixion in the Greek city of Patras. He claimed to be unworthy of crucifixion in the same manner as Jesus and was therefore bound to an X-shaped cross, or saltire, which is now known as St. Andrew's Cross. His feast day is November 30.

Once Andrew was unable to travel, his relics took up the journey, bringing some of his remains to Scotland. When a Pictish king battled the English, he prayed for victory, promising that if said victory were granted, he would make St. Andrew the patron saint of Scotland. The national flag of Scotland, which bears the saltire, tells you how it all turned out. Some believe the elevation of Peter's brother in Scotland was also a jab at the Roman church (founded by Peter), which saw its share of battles with Celtic Christianity.

St. Andrew and St. Francis by El Greco, 1604

It is said that marking your fireplace with St. Andrew's Cross will keep witches from flying down your chimney. (Apparently this was an issue in ancient Britain.) Another tradition claims that if single girls put a branch of sweet basil under their pillow on St. Andrew's Night and someone takes it in their dreams, they will marry soon. Take that with a grain of…basil.

BARTHOLOMEW

Bartholomew presents a puzzle for those counting Jesus' twelve disciples. In the Synoptic Gospels Bartholomew (which means "son of Tolmai") always appears in the company of Philip and is in the various lists of Jesus' twelve disciples. John, however, doesn't mention him, but does include a friend of Philip named Nathanael (which means "gift of God"). It is this Nathanael who famously asks Philip, "Can anything good come out of Nazareth?" when Philip asks him to come and meet Jesus (John 1:45–46). Nathanael's hometown was Cana in Galilee. John doesn't mention anyone named Bartholomew, but then John does not include an actual list of the twelve disciples as the Synoptic Gospels do.

Detail of St. Bartholomew
from Michelangelo's
The Last Judgement fresco in the
Sistine Chapel, 1534-41

Most scholars think Bartholomew and Nathanael are different people, and we have only included Bartholomew here. Still, however, it is curious that John doesn't mention him, especially in the company of Philip. What we can say is that Jesus had many more disciples than the twelve he set apart, and it seems clear from Nathanael's eventual confession of Jesus as the Son of God (John 1:49) that he was a disciple, even if not one of the twelve.

Tradition holds that Bartholomew took a copy of Matthew's gospel to India and, along with Jude, brought Christianity to Armenia. He is also recorded as doing missionary work in Ethiopia, Mesopotamia, Parthia, and Lycaonia. After converting the king of Armenia, Polymius, to Christianity, the king's brother conspired against Bartholomew and he was martyred. Some accounts say that he was beheaded, while others say that he was flayed alive and crucified upside down. Still others claim he was beaten unconscious and thrown into the sea to drown. The flaying is most commonly depicted and it is this tradition that makes Bartholomew the patron saint of tanners. Ewww?

Bartholomew's feast day is June 11 in Eastern Christianity and August 24 in the Roman Catholic calendar. Along with Jude, Bartholomew is the patron saint of the Armenian Apostolic Church.

JAMES (THE ELDER), SON OF ZEBEDEE

As we saw in Session 5, there are a lot of people in the New Testament named James (Jacob in Hebrew), including two of Jesus' twelve disciples. This first James frequently bears the title "the Elder" or sometimes "the Greater," because he was both called to be a disciple earlier and was personally closer to Jesus than the other James. This James is the brother of John, both sons of Zebedee.

Jesus gave the brothers the Greek nickname Boanerges, meaning "Sons of Thunder" (Mark 3:17). While the gospels offer the rationale for Peter's nickname ("the rock"), we don't get an explanation for "sons of thunder." Most assume that it had something to do with their temperament—maybe they were impetuous or quick to anger. However, if they were cousins to Jesus, the fact that he called them sons of thunder could be a reference to old Zebedee's temperament rather than that of James and John.

Saint [James the Greater]
by Carlo Crivelli, ca. 1480

While it's believed that John was the only one of the twelve disciples to live out a natural life, his brother James had the distinction of being the first of the twelve to be martyred (about 44 C.E.) and the only one whose martyrdom was early enough to be recorded in the New Testament writings (Acts 12:1–2). James appears too frequently in the gospels to list all the mentions here, apart from mentioning again that Peter, James, and John were the three disciples of the twelve that were closest to Jesus.

James is the patron saint of Spain, where ancient tradition says he was preaching as early as the year 40 C.E.; his feast day is on July 25 (April 30 on the Orthodox liturgical calendar). "The Way of St. James" has been one of the most popular pilgrimage routes in Europe since the Middle Ages and will take you to Santiago de Compostela (Iago is the Spanish version of the name James, so Santiago is named for St. James), where the relics of St. James are interred.

SALOME

Fresco of Salome (right) bathing Jesus. Cappadocia, 11th Century

The mother of both James and John is most frequently believed to be Salome (not *the* Salome, daughter of Herodias, who danced for the head of John the Baptist), who is present at the crucifixion of Jesus in Mark's account (Mark 15:40) and among the women who went to anoint Jesus' body in the tomb (Mark 16:1). Because Matthew says "the mother of the sons of Zebedee" was at the crucifixion and doesn't mention Salome, they are thought to be the same person (Matthew 27:56).

Some traditions believe her to be the sister of Mary, the mother of Jesus, which could certainly explain why James and John were both among the first disciples called and part of Jesus' inner circle. If they were essentially cousins, Jesus probably had known them for a long time. If Salome was actually Jesus' aunt, that could also explain her boldness in Matthew 20:20–21:

> Then the mother of the sons of Zebedee came to him with her sons, and kneeling before him she asked a favor of him. And he said to her, "What do you want?" She said to him, "Declare that these two sons of mine will sit one at your right hand and one at your left, in your kingdom."

That's quite the favor to ask, even if you are a relative, but seems a little more plausible if this were indeed Mary's sister. If this is Mary's sister, then John may also place her at the Crucifixion in John 19:25. See the boxed discussion "Oh, Mary" on p. 19 for more on this. She is also sometimes referred to as Mary Salome. Adding Mary clears it all up, right?

In 1483, the Portuguese introduced St. James to the Congo, where his feast day is a national holiday. Congolese slaves brought the celebration to the Americas, where it's still celebrated in Haiti and Puerto Rico.

It's said that either James himself or his relics had an encounter with a knight who emerged from the water covered in scallops. For that reason, the scallop (or cockle) shell became the emblem of St. James and was often carried by pilgrims and seen in artwork representing the saint. The association became so close that if you order scallops in a French restaurant today, you will order *coquille St. Jacques*. In Munich instead of Paris? Order *Jakobsmuschel*. In Amsterdam? *Jacobsschelp*. His name is actually part of the word in all three languages.

JAMES, SON OF ALPHAEUS

We talked some about this James in connection with the book of James in Session 5. The Bible tells us that the second man named James among Jesus' disciples was the son of Alphaeus. There's a fellow identified by the Gospel of Mark (Mark 15:40) as "James the Less" or "James the Younger" (depending on your translation) and tradition has identified that James with James the son of Alphaeus. Like the sons of Zebedee, there were two, possibly even three sons of Alphaeus among the twelve disciples. Assuming there wasn't more than one Alphaeus, this James may have been Matthew's brother.

If the connection between James the son of Alphaeus and James the Less is correct, then the mother of this James (according to Mark) is named…wait for it…Mary. According to that same verse, he would also have a brother named Joses. I won't even begin to try to untie the biblical knots by which Mary might be connected to each James. Suffice it to say that we can only be sure that lots of Marys were standing at the cross and at least a couple of them had sons. As we saw in Session 5, opinion is split about whether James the son of Alphaeus is Jesus' brother and/or the James who came to lead the church in Jerusalem, known as James the Just. Roman Catholic tradition believes all three to be the same person.

Apostle James, son of Alphaeus (James the Less). Russian Orthodox icon by craftsmen of Mstyora, 19th Century (Russian Empire)

Unlike James, son of Zebedee, this James gets almost no ink in the gospels. He's mentioned just four times, and in all four instances simply appears in a list of the twelve disciples. So, if he's not James the Less, James the brother of Jesus, James the leader of the church in

Jerusalem, James the author of the book of James, or some combination of those, then we know precious little about him. All the traditions about this James rely on equating him with one of those other men named James.

If you're looking at artwork and want to know which James you're looking at, James the son of Alphaeus will be shown with a fuller's club, a tool used in the making of cloth. He's believed to have been crucified in Egypt while preaching the gospel there. His feast day in the Orthodox tradition is October 9.

JOHN, SON OF ZEBEDEE

As with James, John is a name attached to lots of important people in the Bible. Our discussions of the Gospel of John, the three letters of John, and Revelation examine the debates about just how many of those Johns are believed to be the same person. It's agreed that John the disciple of Jesus is the son of Zebedee and brother of James the son of Zebedee. The possibility that Salome was their mother (and that James and John were cousins of Jesus) was discussed in the entry for James. It's also agreed that John the Baptist is a different John from all the others.

*The head of John the Apostle
by Nikolai Ge, 1863*

We've already mentioned that John is believed to be the only one of the twelve disciples to live out a natural lifetime. (Ten of the others were martyrs and Judas, as we'll see in a moment, took his own life.) It's believed that John died in Ephesus sometime around the year 100 C.E. at about ninety-five years of age.

Like his father and brother, John was a fisherman in Galilee, where they were plying their trade when Jesus called them to become disciples. Along with his brother and Peter, John is part of Jesus' inner circle, and if it is correct to equate John with the person called "the beloved disciple" in John's gospel, he's the only male disciple recorded as being present at the cross. It is this same beloved disciple who is seated next to Jesus at the Last Supper.

In John 19:26, Jesus speaks from the cross to commit his mother into the care of "the disciple whom he loved." Tradition therefore has John caring for the Virgin Mary throughout the rest of her life. After Pentecost, Peter works closely with John in working miracles and spreading the gospel in Judea and Samaria—you've read about that in the beginning chapters of Acts.

When persecution began scattering Jesus' followers, John (and the Virgin Mary) settled in Ephesus. A number of traditions add Mary Magdalene (see her entry below) to their company as well. The Virgin Mary died around 54 C.E. and the tradition claims that, like her son, her grave was empty. The Assumption of Mary represents the belief that she, too, rose from the dead and was assumed bodily into heaven. Others claim that her body was simply taken away so that it would not become an idol, which seems to indicate that, whatever happened, her body was indeed not where it was supposed to have been.

After the death of Mary, John and Mary Magdalene are believed to have traveled together to evangelize and strengthen the churches in the region.

Although John apparently died at an advanced age of natural causes, it wasn't because no one tried to kill him. Acts 4 tells us that he was thrown in prison with Peter, and one of several feast days for John remembers the claim that he was once thrown into a pot of boiling oil and emerged none the worse for wear. This was apparently meant as a public execution in the Colosseum and tradition has it that the entire audience converted to Christianity when John emerged unscathed. The same tradition records that his reward was exile in Patmos.

Later set free, John is said to have trained Polycarp (later the bishop of Smyrna), who in turn trained Irenaeus, one of the early church fathers. It is not without irony that the main mission of Irenaeus became fighting the Gnostics, who adopted the Gospel of John as one of their favorite texts.

John is, of course, venerated as a saint whose feast day is December 27 in the Roman calendar and May 8 in the Orthodox tradition. Both recognize his assumed role as the author of the fourth gospel in his titles.

John is acknowledged in Muslim commentaries on the Qur'an, and Islamic tradition names him as one of three disciples preaching to the people in Antioch. Jumping from the Muslims to the Mormons: Latter-Day Saints believe that Peter, James, and John were all resurrected and appeared to Joseph Smith, the founder of Mormonism.

JUDAS ISCARIOT

In his famous work *The Inferno*, Dante reserves a special place in the ninth level of hell for the traitor, Judas. Judas isn't alone there, but he's the lowest of all the human inhabitants, only edged out by the devil himself. This image from *The Inferno* shows Satan chowing down on three traitors. The two on the sides are Brutus and Cassius. The one in the middle with his head getting bitten off is Judas.

Dante's Lucifer, from *Commedia*, Codex Altonensis, folio 48r, located in
Ex Bibliotheca Gymnasii Altonani (Hamburg)

You may remember that Judas was an esteemed name in Jesus' day. Those who heard it in first-century Palestine would've immediately thought of the war hero, Judas Maccabeus, who brought independence to the beleaguered Jewish nation.

We've already looked at the role such an association might have played in Judas's decision to betray Jesus to the authorities. We'll never know whether his motivation came from greed, impatience, or a more sinister evil, but we do know that the name Judas dropped dramatically from the list of popular baby names after his action.

The Iscariot part of his name is commonly thought to refer to the town of Kerioth, which is the name of a couple of Judean towns. John identifies Judas as the "son of Simon Iscariot" (John 6:71), which could be a reference to the father's birthplace and not necessarily to Judas himself. There are also other theories about the origins of the word "Iscariot," ranging from a word meaning "liar" to a reference to his death. But given the naming conventions of the time, some relation to one of the towns named Kerioth is more likely. At the very least it helps us keep the names straight, since there's also a disciple named Jude (see the next entry).

The New Testament has no wholesome stories about Judas. His is not presented as a story about a good man gone wrong. Even before the betrayal, Judas is presented as being small and petty—but remember that his story was written by people whose perspective was colored by the incidents of Jesus' last days.

Judas doesn't meet a happy end, although the narratives conflict to a certain degree. Matthew has Judas returning the money given him for the betrayal and then hanging himself (Matthew 27:3–10), while Luke (in Acts 1) says he used the money to buy a field and then fell and died when he sort of exploded on impact and his "bowels gushed out." The former makes for a better painting; the latter needs to be saved for the movie.

Some resolve the differences by saying that Judas hanged himself and, when cut loose, exploded on impact. But that doesn't resolve the question of whether he returned the money or bought a field with it. The Matthew passage presents additional problems, since it claims that returning the money fulfilled a prophecy in Jeremiah. Both John Calvin and St. Jerome concluded that Matthew meant to refer to the prophet Zechariah rather than to the prophet Jeremiah, since Zechariah 11:12–13 refers to thirty pieces of silver and Jeremiah doesn't. The discrepancy also caused evangelical icon C. S. Lewis to remark in a 1959 letter to a friend that he had to reject the notion that every statement in Scripture represented historical truth.

Most of us, however, don't need to get lost in the weeds to see that Judas came to an unseemly end. The more interesting discussions about Judas revolve around issues of sin and forgiveness, predestination and culpability. Is Judas damned? If so, is it because of his betrayal or because of his suicide? If he's fulfilling a predestined part in a divine drama, is he off the hook because he's doing God's will? If his betrayal is motivated by some mistaken notion of Jesus' mission, is he still in big trouble? To me, those are much more fruitful discussions than debates over whether Matthew made a mistake in his prophecy citation.

Of course nobody reveres Judas today as a saint, and his depiction in art varies. Sometimes, to acknowledge that he was, indeed, one of the twelve, he's given a halo, but it's usually in a darker hue than the other apostles'. Most often, however, he gets no halo at all. What he does get is a fascinating assortment of artistic treatments. From superhero comics to classical art, from the classical poet Dante to the novelist and playwright Mikhail Bulgakov, from Martin Scorsese's *Last Temptation of Christ* to a thirteenth-century Scottish ballad that blames the whole mess on Judas' sister, the character of Judas is explored, dissected, condemned, redeemed, and investigated.

In every culture and every age where the story is known, the norms of who and what constitute the damned can be seen in the depiction of Judas Iscariot. And as we see the scenarios play out in art, literature, and music, we often find ourselves asking—as Judas did in Matthew 26:25—"Surely not I, Rabbi?"

JUDE (THADDEUS)

Jude the Apostle is the guy you don't want to confuse with Judas Iscariot. John makes sure of this by calling him specifically, "Judas not Iscariot" in John 14:22. It's normally assumed that Jude and Thaddeus are the same person, as there's some evidence that Thaddeus is a nickname. Some lists of the twelve disciples include "Judas son of James" but not Thaddeus (Luke 6:14–16) and others leave out Jude and include Thaddeus

The legacy of St. Jude, St. Jude's Children's Research Hospital, Memphis, TN

(Matthew 10:1–4, Mark 3:14–19). So you sometimes see people calling him Jude Thaddeus or Judas Thaddeus. Luke calls him "Jude of James," and most people interpret that to be Jude, son of James (No! Not another James!), but it could point to a brother as well.

Some scholars believe he's a brother of Jesus and author of the book of Jude. In general Catholics believe this to be the case and Protestants don't, but the line isn't hard and fast. A fourteenth-century Greek historian has suggested that Jude was the bridegroom at the wedding in Cana where Jesus turned the water into wine.

Tradition holds that after Jesus' death, Jude preached in Judea, Samaria, Idumaea, Syria, Mesopotamia, and Libya, with some possible excursions to Edessa and Beirut, where tradition says he was martyred somewhere around 65 C.E. He is often pictured with the axe that took his life or with the fire of Pentecost above his head. Along with Bartholomew, he's a patron saint of the Armenian Apostolic Church.

In the Roman Catholic Church St. Jude is the patron saint of hopeless and impossible causes—that's why he's my favorite saint. If there is someone to pray to, to specifically fix hopeless and impossible causes, then no cause is actually hopeless or impossible. Genius. This attribution, which came from people reporting miracles after praying at his grave, is the reason you often have hospitals named for St. Jude, most famously St. Jude Children's

Research Hospital in Memphis, TN. His feast day is October 28 in the West and June 19 in the Eastern Orthodox Church.

I'm not sure of the message behind the fact that St. Jude is also the patron saint of the Chicago Police Department and am even less sure that having St. Jude as the patron saint of the Clube de Regatas do Flamengo (a Brazilian soccer team) is a way to energize the fans. But I guess you can't give up on them even in the worst losing streak.

MARY MAGDALENE

Yes, indeedy, Mary of Magdala gets her own spot on the list of disciples. While not one of "the twelve," every major Christian tradition interprets the biblical account as giving Mary a position of discipleship and a prominent one at that. Let's review.

Mary Magdalene was not a prostitute, nor does the Bible identify her as a sinner of any kind. All the Bible tells us of her life prior to meeting Jesus was that she had seven demons that Jesus drove out of her (Luke 8:2). We also know from the Bible that she was a woman of means, one of several women who (in the section of Luke 8 that tells about the demons) traveled with Jesus

Magdalena by Gheorghe Tattarescu

and the other disciples and provided for them out of their resources.

Some early traditions confused her identity with the unnamed "sinner" who anoints Jesus' feet in Luke 7:36–50 (and, of course, the only sin women commit is sexual, right?), but every major tradition has since rejected that association. If you hear someone make the mistake of calling Mary Magdalene a prostitute, set them straight. The only "evidence" for that are medieval mistakes that have since been acknowledged as being in error.

The Eastern Orthodox tradition believes Mary Magdalene was a virtuous woman from birth—so pure that she made God's short list for becoming the mother of Jesus, which Satan then thwarted by hitting her with those seven demons.

From the earliest church fathers onward, Roman Catholic tradition has named Mary Magdalene the "apostle to the apostles" because Jesus first appeared to her after his resurrection and instructed her to bring the news of his resurrection to the others.

St. Augustine in the fourth century gave her that title, calling her equal to the apostles. Pope John Paul II concurred, adding "This event, in a sense, crowns all that has been said previously about Christ entrusting divine truths to women as well as men."[4] And Pope Benedict XVI said Mary Magdalene was "a disciple of the Lord who plays a lead role in the Gospels."[5]

There's no equivalent Protestant spokesperson, but as the folks who rallied to the Reformation cry of "sola scriptura!" (Scripture alone), Protestants recognize that Mary is never named as a sinner of any kind in the Bible and is given enormous prestige in its pages, especially in the death and resurrection of Jesus.

Some early traditions believe she was married to Jesus, others believe she was married to John or maybe both since John was possibly a relative who might have taken Jesus' wife as his own upon his death, as was the custom. Though I don't have a problem with either scenario, I think they're both unlikely.

While the notion seems scandalous in many circles today, I don't think it would have been an issue at all in Jesus' day. First-century Jewish rabbis regularly married. We know Peter had a wife because Jesus healed his mother-in-law, and there's no indication that any of the disciples had to become celibate to follow Jesus. Because a married Jesus wouldn't have been a big deal, and because Mary Magdalene was around so much, I think the biblical authors would have mentioned it. A prime place for such a mention would have been in John's gospel, where Jesus transfers care of his mother to John. Mary Magdalene is right there and it would have been natural to do the same for her if she and Jesus were married.

It's also true that the early church believed that Jesus would be returning in glory during their generation. For that reason Paul recommended that followers of Jesus not worry about long-term commitments like marriage and family. Spreading the gospel was the priority because time was short. So I don't think Mary Magdalene was married to John either, even though most traditions place them together in Ephesus.

Finally, why does Mary Magdalene have to be married to anybody? Luke tells us she had resources of her own to share, and her association with Jesus and, later, John would have given her the male "cover" that women needed in ancient settings. Some traditions place her in Ephesus until her death; others have her traveling to Gaul and living out her life in Provence, converting the whole population while she was there. Others have her shipwrecked in Malta. But all have her living out that mandate that Jesus gave to her first (perhaps with some of the other women), before any of the twelve disciples and before any other human being: Go and tell the others that Jesus has risen from the dead.

4 "Mulieris Dignitatem," apostolic letter, August 15, 1988. Vatican.va. 1988-08-15. Retrieved August 13, 2012.
5 Reflection before recitation of the Angelus, July 23, 2006.

Mary Magdalene is revered as a saint in all the traditions that recognize saints. The Catholic Church cleaned up her reputation a bit in 1969 (the same year St. Christopher lost his saintly status), and tacitly acknowledged the error by changing the liturgical reading on her feast day (July 22) from the passage about the unnamed sinner in Luke 7 to Mary's discovery of the empty tomb in John 20.

Mary Magdalene is named fourteen times in the gospels, more than most of the twelve disciples. Some scholars (most notably Elaine Pagels) have suggested that Mary might even be the beloved disciple of John's gospel.

One of the later traditions associated with Mary Magdalene will help you add a religious element to your Easter egg traditions. It is said that she secured an invitation to a feast given by the Roman emperor Tiberius, where she gave him a red egg. How it got to be red is explained in two ways. One is that she had a basket of eggs at the crucifixion and Jesus' blood dripped on them, making them red. I'm not sure why you take eggs to crucifixions, but there you go.

The second explanation: Mary presented a regular egg to Tiberius, using it as a symbol of resurrection and proclaiming, "Christ is risen." The emperor declared the idea about as likely as having the egg suddenly turn red in her hand. The obliging egg did just that.

MATTHEW

Matthew was kind of a surprise pick for a disciple of Jesus. Known occasionally as Levi, he was a tax collector (publican in some translations). That means he would have been literate in both Aramaic and Greek (and perhaps other languages), and that he was part of a despised class of people. In fact, the minute Jesus calls him from his tax booth and goes to Matthew's house for dinner, the scribes and Pharisees are on him for associating with the riff raff. (Matthew 9:9–13, Mark 2:13–17, Luke 5:27–32)

Of course nobody has ever really loved tax collectors, ancient or modern. Just try going to a party and saying, "Hi, I work for the IRS," and you'll understand what I mean. But in Jesus' day,

Inspiration of Saint Matthew
by Caravaggio, 1602

the reasons for hating tax collectors went deeper than today. The system was not only corrupt, it was intentionally corrupt from the get-go.

In Roman provinces, the Romans recruited tax collectors from the local population and then simply told them how much they had to turn over per person to Rome. There was complete freedom to collect as much beyond that as the individual tax collector wanted, just as long as he passed along the required amount to Rome. So tax collectors routinely bilked their own people to line their own pockets with complete immunity from prosecution. That's a formula for wealth, but not popularity.

There may have been honest tax collectors—it was up to the individual, after all. Perhaps Matthew had never taken anything extra and Jesus called him because he was amazed to find an honest tax collector. We don't know, although John does tell us that it was Judas and not Matthew who was in charge of finances for Jesus and the twelve. (John 12:6)

According to the biblical text, Matthew was from Galilee and his tax office (and perhaps his home) was in Capernaum, though the Roman historian Eusebius claims he was from Syria. Matthew is called the "son of Alphaeus," so he may have been a brother to James, son of Alphaeus. Most scholars assume that Matthew is somehow behind the gospel that bears his name, although the book itself claims no author. Some believe he wrote it, while others believe someone else wrote it based on stories and accounts passed on by Matthew.

There's no scholarly agreement on what Matthew did after Jesus' death and resurrection. Most believe he stayed and preached in Judea for some time and that he also went to Ethiopia—Islamic commentary also mentions his presence there with Andrew. Nobody can be certain when or how he died, though it's assumed by some sources that he was a martyr.

Matthew's feast day is September 21 in the Roman calendar and November 16 in the Greek. Bankers claim him as their patron saint, so I'm guessing he's been especially busy of late.

PETER

To get a complete picture of Andrew's brother Peter, we'd have to cut and paste at least all four gospels and the book of Acts into this space. When we first meet him in the gospels, he's a fisherman named Simon, from the town in the Galilee called Bethsaida. When Simon declares Jesus to be the Messiah, Jesus famously changes his name to Peter (or in Aramaic, Cephas), which means "rock."

Altar Frontal at St. Peter's Episcopal Church-on-the-Canal / Buzzards Bay, MA, photo by Charlotte Daigle

Before Jesus' death, however, the only rock-like qualities we see in Peter are his obstinacy and denseness. He denies knowing Jesus after Jesus is arrested—three times—then feels terrible and would've liked to hide under the very rock he was supposed to be.

Along with the sons of Zebedee, James and John, Peter is part of Jesus' inner circle; when the disciples are listed in the gospels, Peter is named first, an indicator of importance in ancient lists. Some of the apocryphal New Testament texts (see Appendix 4 on p. 247) paint a picture of Peter being jealous of Mary Magdalene's relationship to Jesus.

After Jesus' resurrection, it's a new Peter that we see. It's Peter who takes the lead at Pentecost and preaches to those gathered about what he and the other disciples have seen. It's then that Peter becomes the solid rock on which the early church is built. Tradition says he was bishop of the church in Antioch before leaving to become the founder, then bishop, of the church in Rome. Peter is recognized as the first pope, although many question to what degree that role can be compared to today's position.

Ancient accounts by Tertullian and Origen confirm that Peter was martyred about the same time as St. Paul (some believe on the same date of October 13, 64 C.E.), but while Paul was a Roman citizen and had the luxury of a quick beheading, no such option was available for Peter. It was crucifixion for him, but tradition tells us that Peter thought himself unworthy of the same death that Jesus suffered and requested to be crucified upside down. His burial place is believed to be directly below the high altar in what is now St. Peter's Basilica in Rome. Excavations and testing in 1960 revealed bones of a first-century male who was about sixty-one years old.

Most of the arguments about Peter in the centuries that followed his death centered around the emerging claims of the Roman Catholic Church regarding the papacy and apostolic succession (the notion that ultimate church authority began with Peter, and only Peter, and is only legitimate when traced back to him). With divisions between the Catholic and Orthodox traditions—and then throwing Protestants into the mix—there are too many outside agendas in the literature to draw definitive conclusions from later writing.

Peter gets multiple feast days, sometimes with Paul, sometimes with other apostles, sometimes on his own, due to his acknowledged importance across all traditions. Even in Shia Islam, Peter's relationship to Jesus (whom Muslims revere as a prophet and messiah) is likened to the relationship of Ali to Muhammad—a kind of chief deputy. Ali is believed to be the first caliph after Muhammad, and Muslims see Peter's emergence as a leader in the early church in a similar light.

Peter not only gets lots of feasts, he's also patron of lots of places, institutions, and trades. As a sampling, Peter's switchboard is filled with messages from Scranton, PA; Cologne, Germany; Las Vegas, NV; Chartres, France; of course St. Petersburg, Russia, and forty other locations worldwide. He's busy looking after bakers, bridge builders, and cobblers as well as the more predictable fishermen, locksmiths (he has the keys, after all), net makers, and shipwrights.

You call on Peter if you have foot problems or fever and also if you want longevity, although it seems to me that John would be the guy to call for that. And of course he's in charge of the papacy, every school and church bearing his name, as well as Bishop Cotton's Boys' School in Bangalore and the Universalist Church. No word on whether prayers to Peter have an extended wait time due to volume.

PHILIP

Philip hails from the town in Galilee called Bethsaida, also the hometown of Peter and Andrew. His big gospel appearance is in John 1:43–46, where he's called to follow Jesus and goes to find Nathanael (Bartholomew) to add him to the group. John 6:5–6 also relates that Jesus tested Philip's faith by asking him where they should get food to feed the large crowd. Philip responds that six months' wages wouldn't even scratch the surface—and the story of Jesus feeding the five thousand follows. As a result, Philip is the patron saint of pastry chefs. Ah, irony.

Apostle Philip
by Albrecht Durer, 1516

In John 12:20–21, some Greeks approach Philip to ask about Jesus. His Greek name and the fact that Greeks address him have made scholars assume that Philip spoke Greek. Scholars are at odds about whether this is the same Philip who evangelized the Ethiopian eunuch in Acts.

Those who think they're separate people point out that when the role of deacon is established in Acts 6, Philip is one of the new deacons. Since the role of deacon was created to allow the apostles to preach, it seems unlikely that the apostle Philip would've become a deacon. They also point out that when Philip the Evangelist (the guy in Acts) goes to Samaria, he preaches and baptizes, but it takes the arrival of Peter and John to give those folks the Holy Spirit. Scholars argue that Philip the Apostle would surely have been able to do the job himself.

Others, however, think drawing such hard and fast lines wouldn't have been necessary. The deacons may have wanted an apostolic liaison among their ranks, and since Peter and John were coming as official representatives from the church in Jerusalem, Philip may have held back for a more formal occasion. At least two ancient sources equate the two Philips.

Of course, there could've been two Philips and both of them could be represented in Acts. After all, explaining the Scriptures and preaching to an Ethiopian eunuch would've been more the role of an apostle than a deacon. You could have Philip the Apostle doing apostle-like things in Acts and another guy named Philip doing deacon-like things.

We learn in Acts 21:8–9 that Paul visited the family of one Philip who had four virgin daughters who were prophets. The passage calls him "Philip the evangelist," then immediately adds that he was "one of the seven," presumably the seven deacons from Acts 6. Evangelism is more the job of an apostle than a deacon, which says to me that the lines between who did what don't seem to be so hard and fast that you draw definite conclusions about identities.

Philip's feast day is May 3 (Roman) and November 14 (Greek) and he was martyred by crucifixion or beheading in about 80 C.E. in Hierapolis. By some reports, he was crucified along with Bartholomew. In any case, Hierapolis (in modern Turkey) claims him and on July 27, 2011, archaeologists claim to have found his tomb there. Some believe Philip the deacon is buried in Caesarea. Cape Verde, San Felipe Pueblo, Luxembourg, and Uruguay all claim Philip the Apostle as their patron, along with the pastry chefs and (don't ask me why) hatters.

SIMON THE ZEALOT

This disciple may as well have been called "Simon the Obscure" as his name is about all we know about him. "The Zealot" is added in some lists of disciples to distinguish him from Simon Peter, but scholars debate whether "zealot" is an accurate translation of the Greek word.

Tradition in the Eastern Orthodox Church says that it was this Simon, not Jude, who was the bridegroom at the famous water-into-wine wedding at Cana. The Orthodox claim is that his family labeled him a zealot after the wedding, when he ran off and followed Jesus. The Hebrew word translated here as zealot is *qana*. Some think that's a reference to Cana and not to zealotry at all. Simon has even been called "the Canaanite."

St. Simon (the Zealot) by Albrecht Durer, 1523

There was actually a formal group of revolutionaries called the Zealots, but they didn't exist until thirty to forty years after the gospel events. Depending on how you date the gospels, though, it could be that this Simon joined the Zealots later in life and that the title was added somewhat later to help set him apart. Some kind of revolutionary association is the approach taken in popular presentations of Simon, including *Jesus Christ Superstar* and the miniseries *Jesus of Nazareth*. Other scholars think Simon's zealotry was just a personality trait and that he was especially zealous about Jewish law.

Mark 6:3 lists a person named Simon as one of Jesus' brothers, and Catholic tradition sometimes adopts that view (from different mothers). Other Catholic scholars have equated him with Simeon of Jerusalem, the son of Clopas, who led the church in Jerusalem after James was martyred. If it's true that Clopas was the brother of Jesus' father, Joseph, and Simeon of Jerusalem is Simon the Zealot (or maybe zealous), then perhaps they were cousins rather than brothers.

Tradition links Simon with Jude Thaddeus as an evangelism team, and as we've seen there is also the possibility that Jude was a brother of Jesus, or at least related in some way. If they were relatives, it would make sense for them to team up. They're also buried together in the same tomb in St. Peter's Basilica. Some people think Simon actually is Jude Thaddeus. Or was.

But none of that is stated in the gospels directly. We just want to know who these folks were and so we tend to fill in the blanks. We may be right, we may not. But we can all agree that there are a lot of blanks with Simon the Zealot. Christian tradition says he preached in Egypt, Persia, Armenia, and Lebanon. Muslim tradition chimes in with a vote for North Africa, recording that he preached to the Berbers. It's said Simon was martyred with a saw, with which you often see him pictured. His feast day is October 28 in the West and May 10 in the Coptic Church. He is the patron saint of—you guessed it—sawyers.

THOMAS

Apart from seeing his name on a list, all of what we know of Thomas comes from the Gospel of John, who tells us that Thomas was also known as *Didymus*, Greek for twin. Since the name Thomas comes from the Aramaic word for twin, chances are pretty good that Thomas was a twin. But whose?

Incredulity of Saint Thomas by Caravaggio, 1602

Well, as you've seen, when we get to these disciples that we don't know much about, lots of people think we have them mixed up. There are those who think Thomas is the same person as Jude Thaddeus. He's sometimes called Judas Thomas. Some think he's Simon the Zealot. Maybe one of them is his twin. One of the ancient texts found at Nag Hammadi, *The Book of Thomas the Contender*, claims Jesus was his twin. Obviously the latter presents some problems.

From John, however, we learn that Thomas isn't afraid to speak up and say things that were probably on the minds of at least some of the others. After the death and raising of Lazarus, with the religious leaders cranky and the disciples reluctant to go back to the area, Jesus announces that they're going anyway. It's Thomas who says, maybe with a resigned sigh, "Let us also go, that we may die with him." (John 11:16)

When Jesus created our funeral liturgies by saying that there were many mansions (rooms, dwelling places, depending on your translation) in his Father's house and he would prepare a place there for his disciples, he adds, "You know the way to the place where I am going." The disciples must all have been thinking it, but it's Thomas who speaks up and says, "Lord, we do not know where you are going. How can we know the way?" (John 14:4–5)

But Thomas is best remembered for his question of the resurrected Jesus. John reports that Thomas wasn't with the other apostles on Easter morning. (John 20:24) When the others tell Thomas the news, he doesn't believe them. "Unless I see the mark of the nails in his hands, and put my finger in the mark of the nails and my hand in his side," he declares, "I will not believe." (John 20:25) It took a week, but Jesus showed up again when Thomas was with the others and he got his chance to poke and prod. At last Thomas believed, but he was forever after known as "doubting Thomas."

Later traditions are united in the claim that Thomas' main mission later on was in India, and the apocryphal *Acts of Thomas* provides details that may or may not be accurate. In 52 C.E., Thomas supposedly sailed to India, where, branching out from Jewish colonies there, he's said to have founded many churches along the Periyar River, converting some seventeen thousand people across all four social castes. Although some scholars don't think he went to India at all, there's a long list of ancient sources placing him there. Even in Edessa he was known in hymns as "The Apostle of India." For a discussion of the apocryphal book *The Gospel of Thomas*, see Appendix 3, p. 245.

Legend has it that on the way to India he met the biblical magi (aka the three kings of the Christmas story); another tradition claims that, divinely transported from India to her tomb, he was the only witness to the Assumption of Mary.

Christian tradition says he was martyred with a spear (some say four spears) either in India or in Persia about 72 C.E. In the thirteenth century, Italian traveler Marco Polo claimed he was told that someone hunting peacocks accidentally killed Thomas with an arrow near his home in Chennai, India. A part of me thinks that's just weird enough to be true—but Marco Polo also claimed to have found Adam's tomb in Ceylon. Others claim Thomas died of natural causes. St. Thomas Mount is a small hill near the Chennai airport and is a holy site for Christians, Muslims, and Hindus.

Either Thomas' remains were brought to Edessa in the third century by a merchant named Khabin and buried there or he was martyred in Edessa (the ancient Persian site in modern Turkey, not the Greek city) and buried there. But traditions are in agreement that he had a strong mission in India and was at least mostly buried in a shrine at Edessa. That shrine, however, was sacked in 1144 and the remains of Thomas found themselves on the way to Italy, where they now rest in a town named Ortona in the Abruzzo region.

St. Thomas has an entire branch of Christianity named for him—the St. Thomas Christians (or Nasrani) of India. He's the patron saint of architects, since he was a builder by trade. He has three feast days: July 3 for Catholics, October 6 for Eastern Orthodox, and December 21 for the Indian Orthodox and Anglicans.

APPENDIX 3

CANON FODDER: APOCRYPHAL BOOKS OF THE NEW TESTAMENT

As we've seen throughout this course, it took some time to validate the twenty-seven books of the New Testament as Holy Scripture. Some books had an easier time than others, but a few were still being questioned by Christian leaders like Martin Luther more than a thousand years after their composition.

There were at least four serious attempts to determine the books of the New Testament canon. The oldest surviving list is a fragment known as the Muratorian Canon, named after the man (L. A. Muratori) who discovered the fragment, a Latin translation of an earlier Greek manuscript, in the

Last page of the Canon Muratori, as published by Tregelles in 1868

eighteenth century, hidden away in a library in Milan. The early church pillars, Origen and Eusebius, each produced a list of books they believed should comprise the Christian canon, but the one that stuck was put together by Athanasius in the fourth century.

Apart from the twenty-seven books that Athanasius recommended and that became our New Testament, there have always been other writings that have been respected and read by various Christian communities. We've seen in the Old Testament that a collection of writings known as the Apocrypha is accepted as fully part of the Bible by the Catholic and Orthodox traditions while the Protestants see them as optional reading. But the collection known as the Apocrypha are all writings from the Old Testament period.

When it comes to writings after the birth of Jesus, there's no formal acceptance of any works beyond the twenty-seven books in our Bibles today. In the early church, however, that was not the case. There were many, many works circulating across the first few centuries that described the life and teachings of Jesus, the apostles, or others. They were read and studied in early Christian communities much as churches today might study the writings of more contemporary pastors, teachers, and theologians. You probably have your own list of writings outside the Bible that have been important to your faith and life.

But a few of these ancient writings rose above the heads of the others. Some of them are actually named in those early canonical lists, even though they ended up not making the final cut, and some of their authors belong to a special category of early church authority called the Apostolic Fathers. Other writings were singled out by the early church as being recommended reading for all Christians, even though they weren't given the status of Holy Scripture. It's this special set of books, those held in high regard and read widely across the early church, that we'll look at here.

The Shepherd of Hermas

Known sometimes just as The Shepherd, this work sits at the top of this list because it seems that the only reason it didn't become part of the New Testament was that nobody could trace it to the authority of one of the apostles. It was read widely in the ancient church, and some church fathers (like Irenaeus, for example) thought it should go in the canon. Even those who didn't put it in the canon listed it as recommended reading for every Christian. (Tertullian didn't like it, but he seems to have been in the minority.)

The relatively long work was written by Hermas, a former slave who may have been the brother of Pius, the bishop of Rome. Others believe the author to be the same Hermas that Paul mentions in Romans 16:14, who would have lived sixty to seventy years before the time of Pius. The shepherd of the title is an angel who appears to Hermas and facilitates a series of visions.

The visions, however, aren't nearly as mysterious as the apocalyptic visions in Revelation and elsewhere. Instead, they're more like parables, many of which are centered on a vision of a stone tower (representing the church) and the various kinds of rocks (representing people), which are used, reserved, or cast away during its construction. This book has a great bonus, too: Hermas repeatedly asks the angel for—and gets—explanations of the visions. If John had been as assertive when recording Revelation, we wouldn't be so perplexed by his vision today!

The main topic of The Shepherd is the nature of repentance and what happens when Christians fall into sin. This is a work about the church and how to faithfully live within it, not a story about the lives of the apostles or a gospel about Jesus. It was hands down the most popular book among Christians during the second through the fourth centuries C.E.

The Shepherd of Hermas was first written (in Greek) in Rome sometime during the late first or early second century C.E., and was soon translated into Latin. Because the church leadership generally approved of the work, we have good copies that have survived and you can easily find it online or even order a bound copy from Amazon.

The Didache

Next on the list of influential documents that couldn't quite squeeze into the canon of the New Testament is this church manual whose name, Didache (pronounced did-ah-kay'), literally means "the teaching." Written about the same time as The Shepherd of Hermas, this is a much shorter work that claims in its first line to be "The teaching of the Lord through the twelve apostles to the Gentiles."

The work is referenced in many ancient writings and, again, there were a good number of respected early church leaders who lobbied for its inclusion in the canon. The document was long lost, however, until a copy was found in a monastery library in Constantinople in 1873. (Really, people, fund your libraries so people can dig and see what they have in their collections. There's all kinds of interesting stuff in there.)

The anonymous author seems to be familiar with either the Gospel of Matthew or the sources that Matthew used. A good chunk of the early part of the work echoes instruction in the Sermon on the Mount from Matthew 5–8. It also appears that the author wasn't familiar with a highly structured church hierarchy—that's why scholars tend to date it around 110–120 C.E.

After reviewing basic ethical teaching, the text goes on to talk more specifically about baptism and Holy Communion (called the "thanksgiving meal"). The final sections discuss apostles and prophets, how to tell the true ones from the false, and how to treat them. Last, there are words that address the expectation of the second coming of Christ and the resurrection of the dead.

The discovery of an actual text of the Didache gave scholars a direct line to the ritual practices and expected behaviors of the earliest Christians. You can easily find copies in English translation both online and in print.

The Apocalypse of Peter

A number of writings of the period fit the genre of apocalypse. The Apocalypse of John, better known as Revelation, is the only one of these to make it into the New Testament, but the Apocalypse of Peter came close. There are several documents that bear that name, but the one most widely respected and circulated was found in 1887 in the tomb of a Christian monk and later in an Ethiopian translation.

A different work, now called the Gnostic Apocalypse of Peter, circulated among the Gnostics and was found with the Nag Hammadi texts (fifty texts used by the Gnostics and excavated in Egypt in 1945).

The Muratorian Canon mentioned previously says, "We receive only the apocalypses of John and Peter, though some of us are not willing that the later be read in church." Apparently a lot of people read it outside of church, however, and would have found it a lot easier to understand than John's vision. If you're familiar with Dante's *Divine Comedy*, then the Apocalypse of Peter will strike the same chords. Most of the work involves Jesus showing Peter the specific joys of heaven and pains of hell, with the latter carefully worked out to be punishments befitting the particular sins of each person.

The work ends with Peter recounting the scene of Jesus' Transfiguration that we know from the gospels with some additional detail. It quotes from a work written about 100 C.E. and thus is most commonly dated after that time.

The Acts of Paul

Along with The Shepherd of Hermas and the Didache, Eusebius singles out the Acts of Paul as a contender for belonging in the canon of Scripture. The Acts of Paul includes a number of works often separated into different documents. They include the Acts of Paul and Thecla, the Third Letter to the Corinthians, a letter from the Corinthians to Paul, and an account of Paul's martyrdom. We don't have the whole thing, so there were probably other sub-works that belong on that list.

My favorite story provides the background for Paul's claim in 1 Corinthians 15:32 that he fought with wild beasts in Ephesus. Many take that to be a reference to the riot in Ephesus described in Acts 19:23 and following with "beasts" used metaphorically. But in the Acts of Paul, in a feat that would have made St. Francis proud, St. Paul baptizes a lion. Apparently the lion is granted powers of speech so he can understand and respond to the gospel message. Later, that same lion ends up in a gladiator's ring in Ephesus, and Paul finds himself faced with his converted buddy. The lion, in recognition of Paul's graceful act, does no harm to Paul.

There were works called the "Acts of…" for just about every one of the apostles, but, as in the canonical book of Acts, it was the stories of Paul that rose to the top of the charts. Tertullian again opposed this book, claiming he had found and extracted a confession from the person who forged it. But Tertullian also was not a fan of the fact that the work contained permission for women to preach and to baptize, so there's that.

Although there are many works within the Acts of Paul, all appear to fit together and are believed to have been penned by the same author, who pulled together various oral traditions and other stories about Paul's life and ministry. Whoever did it either didn't know about the Acts of the Apostles as we have it in the canon or at least didn't see this collection as needing to fit into that narrative. There are no references to the canonical book of Acts. The letters from and to the Corinthians in this collection can be found in some editions of the Armenian Bible.

It's easiest to find this work online in its smaller pieces, but the whole is available as well.

The Letter of Barnabas

One last work deserves mention here with the also-rans. While not mentioned in the lists described above, it was included in one of the oldest handwritten copies of the Greek Bible that we know of, the Codex Sinaiticus (or Sinai Bible). This Bible, created in the fourth century, includes both The Shepherd of Hermas and the Letter of Barnabas, along with the regular twenty-seven books of the New Testament.

The letter is traditionally associated with Paul's traveling companion, Barnabas, although the work itself is anonymous. Twenty-one chapters long, it shows familiarity with the Didache and refers to the destruction of the Temple in 70 C.E. Most scholars think it was written in the first few decades of the second century.

The subject matter offers a glimpse into the mounting Jewish-Christian tensions we talked about in Sessions 2 and 3. As Christianity separated itself more and more from its Jewish roots, works like the Letter of Barnabas laid out in detail how Christians were right and Jews were wrong in their beliefs. This letter takes things a bit further by claiming that the Jews were never really God's people and that they've misunderstood their own Scriptures from the beginning. It's not something you want to pull out for your next interfaith gathering.

However, its wide circulation in the early centuries of the church explain a lot about Jewish-Christian relations both then and in the decades and centuries that followed. To the extent that the canonical New Testament texts were either composed or edited in the early second century C.E., we can see possible explanations for wording that implies a hostility toward all Jews back in an era when Christians were actually Jews debating whether Gentiles had a place among them.

Other Works

Many, many other works could have been included here. In recent times a number of the Gnostic texts from Nag Hammadi have had their day in the sun, thanks to *The Da Vinci Code* by Dan Brown and published scholarship about the texts. Like the Dead Sea Scrolls, they were found so recently that they've had more publicity when scholars have delved into them and issued new translations.

There are a number of print (and probably digital) collections where you can read literally hundreds and hundreds of pages of these extra-biblical works. They come under names like *The Other Bible, The Lost Scriptures, The Nag Hammadi Library, The Gnostic Gospels*, and many others. Many of the other books were also highly influential across the centuries, including the proto-gospel of James with its wonderful stories of Jesus as an infant and even the birth of Mary.

Just one word of caution: We've seen that the books of the Bible didn't descend from the hand of God as a set. People debated the merits of both the Old and New Testament books and those sets were not always as carved in stone as they are now. In fact, given the differences even in today's Bibles, they're *still* not as carved in stone as some would think.

However, once you realize that human beings had a role (however divinely inspired) in collecting these materials and naming the set that would be authoritative, people can get suspicious. What if some got left out for less than holy reasons? It's a valid question, but one that can open us up to an error that is equally problematic.

If you start down the path of thinking as a conspiracy theorist would about which texts were in and which were out, you can end up assuming that the exclusion of a book automatically means that it's way more credible than the ones that were included. This sentiment can be magnified if the excluded text is called something enticing, like the *Secret Gospel of Mark* or *The Secret Book of John* or *The Gospel of Truth*. It's easy to latch onto those other works and assume that the traditional gospels were trying to cover up what really happened—and if we can just get our hands on these other books, we'll have the real story.

If you look at the current canon with a skeptical eye, don't throw out that skepticism when it comes to other writings. While there may have been some political and theological wranglings in determining the canon we have, it's also possible that the works we have were included for some very good reasons. Let's take the frequently mentioned *Gospel of Thomas* as an example.

The *Gospel of Thomas* (a quick Internet search will turn it up) consists of 114 sayings with no narrative framework—just statements lined up like proverbs, one after another. The *Gospel of Thomas* contains sayings of Jesus that we have in the canonical gospels. A conspiracy theorist approach to the canon looks for verses that are not represented in the canon and thinks there was a political motive for excluding the *Gospel of Thomas* based on the content of those other verses. Maybe so.

But it's also possible that those who decided on the four gospels we have in the canon found them much more complete and interesting versions of the same information we have in the *Gospel of Thomas*. In other words, 114 unconnected verses might have just seemed boring when you could have the full portraits sketched out in Matthew, Mark, Luke, and John.

Ultimately when considering these issues, I remember the words of my seminary professor, Luke Timothy Johnson. Holding up his Bible, he said, "These books aren't the only truth there is. This just represents the only truth we can agree on." That perspective has served me very well over the years. Clearly there are books outside our canon that nourished the faith and strengthened the resolve of Christians for centuries. We can question whether Paul converted a talking lion, but we have a talking ass in the canonical book of Numbers, so that story isn't a deal-breaker.

What we can say is that the set of texts we have in the Bible sitting in your lap is the set of texts that Christians have come to agree on. It is these texts, and not others, where we turn to settle our disputes and guide our faith and practice when we gather as the church. But Christians have always believed that God speaks in many voices and through many agents, from the whirlwind in Job through the very human apostles who carried the gospel to the New Testament world. As individuals, we'll find God's truth in many places. As the church, however, we've agreed to eat from the feast of the canon as it's been passed down to us.

Enjoy the meal.

APPENDIX 4

WHO KILLED JESUS? A VOLATILE ISSUE EXPLAINED

Ultimate Responsibility

The accounts of Jesus' trial and crucifixion in the gospels have differences, but there are two things common to all of them: When Jesus is arrested he is first brought to the Sanhedrin (see p. 48) for questioning and the Sanhedrin turns him over to Pilate, who ultimately orders the crucifixion. Three of the four gospels describe Judas as working out his betrayal with the "chief priests," and all four claim that Pilate was uneasy about his sentence.

Sketch for the Crucifixion
by Thomas Eakins, 1880

So the first thing to note is that, as a technical matter, it was Roman authority that ordered the crucifixion of Jesus and Roman soldiers who did the deed. We know from our own experience with government that it doesn't matter if a particular judge has misgivings about handing down a death sentence or if a particular governor thinks a death-row inmate is probably innocent. If the sentence is given and the order signed, the judge and the governor bear the responsibility for the execution. As a matter of history and according to the gospels, the Romans killed Jesus.

Now before we go on, stop and think about this. The gospels do paint a nuanced picture, but they also are clear that Pilate ordered the crucifixion of Jesus and that his soldiers carried out the orders. And yet nobody goes around today taunting Italian-American children by calling them "Jesus killers." Rome was not sacked by Christians hollering that the Romans killed Jesus. If you find yourself getting defensive and claiming anti-Semitism is not at the root of the persecutions I described at the end of Session 2, think again. If it were strictly a matter of the Bible, the Italians would be feeling it, too.

There has been no persecution of Italians and no huge backlash against even ancient Rome because, under normal circumstances, we recognize that the actions of one Roman prefect in one Roman province are just that. Even if it were the emperor himself who had given the order, we'd recognize that history's record of "the Romans killed Jesus" meant the actions of the government and not every single Roman, and certainly not every contemporary person who could trace ancestry to first-century Italy.

The fact that people today who hear "the Jews killed Jesus" think that can justify either the abuse of Jewish-American children or the slaughter of any and all Jews when the same doesn't apply to Italians reveals the depth of our anti-Semitism, not the depth of our biblical knowledge. But let's go back to the text for a moment.

While laying ultimate blame at the feet of the Romans, it's also clear that the gospel writers believed that the chief priests, and perhaps the Sanhedrin as a body, encouraged and enabled Jesus' crucifixion by arranging (and perhaps paying) for Jesus' betrayal and providing political charges against him. Adding fuel to this fire is Matthew's gospel. After explaining that Pilate offers to free a prisoner in honor of Passover, Matthew and Luke tell us that the crowds choose another man (Barabbas) over Jesus. Then Matthew adds the following in Matthew 27:24–26:

> So when Pilate saw that he could do nothing, but rather that a riot was beginning, he took some water and washed his hands before the crowd, saying, "I am innocent of this man's blood; see to it yourselves." Then the people as a whole answered, "His blood be on us and on our children!" So he released Barabbas for them; and after flogging Jesus, he handed him over to be crucified.

With the gospel accounts (which, remember are not, by their own admission, neutral accounts) claiming the Jewish leadership aided and abetted the whole affair; with Matthew recording the mob response; and with several gospel writers and the author of Acts using general terms like "the Jews" instead of narrowing things down to the actual individuals responsible—things can get ugly, and they have.

We've already talked about the inconsistency of holding all Jews responsible for Jesus' death while letting all Italians off the hook—not to mention the clear nonsense of doing either. But there is also a second gross misunderstanding that underlies the charge of "the Jews killed Jesus." That phrase implies that "the Jews" killed the Christian leader, Jesus. The problem is that at the time of Jesus' execution, there are no Christians.

With the exception of the Roman leadership, everybody involved is Jewish. Jesus, his disciples, the chief priests, the Sanhedrin—everybody. Joseph of Arimathea is thought to have been a member of the very Sanhedrin that turned Jesus over to Pilate, and yet he gave his own burial chamber to Jesus, a gesture of honor and respect. This was entirely a Jewish matter in a Jewish colony of Rome. *No Christians were involved. No Christians were harmed. No Christians existed.* Even if you narrowly define "Christian" as someone who believed in Jesus' resurrection, you wouldn't have had any Christians at his crucifixion, since the resurrection hadn't happened yet.

THE THEORIES

But why do the gospels claim that the Jews have any responsibility at all? For starters, remember that the sect living in Qumran was started by Jewish priests who believed that the priesthood in Jerusalem had become corrupt. With the mix of religious and political power that existed at the time, such corruption wouldn't be surprising, and the gospel accounts may well be evidence of it. In other words, the specific intrigues and betrayals of the Jewish leaders in the gospels may well be true. It doesn't take a huge stretch to imagine why they might want Jesus to go away, by whatever means necessary.

But why use general language like "the Jews" when what you mean are a few bad eggs? There are a number of theories.

Language Conventions

In this view, "the Jews" is used generally to represent the Jewish leadership of the time simply because it's a common use of language. We see this every day. If an American president decides to go to war, historians record that "the Americans" went to war. In the history books it's "the Americans" who dropped the bomb on Hiroshima and Nagasaki, and those who read history are supposed to recognize that such language is referencing the American government, not every single American.

However, if you've ever traveled abroad during a time when American political action is unpopular overseas, you know that the perception is that you personally are complicit in whatever the government is up to at the time. And, especially in a democracy, perhaps we are. When I traveled to Germany with a college group, I discovered that if I spoke German and wasn't immediately perceived as being American, I received markedly better treatment than my friends who had to rely on English with an American accent. I was actually even charged less for things like checking a coat in the theater than my (more clearly American) friends.

Anti-American sentiment, wherever it's encountered, represents people making the leap that the actions of some Americans are approved by—and are likely to be repeated by—all of us. But we certainly do it, too. Americans have assumed that the terrorism of Muslim extremists represents the beliefs and attitudes of every Muslim. (And did you notice that I generalized about Americans there?)

It's common to speak and write in generalities about group or national actions that represent only that group's leadership. But it's also common for members of a group to be thought of, rightly or wrongly, as being complicit in the actions of their leaders. Biblical language could be either an objective account that uses such conventions or a more biased assumption that the actions of the leaders are reflective of the people they govern.

Sibling Rivalry

It's also true that as Christianity and Judaism began to split into different religions, animosity between them grew. Even during the life of St. Paul (who was a Pharisee and proudly Jewish from birth to death), there are significant tensions building between those Jews who were coming to view Jesus as the Messiah and those who weren't. As Gentile converts swelled the ranks and were allowed to become Christian while remaining Gentiles (read about the Council of Jerusalem on p. 176), the tensions of changing demographics also played a role.

More traditional branches of Judaism began to toss those who adhered to this new teaching out of the synagogues as a kind of heretic, and as time went on there was actual violence between the groups. The hatred and violence between Catholics and Protestants across the centuries represent a similar kind of intra-religious conflict. It is during these later years of tension between traditional Judaism and the Jewish Christians that the gospel writers are recording their versions of the life of Jesus. Their writing often reflects the tensions of that later time, not just the reality during Jesus' lifetime.

Paul himself is part of the debate on both sides of the equation. We first meet him in the book of Acts as he hunts down other Jews who are part of this new faction called "the Way." Acts 9:1–2 tells us that Paul, "*still breathing threats and murder against the disciples of the Lord, went to the high priest and asked him for letters to the synagogues at Damascus, so that if he found any who belonged to the Way, men or women, he might bring them bound to Jerusalem.*"

Note that Paul is looking for these "disciples of the Lord" in Damascus synagogues. These disciples are Jews, just like Paul, and just like the high priest who sanctions their arrest. Even in Acts, there are still no Christians. The Bible tells us that the disciples were first called Christians during the ministry of Paul and Barnabas in Antioch (Acts 11:26), at least fourteen years after Paul's conversion. And even then, those early "Christians" still considered themselves Jews. "Christian" was just the name chosen for their particular branch of Judaism, standing beside the names of other groups like the Essenes, Pharisees, and Sadducees.

It isn't long, however, before we see Paul on the other side. In the very next verse he has a conversion experience that literally knocks him off his horse and forever alters the religious landscape. After his vision on the Damascus Road, he still calls himself a Jew but is now hunted down by the particular Jewish groups he once represented.

But how is that hunt described in Acts 9? "After some time *the Jews* [emphasis mine] plotted to kill him…but his disciples took him by night and let him down through an opening in the wall, lowering him in a basket." The language in Acts makes it sound like it's "the Jews" vs. "the disciples," even though they are all professing Jews. Eventually Paul is called before the Sanhedrin to account for his belief in Jesus, and it doesn't go terribly well.

Similar issues can be found in many places in the Gospel of John. Language in the Fourth Gospel, which most scholars believe to have been written long after the other three, reveals the extent of the animosity at the time of writing, frequently lumping all who oppose Jesus together as "the Jews." Jewish disciples of Jesus would have understood the complex relationship, but that nuanced understanding became lost over time as a branch of Judaism ultimately became the separate religion called Christianity.

As the distinction between Jews who believed in Jesus and Jews who didn't grew, a larger and uglier shift started to occur. What was once a conflict between a popular Jewish rabbi and a political class of (probably corrupt) Jewish priests started to get described as something that "the Jews" did to Jesus.

Self-Preservation

Another theory holds that the Christians wanted to distinguish themselves from their Jewish heritage, essentially to save their skins. After the Jewish uprising that resulted in the Romans crushing Jerusalem and razing the Temple in 70 C.E., Roman-Jewish tensions were even higher than they had been under the simpler occupation of the first part of the century.

Christians already had the same religious conflicts with Rome that traditional Jews had— that is, they would not acknowledge that Caesar was divine and give the required yearly assent to that principle. Already in hot water for this, they weren't eager to be seen as political revolutionaries as well, especially since they now had Gentile believers from across Asia Minor in the mix.

Given that, some believe that the gospel writers presented their accounts in a way that minimized Roman involvement and maximized Jewish responsibility simply as a matter of self-preservation. If you put this theory into a cartoon, you'd have a band of unarmed, simple Christians standing in front of the full force of a Roman legion saying, "Heh, no hard feelings about the Jesus thing. We know Pilate didn't want to do it. The Jews made him. Uh, can we go now?"

If you take Mark as the earliest gospel to be written and John as the latest and trace the portrayal of Pilate down the line, you'll see that the later the gospel, the weaker Pilate becomes. The writers wanted to send the signal to Rome that, although this Christian movement may have a substantial religious issue to resolve with the Empire, they weren't out to overthrow the government. Christians wanted to be sure the Romans understood that they were not "the Jews" as a political entity.

Making Sense of History

We saw in our examination of the Old Testament in Course 2 of this series that many of the Old Testament texts look back on prior events to find perspective and meaning. This was especially true when they examined how God could have allowed the complete destruction of Jerusalem by Babylon in 586 B.C.E. and the subsequent exile of Jews to Babylon. As a result of this examination, we have the books of Chronicles, in which the exiles retell the Jewish history of the books of Kings in a way that laid blame on the idolatry of the people and the sins of many of their kings. Why did we have to suffer? Well, let's look back. Obviously we sinned greatly and God had to punish us.

Some see the placing of blame for the death of Jesus on the Jews resulting from the same kind of self-examination that created Chronicles. This time, however, it was about the destruction of the temple in Jerusalem by the Romans in 70 C.E. How could God let such a thing happen? It must have been because the Jews (as the political leaders of the Jewish nation) killed Jesus, just like God had punished Israel for its evil kings and the spread of idolatry among the people back in the day. Once again, Israel had killed its prophets and God was angry.

Theological Understanding

These theories are all a bit cynical, but there's also a more hopeful theory based in possible theological motivation. (Remember that theology simply means the talk and belief about God, human beings, and their relationship.) I was raised in churches that taught me that "Jesus died for my sins," which frequently took the form of laying the blame for Jesus' death squarely on the shoulders not of the Jews or the Romans but on all of humanity. In other words, Jesus had to die because people from Adam on down had sinned and, in the tradition of Leviticus, the shedding of blood was necessary for the remission of sins. That theory of atonement is discussed more in Session 3 on p. 95.

For our purposes here, however, some believe that the gospels' laying responsibility for Jesus' death on "the Jews" as a whole doesn't represent any kind of attempt to separate Christians from traditional Judaism. Instead, they suggest, it represents the theological belief that it was the sins of the people that made Jesus' death necessary and Jesus' love for all that made him a willing participant in God's act of salvation. This theory claims that the general language of "the Jews" was Jewish Christians saying, in effect, "We killed Jesus." With this twist, the cry of the Jewish mob in Matthew that puts Jesus' blood on themselves and their children becomes ultimately a prophetic statement about the same saving power of the blood of Jesus that's woven throughout Christian hymnody.

Especially in the Gospel of John and in Paul's writing, we see threads of teaching that Jesus makes us all one, without distinction. Jesus' prayer in John asks of God "that they may be one, as we are one." (John 17:11) Paul talks about the different gifts but ultimate unity of the Body of Christ and says in 1 Corinthians 15:22, "For as all die in Adam, so all will be made alive in Christ." In Romans 11:26 he makes it clear that all Israel will be saved—not just Jewish and Gentile believers, but even those Jews he currently believes are on the wrong side of the Jesus fence.

Some believe that the language that's become problematic was initially meant to bring Christians and other branches of Judaism back together, all sinful people saved by the blood of the Lamb of God—blood that was shed willingly by Jesus in accordance with God's will. That theology takes the blame off both Jews and Romans as political entities and puts it on every person who has ever sinned. Including us.

The Bottom Line

Whether the language of the New Testament originally was meant to unite or divide, however, ends up being beside the point. Whether it was a political act of self-preservation, resentment over growing persecution, a retelling of history, or something else can't erase the damage done. You can repeat all you want that the swastika was originally just an artistic representation of a cross, but the fact that it became the symbol of Nazi horrors makes it necessary to ditch the thing for the love of our common humanity.

Such atrocities have been visited on Jews because of the interpretation of the New Testament language about "the Jews" that a number of churches will not read aloud portions as it is written, substituting, "leaders" or "priests" or something else more specific wherever the New Testament writers name "the Jews." We all need to do our part to stop anti-Semitism in its tracks and to keep those who don't know the history and background of the Bible from hearing it incorrectly in our communities.

Jesus, the Jewish rabbi, was betrayed by a Jewish disciple named Judas, who was probably encouraged by a group of corrupt Jewish priests in positions of power. Roman authorities ordered and carried out the execution, which was mourned by Jesus' Jewish followers and disciples. Both Judas and Pilate later committed suicide. According to Luke, as Jesus was hanging on the cross, he said, "Father, forgive them; for they do not know what they are doing." (Luke 23:34) Too often, we still don't know what we're doing.

Exploring the Bible
THE DICKINSON SERIES

Please return this evaluation to:
Massachusetts Bible Society, 199 Herrick Rd.,
Newton Centre, MA 02459
or e-mail to dsadmin@massbible.org.

Course (circle one):   I   II   III

Why did you take this course? Were your expectations met?

Did you do this study with a group or on your own?   ☐ **Group**   ☐ **Alone**

Did you take this course for certification
or CEUs?
If yes, please be sure that all of your written work
is submitted to the Massachusetts Bible Society by
either yourself or your group leader at the conclusion
of the course.
☐ **Yes**   ☐ **No**

Did your group have a mix of "Extra Mile" and informal students? ☐ **Yes** ☐ **No**

    If "yes," did you find the mix helpful? ☐ **Yes** ☐ **No**

    Why or why not?

Who was your group leader? _____

Scale: 1 - most negative, 10 - most positive

Please rate your leader on the following using a scale of 1-10.

_____ Creating a welcoming and inclusive environment

_____ Keeping the class sessions on track

_____ Beginning and ending on time

_____ Handling conflicting opinions with respect

_____ Being prepared for class sessions

Scale: 1 - most negative, 10 - most positive

Please rate your physical setting for your group on the following using a scale of 1-10.

_____ The space was free of distractions and interruptions

_____ The space was physically comfortable and conductive to learning

_____ The group could easily adjust to different configurations

_____ It was easy to see instructional materials and group members

_____ Restroom facilities were easily accessible

_____ The space was accessible to those with disabilities

Do you have a particular faith tradition or spiritual orientation? If so, how would you name it?

Did you feel that your opinions and perspective were respected in the following areas:

Course materials? ☐ **Yes** ☐ **No**

Class discussions? ☐ **Yes** ☐ **No**

By the group leader? ☐ **Yes** ☐ **No**

If you were an "informal student" (i.e., not a student
seeking certification or CEUs), how much of the
homework and reading did you complete? Please
describe on a scale of 1-10, with 1 being virtually
none and 10 being all of it.

_____

Did you do any of the Extra Mile assignments?   ☐ **Yes**   ☐ **No**

Scale: 1 - most negative, 10 - most positive

Please rate the quality of the homework assignments using a scale of 1-10.

_____   It was easy to understand the assignment

_____   The work could reasonably be completed between sessions

_____   I learned important things from doing the homework

_____   I did not feel pushed to come to a particular conclusion

Please answer the following questions:

Did you visit the Exploring the Bible Facebook page or follow us on Twitter
@ExploreBible? Do you find these tools useful in staying connected to the
Exploring the Bible community? Are there other ways you would prefer to
be connected? If you would like to be on the Exploring the Bible e-mail list,
please include your e-mail address in the space below.

Did this study answer any questions you had at the beginning? What were some of the most important questions that were answered for you?

Did anything disappoint you in this study? Was there something you expected that was not provided? Questions you really wanted answered that were not?

What new questions do you have upon completion that you did not have at the beginning? Do you find those new questions exciting or frustrating?

Did you learn anything of interest to you from this study? If you studied with a group, indicate how much of that came from the material provided and how much from the group discussion.

Have your impressions/beliefs/thoughts about the Bible changed as a result of this study? In what way?

Would you recommend this study to a friend?

How would you rate this study using a scale of 1-10, with 1 being not at all helpful and 10 being exceptionally helpful.

Other thoughts, comments, or suggestions?

Please return this evaluation to:
Massachusetts Bible Society, 199 Herrick Rd.,
Newton Centre MA 02459
or e-mail to dsadmin@massbible.org.

APPENDIX 6

MASSACHUSETTS BIBLE SOCIETY STATEMENT ON SCRIPTURE

The Massachusetts Bible Society is an ecumenical, Christian organization with a broad diversity of scriptural approaches and interpretations among its members and supporters. The following statement on the nature of Scripture represents the guiding principle for our selection of programming and resources, but agreement with it is neither a pre-requisite for membership nor a litmus test for grant recipients.

> *The Bible was written by many authors, all inspired by God. It is neither a simple collection of books written by human authors, nor is it the literal words of God dictated to human scribes. It is a source of religious truth, presented in a diversity of styles, genres, and languages and is not meant to serve as fact in science, history, or social structure.*

> *The Bible has authority for communities of faith who take time to study and prayerfully interpret its message, but it is also important for anyone who wants more fully to understand culture, religious thought, and the world in which we live.*

> *Biblical texts have been interpreted in diverse ways from generation to generation and are always filtered through the lens of the reader's faith and life experiences. This breadth and plurality, however, are what keep the Bible alive through the ages and enhance its ongoing, transformative power.*

APPENDIX 7

A COVENANT FOR BIBLE STUDY

We covenant together to deal with our differences in a spirit of mutual respect and to refrain from actions that may harm the emotional and physical well-being of others.

The following principles will guide our actions:

- We will treat others whose views may differ from our own with the same courtesy we would want to receive ourselves.

- We will listen with a sincere desire to understand the point of view being expressed by another person, especially if it is different from our own.

- We will respect each other's ideas, feelings, and experiences.

- We will refrain from blaming or judging in our attitude and behavior towards others.

- We will communicate directly with any person with whom we may disagree in a respectful and constructive way.

- We will seek feedback to ensure that we have truly understood each other in our communications.

Additional agreements for our particular group:

APPENDIX 8

HELP! I HAVE QUESTIONS!

- If the question is specific to a particular Bible passage, look in the notes associated with that passage in your study Bible. Are there notes that address the question?

- Does someone else in your group have a different study Bible? Does it have any helpful notes?

- Google is your friend. It is quite likely that if you type your question into an Internet search engine verbatim, you will come up with more "answers" than you thought possible. Ditto for just putting in a Bible verse reference. These results, however, are unfiltered and will range from well-informed responses to the conclusions of the truly unbalanced or the simply ignorant. It is sometimes difficult to tell the difference if you don't have a biblical education yourself, so approach this option with caution. It will, however, give you a sense of the range of ideas out there.

- Submit the question to the Ask-a-Prof service of the Massachusetts Bible Society. This is a free service that takes your question to thirty-five professors from seminaries and universities across the US and the UK. Participating professors come from a variety of denominations and faith traditions and represent both liberal and conservative viewpoints. You can read more about them and ask your question at massbible.org/ask-a-prof.

- "Like" the Exploring the Bible page on Facebook to discuss your questions with students in other groups and the Massachusetts Bible Society staff.

- Ask your group leader or another religious leader you trust for help.

- Remember that not all questions have "answers" per se. Sometimes a variety of opinions will be the best you can do.

APPENDIX 9

GLOSSARY

A.D.
Abbreviation for the Latin *Anno Domini*, meaning "in the year of the Lord." A system of notating time, generally used with B.C.

Antichrist
With a small "a" it is one who denies or opposes Christ. With a capital "A" it refers to a great antagonist expected to fill the world with wickedness but to be conquered forever by Christ at his second coming.

Apocalypse (adj. apocalyptic)
One of the Jewish and Christian writings of 200 B.C.E. to 150 C.E. marked by pseudonymity, symbolic imagery, and the expectation of an imminent cosmic cataclysm in which God destroys the ruling powers of evil and raises the righteous to life in a messianic kingdom.

Apocrypha
Books included in the Septuagint and Vulgate but excluded from the Hebrew Scriptures and Protestant books of the Old Testament.

Ark
Something that affords protection and safety. Two different forms of this are prominent in the Bible. One is a boat—Noah's Ark—and the other is a sacred box—the Ark of the Covenant.

Babylonian Captivity (or Exile)
The period in Jewish history during which the Jews of the ancient Kingdom of Judah were captives in Babylon—conventionally 586–538 B.C.E. although some claim a date of 596 B.C.E.

B.C.
Abbreviation for "Before Christ." A system of notating time, generally used with A.D.

B.C.E.
Abbreviation for "Before the Christian Era" or "Before the Common Era." An academic and faith-neutral notation of time. Generally used with C.E.

Canon
An authoritative list of books accepted as Holy Scripture. The word is from the Latin meaning "rule" or "standard."

Catholic
With a small "c," the word means "universal." It is used this way in the Apostles' Creed. With a capital "C" the word denotes the Roman Catholic Church.

C.E.
Abbreviation for "Christian Era" or "Common Era." An academic and faith-neutral notation of time. Generally used with B.C.E.

Codex

A manuscript book especially of Scripture, classics, or ancient annals. A codex is bound like we are used to in a modern book instead of the more common scroll.

Codex Sinaiticus

A fourth-century, hand-written copy of the Greek Bible.

Concordance

An alphabetical index of all the words in a text or corpus of texts, showing every contextual occurrence of a word.

Conquest

The period of Jewish history described in the biblical book of Joshua. Many scholars believe the settlement of the Hebrews in Canaan took place over a much longer period of time and with less bloodshed than is depicted in Joshua. They would say that there was no actual "conquest" at all.

Covenant

A formal, solemn, and binding agreement.

Creationism

The doctrine or theory holding that matter, the various forms of life, and the world were created by God out of nothing in a way determined by a literal reading of Genesis.

Deuterocanonical

Of, relating to, or constituting the books of Scripture contained in the Septuagint but not in the Hebrew canon. Primarily Roman Catholic and Orthodox usage for the texts known to Jews and Protestants as the Apocrypha.

Diaspora

A scattered population originating from a single area. In this course the word refers specifically to Jews living outside of Israel.

Dispensationalism

A system of Christian belief, formalized in the nineteenth century, that divides human history into seven distinct ages or dispensations.

Evangelical

When used with a capital "E," this refers to those in Christian traditions that emphasize a high view of biblical authority, the need for personal relationship with God achieved through a conversion experience (being "born again"), and an emphasis on sharing the gospel that Jesus' death and resurrection save us from our sins. The tradition generally deemphasizes ritual and prioritizes personal experience.

Gilgamesh
A Sumerian king and hero of the *Epic of Gilgamesh*, which contains a story of a great flood during which a man is saved in a boat.

Hapax Legomenon (pl. Hapax Legomena)
A word or form of speech occurring only once in a document or body of work.

Hasmonean Dynasty
Those who ruled Judea in the late second century B.C.E. This represented a brief period of independence between the occupying forces of Greece and Rome and is described in the books of the Maccabees.

Hyksos
Of or relating to a Semitic dynasty that ruled Egypt from about the eighteenth to the sixteenth centuries B.C.E.

Inerrancy
Exemption from error. Infallibility.

Jerome
(ca. 347 C.E.–30 September 420 C.E.) A Roman Christian priest, confessor, theologian, and historian, who became a Doctor of the Church. Best known for his translation of the Bible into Latin (the Vulgate). Recognized by the Roman Catholic and Eastern Orthodox churches as a saint.

LXX
See *Septuagint.*

Mainline
Certain Protestant churches in the United States that comprised a majority of Americans from the colonial era until the early twentieth century. The group is contrasted with evangelical and fundamentalist groups. They include Congregationalists, Episcopalians, Methodists, northern Baptists, most Lutherans, and most Presbyterians, as well as some smaller denominations.

Marcion (of Sinope)
(ca. 85–160 C.E.) An early Christian bishop who believed the God of the Hebrew Scriptures to be inferior or subjugated to the God of the New Testament and developed his own canon of Scripture accordingly. He was excommunicated for his belief.

Masoretes
Groups of Jewish scribes working between the seventh and eleventh centuries C.E. They added vowel notations to the Hebrew Scriptures.

Mordecai Nathan (Rabbi)

Philosopher rabbi of the fifteenth century C.E. who wrote the first concordance to the Hebrew Bible and added numbered verse notations to the Hebrew Bible for the first time.

Orthodox

With a capital "O" referring to the Eastern Orthodox Church (and its various geographic subdivisions), the Oriental Orthodox churches (and their subdivisions), and any Western Rite Orthodox congregations allied with the above.

Ossuary

A depository, most commonly a box, for the bones (as opposed to the entire corpse) of the dead.

Pentateuch

The first five books of the Bible: Genesis, Exodus, Leviticus, Numbers, and Deuteronomy.

Pharisee

A member of a segment of Judaism of the inter-testamental period noted for strict observance of rites and ceremonies of the written law and for insistence on the validity of their own oral traditions concerning the law.

Protestant

Used here in the broadest sense of any Christian not of a Catholic or Orthodox church.

Pseudepigrapha

In biblical studies, the Pseudepigrapha are Jewish religious works written ca. 200 B.C.E.–200 C.E., which are not part of the canon of any established Jewish or Christian tradition.

Rapture

The term "rapture" is used in at least two senses in modern traditions of Christian theology: in pre-tribulationist views, in which a group of people will be "left behind"; and as a synonym for the final resurrection generally.

Robert Stephanus

Protestant book printer living in France in the sixteenth century who divided the chapters of the New Testament into the verses we have today.

Septuagint or LXX

An ancient Greek translation of the Hebrew Scriptures. Translation began in the third century B.C.E. with the Pentateuch and continued for several centuries.

Stephen Langton

Theology professor in Paris and archbishop of Canterbury in the thirteenth century who first added chapter divisions to the Bible.

Supersessionism

The idea that God's covenant with Christians supersedes and therefore displaces God's covenant with Israel.

Synoptic Gospels

From the Greek meaning to "see alike," the Synoptics are Matthew, Mark, and Luke.

Testament

With a capital "T" it means either of the two main divisions of the Bible: the Old Testament or the New Testament. With a small "t" the word simply means a covenant or agreement that is formalized in writing and witnessed.

Tetragrammaton

The four consonants in Exodus 3:14 (YHWH) that comprise God's name.

Vulgate

The late fourth-century Latin translation of the Bible done by St. Jerome.

THE **IDEAL DVD PAIRING** FOR

Exploring the Bible

Produced by the Massachusetts Bible Society and The Walker Group, LLC, the 28-minute video **One Book, Many Voices** will let you hear directly from scholars, clergy, and just regular folks helping you to reflect on these questions:

- **HOW DO YOU UNDERSTAND THE BIBLE?**
- **CAN WE TRUST WHAT IS IN THE BIBLE?**
- **IS THERE A RIGHT OR WRONG WAY TO READ IT?**

To view the trailer and/or order a physical copy of the DVD, go to **massbible.org/DVD**. To buy or rent a streaming download, either search amazon.com for "One Book, Many Voices" or scan the QR code with your smart phone.

Help More People Explore the Bible

Your gift of $25, $50, $100, or more supports *Exploring the Bible* scholarships, study Bibles for those in need, and helps keep our training events at a reasonable cost.

$ _____   ○ One-Time Donation   ○ Recurring

Name _____

Address _____

Phone _____   Email _____

Credit Card Number _____   ○ Check Enclosed

Expiration Date _____   Security Code _____

Mail this completed form to:
Massachusetts Bible Society
199 Herrick Rd., Newton Centre, MA 02459

You can also donate by calling 617.969.9404,
by e-mail at dsadmin@massbible.org, or online at exploringthebible.org.

Made in the USA
Middletown, DE
15 August 2016